Dickens

AND

MASSACHUSETTS

✦

Dickens

AND
MASSACHUSETTS

The Lasting Legacy of the
Commonwealth Visits

✦

Edited by

DIANA C. ARCHIBALD
AND
JOEL J. BRATTIN

University of Massachusetts Press
Amherst and Boston

ISBN 978-1-62534-136-5 (paperback); 135-8 (hardcover)

Designed by Dennis Anderson
Set in Adobe Caslon Pro
Printed and bound by Sheridan Books, Inc.

Library of Congress Cataloging-in-Publication Data

Dickens and Massachusetts : the lasting legacy of the Commonwealth visits /
edited by Diana C. Archibald and Joel J. Brattin.
   pages cm
  Includes bibliographical references and index.
  ISBN 978-1-62534-135-8 (hardcover : alk. paper)—ISBN 978-1-62534-136-5
(pbk. : alk. paper)
   1. Dickens, Charles, 1812–1870—Travel—Massachusetts. 2. Dickens, Charles,
1812–1870—Appreciation—Massachusetts. 3. Dickens, Charles, 1812–1870—
Knowledge—United States. 4. Dickens, Charles, 1812–1870—Social and
political views. 5. British—United States—History—19th century. 6. Novelists,
English—19th century—Biography. I. Archibald, Diana C., editor, author.
II. Brattin, Joel J., 1956– editor, author.
  PR4582.D53 2015
  823'.8—dc23

2014050151

British Library Cataloguing-in-Publication Data
A catalogue record for this book is available from the British Library.

CONTENTS

ACKNOWLEDGMENTS

THIS BOOK is a legacy of the Dickens bicentenary in 2012, when many individuals and institutions worked together to examine the relationship between Dickens and Massachusetts and to share our findings with a wide and varied audience. First of all, therefore, we acknowledge the contributions of many to the Dickens in Lowell project, especially its exhibition, which served as an incubator for much of our scholarly work. Institutional support was provided by the Lowell National Historical Park, the University of Massachusetts Lowell, the Tsongas Industrial History Center, the Charles Dickens Museum, Worcester Polytechnic Institute (WPI), Middlesex Community College, the Cultural Organization of Lowell, the Center for Arts and Ideas, and the Center for Lowell History. Major funders included the Theodore Edson Parker Foundation, the University of Massachusetts President's Office Creative Economy Initiative, the Lowell National Historical Park, and the University of Massachusetts Lowell College of Fine Arts, Humanities, and Social Sciences. Complete information about our other partners and sponsors can be found at www.uml.edu/dickens.

Of the many individuals who facilitated and encouraged this work, we gratefully acknowledge Dean Emerita Nina Coppens (1950–2013) of the University of Massachusetts Lowell, who was the exhibition's first and most steadfast supporter, providing seed money, advice, and inspiration. We also gratefully acknowledge the superintendent of the Lowell National Historical Park, Celeste Bernardo, and former superintendent, Michael Creasey, for their enthusiastic and magnanimous backing of our project. The gallery exhibition's co-curator, David Blackburn, chief of cultural resources and programs at Lowell National Historical Park, and museum specialist Jack Herlihy deserve hearty praise and thanks for their expertise in exhibition planning and development, and we thank their colleagues at the park for their contributions as well: Christine Wirth,

Greg Chagnon, Enrique Melendez, Marc Mousseau, Margaret Neptune, and Phil Lupsiewicz. Our exhibition designer, Chris Danemayer of Proun Design, created a beautiful design for our gallery exhibition, helping us to translate scholarly research into a public humanities project suitable for lay as well as expert audiences. We also thank Professor Kristin Boudreau, chair of WPI's Department of Humanities and Arts, for her unflagging and generous support, and Professors Anthony Szczesiul, chair, and Melissa Pennell, former chair, of the University of Massachusetts Lowell's English Department for their kind assistance and backing of this project over the last several years.

We wish to acknowledge the valued contributions that three scholars in particular made to an early version of the exhibition narrative included in this book: Lillian Nayder (Bates College) drafted sections on Catherine Dickens, Natalie McKnight (Boston University) initially developed the section on Dickens's visit to Lowell, and Christie Jackson (Old Sturbridge Village) offered material for the portion of the script devoted to crossing the Atlantic. Each of these scholars assisted in developing the exhibition's themes and story. Both Nayder and McKnight also contributed essays to this volume and have been steadfast supporters of this project over the years. Other faculty who assisted include University of Massachusetts Lowell American Studies professors Michael Millner and Jonathan Silverman, plastics engineering professor Stephen Johnston, and art professor Ellen Wetmore. Several University of Massachusetts Lowell student research assistants helped with initial efforts to find suitable material for this project; we acknowledge with thanks the work of Kaitlynne Carney, Jennifer Gannon, John Lutkevich, Diane Belfiore, Jenna Reed, Ariel Werbicki, and Falicia Wyman. We also appreciate the help of Beth Brosnan, Lori Mortimer, Dane Netherton, and Turner Netherton in working on the exhibition and the Dickens in Lowell project.

Both for the gallery exhibition and the illustrations in part I of this book, we are indebted to several institutions and individuals. We wish to extend our warm thanks to Mark Dickens for his early and enthusiastic support of our work, and for his prompt and kind permission to use several works in our book, including original letters, drawings, photographs, and an autographed book. We are particularly grateful to the Charles Dickens Museum for the loan of precious artifacts for the exhibition. Former museum director Florian Schweizer provided excellent support, suggesting additional artifacts that would enhance our exhibition goals and working with us over the course of three years to plan the exhibition. We acknowledge Louisa Price, curator at the Dickens Museum, for her kind and generous assistance as well. We are also indebted to Jan Seymour-Ford at the Perkins School for the Blind for offering useful information and facilitating the loan of several precious Laura Bridgman artifacts. We thank the Worcester Polytechnic Institute Curation, Preservation, and Archives Department, George C. Gordon Library, for providing the digital capture of images; specifically, Margaret Anderson, Kathleen Markees, and Molly Bruce deserve thanks for their assistance in selecting and mounting many artifacts in the gallery exhibition and arranging for reproductions for use in this book. We appreciate the assistance of David Daly and Anita Israel of Longfellow House–Washington's Headquarters National Historic Site with the loan of materials as well as providing additional information. Kind thanks go to Lauren Hewes, Jaclyn Penny, and Thomas Knoles from the American Antiquarian Society for facilitating our research as well as artifact reproduction and loans. We are grateful to the other institutions that allowed us to borrow or reproduce images: the Boston Museum of Fine Arts, the Boston Public Library, the New York Public Library, the Lowell National Historical Park, the Lowell Historical Society, the Library of Congress, the Liverpool Record Office at the Liverpool Libraries, FultonHistory.com, Getty Images, and the Metropolitan Museum of Art.

In addition to the institutions and individuals noted above, contributors of the chapters in part II of this book wish to thank those who facilitated their research and reproduction of images. We gratefully acknowledge Mark Dickens and the Trustees of the Victoria and Albert Museum for their kind permission to quote from Dickens's manuscript, and the Dickens Society for kind permission to publish chapter 5, a preliminary version of which appeared in *Dickens Quarterly* 20, no. 3 (September 2003): 153–65. We also appreciate the help of Rowan Watson, Jim Monaco, and Jessica Colati with research for chapter 5. We wish to thank Margaret Humberston, head of library and archives at the Springfield Museums; Christina Vida, curator of collections and interpretation, Windsor Historical Society, Windsor, Connecticut; Richard Colton, historian, and Alex MacKenzie, curator, at the National Park Service Springfield Armory National Historic Site; and Ray Kelly and Jim Gleason at the *Springfield Republican* for assistance with chapter 6 of this book.

Finally, we wish to thank the staff at University of Massachusetts Press who have helped to bring this book project to completion. Brian Halley, our editor, has been a tremendous help; we appreciate his faith in the project and his excellent advice. We are grateful to the outside readers of the manuscript for their suggestions and encouragement. Editorial staff

Carol Betsch and Mary Bellino provided practical support for manuscript preparation, and Margaret Hogan provided thorough and helpful copyediting. Working with the University of Massachusetts Press has been a pleasure, and we deeply appreciate the opportunity to offer our book under their imprint.

Dickens

AND

MASSACHUSETTS

✦

Introduction

Dickens and Massachusetts, the Republic of His Imagination

Diana C. Archibald

✦

FOR MANY today, Charles Dickens seems to be the quintessential English-man, a Londoner through and through. Dickens, however, was a world traveler who toured many European countries, living abroad for extended periods in France and Italy. Notably, he also traveled to North America twice, visiting and enjoying Massachusetts as a part of his itinerary in both 1842 and 1867–68. Many scholars have written about the American trips, with some disagreement about how to interpret Dickens's attitudes toward the republic and how to read his corresponding literary works.[1] Some scholars believe Dickens's forays outside the imperial center only served to highlight or reinforce his British ideals and values. For instance, Jerome Meckier, in *Innocent Abroad*, claims that in 1842, Dickens "discovered his fundamental Englishness, becoming more British and less equalitarian each day he spent in the United States."[2] Meckier further contends, "Dickens found a self-centered society that seemed militantly materialistic, many of its dollar-serving citizens not just brazen in their acquisitiveness but so unrefined and uncivil by British standards as to appear savage, without a trace or prospect of nobility."[3] Many critics follow suit and focus on Dickens's negative portrait of the young republic, either in his travel book *American Notes for General Circulation* or in his novel *Martin Chuzzlewit.* For example, David Stevens cites "Dickens' own inability to think outside the box of English cultural mores or to encounter in America anything other than a bastardized, even sloppy, version of Britain itself." Stevens sees the positive representation of Boston in *American Notes* as "cursory" and "largely a tourist's view," and argues that "the American experience offered no model for British reform."[4] Even those such as Michael Slater and Juliet John, who take a more nuanced view of

Dickens's relationship with the United States, tend not to recognize the distinct and powerful place of Massachusetts in Dickens's life and work.[5] Many scholars, then, underestimate the importance of Massachusetts, as if it were not really a significant part of Dickens's American experience; such readers treat evidence of positive perception of the commonwealth as relatively unimportant in assessing Dickens's relationship with the United States. This book demonstrates that these visits are more significant than heretofore recognized, and that the people, places, and institutions of Massachusetts left a lasting impact on Dickens.

The dominant discourse has emphasized Dickens's profound disillusionment with the New World; many critics cite Dickens's letter to his friend William Macready written from Baltimore, Maryland, on 22 March 1842 as evidence that Dickens disliked America. He wrote there, "I *am* disappointed. This is not the Republic I came to see. This is not the Republic of my imagination."[6] Indeed, as many have noted, Dickens found fault with much in the new country—the powerful and unscrupulous press, the ubiquitous spitting of tobacco juice, and the horrors of slavery, among other things. His 1842 travel book *American Notes for General Circulation* outlines some of these negative reactions to the United States, though calling that work "anti-American" would be going too far.[7] Indeed, much of the book is straightforward description, and the early chapters dealing with Massachusetts are filled with strong praise. Such holds true in Dickens's letters as well. Even the Macready letter undercuts its criticism with notable exceptions, most of which are Massachusetts-based. Dickens wrote, "In every respect but that of National Education" he felt disappointed, but two sentences later he noted exceptions, those things which did *not* disappoint: "its education of the people, and its care for poor children." As the editors of the Pilgrim *Letters* observe, four out of the five institutions for poor children that Dickens had visited by the time he wrote that letter were in Massachusetts, and of the educational institutions he had seen, none garnered higher praise than "the University of Cambridge" (Harvard).[8] The "pang" and "hesitation" Dickens felt at "reject[ing]" America was due to these exceptions; they are presumably the reason he burned the first letter of criticism that he had written to Macready.[9] Massachusetts was the republic he came to see, the one he had imagined and of which he had dreamt.

In another letter to Macready, Dickens wrote, "Boston is what I would have the whole United States to be."[10] Here was his ideal realized; here was a bald statement of his preference. Elsewhere, too, Dickens seems to single out Massachusetts as exceptional and noteworthy. In *American*

Notes, for example, he offers high praise for the commonwealth: "Above all, I sincerely believe that the public institutions and charities of this capital of Massachusetts are as nearly perfect, as the most considerate wisdom, benevolence, and humanity, can make them. . . . It is a great and pleasant feature of all such institutions in America, that they are either supported by the State or assisted by the State; or (in the event of their not needing its helping hand) that they act in concert with it, and are emphatically the people's."[11] Given the classical understanding of a republic—in which citizens govern for the public good—Massachusetts fit that definition well. Boston was in many ways the intellectual and artistic center of the young republic, and Dickens's admiration for the people and institutions of Massachusetts resulted in much more nuanced and conflicted feelings about the country than heretofore recognized. To dismiss Dickens's praise for Massachusetts and discount its generative legacy for him is to paint a skewed picture of Dickens's relationship to the United States, a distorted image that many scholars have accepted without question.

Contrary to Meckier's stance that the 1842 American trip was a "nasty formative experience," this volume contends that Dickens's positive encounter with Massachusetts was no mere anomaly but rather a transformative experience that influenced him for many years to come.[12] Indeed, as Natalie McKnight argues, Dickens, after his 1842 encounter with Massachusetts, "became a more focused, more self-conscious author driven by a desire to produce novels that were both beautiful and purposeful."[13] A reassessment of his relationship to the commonwealth is required to gain a more sophisticated and accurate understanding of the role his two visits to America played in Dickens's life and works. This volume demonstrates the many ways in which Massachusetts functioned as an alternate America, meeting and even exceeding Dickens's expectations for his imagined republic.

Offered at a time when interest in Charles Dickens has become heightened by his 2012 bicentennial and a few recent biographies, this book provides insight from several leading scholars who have begun to reassess the place of Massachusetts in biographical and literary studies of Dickens. The anchor for this collection appears in part I, the full-length narrative for the award-winning public exhibition *Dickens and Massachusetts: A Tale of Power and Transformation,* which was on display from 30 March to 20 October 2012 at the Boott Gallery, Lowell National Historical Park, in Lowell, Massachusetts.[14] Created in honor of the bicentenary of Dickens's birth to explore his connections to Massachusetts, this exhibition received international acclaim from academic and lay visitors alike. Scholars came from as far away as Qatar and Japan, as well as the United Kingdom, Canada, and cities across the United States, to see the exhibition, described by one visitor as an "outstanding visual and textual overview of Dickens and his relationship to the U.S. The original artifacts were wonderful to encounter. . . . There should be some way to preserve the exhibition permanently; it is truly extraordinary." This volume, in part, answers that call for preservation. The exhibition, however, necessarily included only fractions of the master narrative in order to keep text panels in the small gallery a manageable size. In this book, the entire manuscript is available for the first time, and will be of interest to readers since it includes not only the materials used in the exhibition but also much cultural and literary context and a fuller argument about the importance of Massachusetts to Dickens. We also include most of the images from the exhibition, offering readers a view of the exhibition's key artifacts, many of which are not readily available to the public or are scattered across different institutions throughout the United States and Great Britain. The inclusion of the master script in this volume not only helps to "preserve the exhibition permanently" but also to extend the breadth and depth of the exhibition's story to include much new material. Those readers interested in taking a virtual tour of the *Dickens and Massachusetts* exhibition can see the gallery text panels and color images of the artifacts as well as short video explanations online at http://library.uml.edu/dickens.

The exhibition narrative in part I of this volume provides an overview of Dickens's relationship with the commonwealth, telling a tale suitable for experts and lay readers, Dickens enthusiasts and scholars, and those interested in American history. It is our belief that public humanities projects can and should be both scholarly and broadly accessible, and that it is a worthy goal to share research not only with peers but also with a lay audience. Given these ambitions, the exhibition narrative contains some material originally targeted for those without specialized knowledge as well as more arcane information. Taken as a whole, part I presents a broad biographical and historical overview that provides context for the more sharply focused essays in part II. These chapters demonstrate the literary legacy of Massachusetts in Dickens's works, and explore biographical and historical topics as well. They break new ground in examining the importance of Dickens's connection to the commonwealth and participate in a scholarly conversation with each other and with the exhibition narrative that offers readers a complex and rich understanding of the topic of Dickens and Massachusetts.

Part II begins with Natalie McKnight and Chelsea Bray's "Dickens, the Lowell Mill Girls, and the Making of *A Christmas Carol*," which makes the boldest case for Massachusetts's lasting legacy for Dickens. In this piece, McKnight and Bray demonstrate the connections between the Lowell mill girls' publication *The Lowell Offering* and Dickens's *A Christmas Carol*, arguing that the Massachusetts publication influenced the production of Dickens's most famous tale. They examine why Dickens referred to his visit to Lowell as "the happiest day he had passed in the country," explaining how the day trip to the young mill city shaped not only his conception of industry but also his writing.[15] In fact, they go so far as to claim that "his day in Lowell . . . had a greater positive impact on his writing than any other place he visited on his tour." A meticulous reading of all of the issues of the first two years of the *Lowell Offering* yielded remarkable evidence showing a "preponderance of thematic, imagistic, structural, and phrasing similarities between many of the essays and stories" of the *Offering* and *A Christmas Carol*.

André DeCuir's "Visions of Lowell, Light and Dark, in *Our Mutual Friend*" similarly takes as its subject the legacy of the Lowell visit on Dickens's fiction. This chapter examines the intertwining of idyllic images inspired by Lowell with a fascination with the psychology of murderers in *Our Mutual Friend*. DeCuir claims that the character Lizzie Hexam is placed "in a Lowellesque mill of 1842, complete with a youthful, childlike river," and that Betty Higden, the innocent old woman who dies in Lizzie's arms, is also associated with this pristine past. The essay draws further parallels between Marcus Stone's illustration "The Parting at the River," published in the first edition of *Our Mutual Friend*, and Dickens's descriptions of the mill girls in *American Notes*. It is in this Lowell-like setting that Dickens allows his villain Bradley Headstone to attempt murder, thereby heightening the contrast between good and evil that Dickens also makes explicit in *American Notes*. DeCuir argues that "Dickens's novel throws into stark relief, against the fading backdrop of romantic art mixed with his memories of Lowell, the polluting 'defilements' that come not from factory runoff but from what haunted Dickens in the latter part of his career—the fragile and potentially dangerous human psyche."

The next two chapters move away from Lowell to Boston institutions and friendships. "Dickens's Visit to the Perkins School and 'Doctor Marigold'" by Diana C. Archibald considers the influence of the Perkins School for the Blind in Boston on Dickens's understanding of deafness and deaf culture. Archibald contends that the Christmas story "Doctor

Marigold's Prescriptions" is "notably progressive for its day," with a relatively enlightened portrayal of a signing deaf character and her adoptive father. The essay contextualizes the story within the oralist movement of the 1860s, a radical effort to forcibly restrict deaf students from learning sign language. Dickens took a minority position, falling on the side of those who saw "finger language" as a natural and suitable mode of expression. Further, Dickens allows Sophy, his deaf heroine, to marry a deaf man and have a child, another unusual breach of literary tradition. Archibald marks the echoes in "Doctor Marigold" of the Perkins School and Laura Bridgman, the famous American deaf-blind student about whom Dickens writes in *American Notes*. The school that educates Sophy bears a stronger resemblance to the Perkins School than the supposed London model for the institution. Further, the sentimental ending of the story, in which we learn that Sophy's child is hearing, avoids some of the bias against disability by having the child not only speak English but also speak fluently in signs, participating actively in the deaf culture to which she belongs.

Lillian Nayder's chapter, "Dickens, Longfellow, and the Village Blacksmith," reveals the intertextuality of Longfellow's poem "The Village Blacksmith" and Dickens's *Great Expectations*. Nayder demonstrates how Dickens's friendship with the Boston poet influenced his own literary production. Longfellow wrote his *Poems on Slavery* in 1842 on the voyage home from England after visiting Dickens and discussing his antislavery views in *American Notes*. Dickens, likewise, was influenced by Longfellow's "The Village Blacksmith," which he admired for its ability "to foster a nostalgia that questions the value of social change while also acknowledging the resistance to memory triggered by social and personal loss." Nayder contrasts Longfellow's loss of his wife in a terrible accident with Dickens's separation from his wife, Catherine, revealing how these personal circumstances played a part in the literary productions of the two authors, albeit to different ends. Relying on textual and historical evidence, the chapter demonstrates how Dickens deepens and transforms the nostalgia of Longfellow's poem within *Great Expectations*, which, like the poem, features a forge, a blacksmith, and a dead wife.

The last three chapters in part II focus on historical and biographical questions rather than on the legacy of Massachusetts in Dickens's fiction. "Slavery in Dickens's Manuscript of *American Notes for General Circulation*" by Joel J. Brattin discusses Dickens's attitudes toward slavery and the influence of Massachusetts figures and texts as revealed in the manuscript of *American Notes*. As Brattin demonstrates, Dickens mentions

Massachusetts at key moments in the travel book, "often as a way to highlight the contrast with what he found elsewhere" in the country. Although Dickens purposely avoids naming individuals in the book, he alludes to well-known antislavery figures from Boston such as Dr. William Ellery Channing and William Lloyd Garrison. Further, as Brattin demonstrates through meticulous comparisons of manuscript and text, Dickens relied heavily on "the abolitionist work of Theodore Dwight Weld, a New Englander with strong ties to Massachusetts." Manuscript analysis shows clearly Dickens's disgust with slavery and commitment to speaking out against the hypocrisy of this injustice.

Kit Polga fills a significant gap in the scholarship in "Dickens's Visits to Springfield, Massachusetts, in 1842 and 1868." While some previous work has been published about Dickens's connection to Lowell and Boston, his two visits to Springfield, Massachusetts, have garnered almost no critical attention. This chapter argues that "Dickens's first visit was emblematic of his eagerness to experience America, while his second visit reflected the genius and vulnerability of the mature writer who had transformed himself into a performer, bringing his characters alive to his American readers." Through close examination of the historical records, illustrations, diaries, and letters, Polga discusses what Dickens saw and did while passing through the city on his birthday in 1842, and surmises what impressions such sights were likely to have made on the author. Twenty-five years later, when Dickens returned for his reading tour, "Springfield had been transformed from a sleepy town to a bustling industrial and residential metropolis." It was in Springfield on 21 March 1868 that Dickens wrote another letter to Macready, this time praising the country he once maligned: "You would find the general aspect of America and Americans, decidedly much improved."[16]

Iain Crawford's "Dickens, Martineau, and Massachusetts: The Republic They Came to See" concludes the collection, offering a marked contrast to the first chapter of part II. While McKnight and Bray see Lowell's profound influence on Dickens, Crawford contends that the value of *The Lowell Offering* "was not as a vehicle for creative or intellectual expression but rather as an agent of social discipline." He claims that Dickens renders the mill girls in a way that "epitomiz[es] the selflessness he so often privileges in his accounts of female characters" while simultaneously reducing "both their agency and individual autonomy." Crawford's work brings a fresh perspective to Dickens's views on America by careful contrasts with the work of Harriet Martineau. Showing the parallels and divergences of the two contemporaries' writings about America, Crawford brings a greater context to our understanding of Dickens's relationship to the commonwealth and his attitudes toward women, education, and the press. The chapter demonstrates how these two authors' responses to America were integral to the plans they made for future work when they returned home. Further, Crawford argues, "The republic they came to see, and especially the commonwealth that made such an impact upon them, thus helped to form crucial elements of the underlying conflict" between them that would break out into an open clash years later.

Taken as a whole, this volume presents a coherent tale of Dickens and Massachusetts. From the exhibition narrative of part I with its varied and rich illustrations and intriguing biographical and historical background, to the specialized chapters of part II with their careful analyses of literary and historical evidence, the book shows the important place the Commonwealth of Massachusetts held in the transatlantic world of the nineteenth century, a world of which Charles Dickens was a central—and vital—part.

Notes

1. Many critics have written about Dickens's American visits, including Michael Slater, "Introduction," in *Dickens on America and the Americans,* ed. Slater (Austin: University of Texas Press, 1978), 1–67; Sidney P. Moss, *Charles Dickens' Quarrel with America* (Troy, N.Y.: Whitson Publishing, 1984); Gerhard Joseph, "The Labyrinth and the Library: A View from the Temple in *Martin Chuzzlewit," Dickens Studies Annual* 15 (1986): 1–22; John Hildebidle, "Hail Columbia: Martin Chuzzlewit in America," *Dickens Studies Annual* 15 (1986): 41–54; David Parker, "Dickens and America: The Unflattering Glass," *Dickens Studies Annual,* 15 (1986): 55–64; Alexander Welsh, *From Copyright to Copperfield: The Identity of Dickens* (Cambridge, Mass.: Harvard University Press, 1987); Patricia M. Ard, "Charles Dickens' Stormy Crossing: The Rhetorical Voyage from Letters to *American Notes," Nineteenth Century Prose* 23 (1996): 34–42; Sidney P. Moss and Carolyn J. Moss, *American Episodes involving Charles Dickens* (Troy, N.Y.: Whitson Publishing, 1999); Robert Lougy, "Nationalism and Violence: America in Charles Dickens's *Martin Chuzzewit,*" in *Dickens and the Children of Empire,* ed. Wendy S. Jacobson (New York: Palgrave, 2000), 105–15; Nancy Aycock Metz, *The Companion to* Martin Chuzzlewit (The Banks, Mountfield, near Robertsbridge, Eng.: Helm Information, 2001); Jeremy Tambling, *Lost in the American City: Dickens, James, and Kafka* (New York: Palgrave, 2001); Efraim Sicher, *Rereading the City Rereading Dickens: Representation, the Novel, and Urban Realism* (New York: AMS, 2003); John M. L. Drew, *Dickens the Journalist* (New York: Palgrave Macmillan, 2003); Amanda Claybaugh, *The Novel of Purpose: Literature and Social Reform in the Anglo-American World* (Ithaca, N.Y.: Cornell University Press, 2007); and Juliet John, *Dickens and Mass Culture* (Oxford: Oxford University Press, 2010).

2. Jerome Meckier, *Innocent Abroad: Charles Dickens's American Engagements* (Lexington: University Press of Kentucky, 1990), ix. Not all critics agree; see, for instance, an earlier scholar, Louie Crew, in "Charles Dickens as a Critic of the United States," *The Midwest Quarterly* 16 (1974): 42–50, who recognizes, like Meckier, that the 1842 trip was "a crisis in which Dickens was forced to confront his own Englishness and his own middle-class lifestyle," but who contends that Dickens remained equally critical of the English and deeply interested in the "other America" (45). Slater, too, sees Dickens's relationship with Americans as being consistent with his other "love/hate relationship[s]" (*Dickens on America*, 67).

3. Meckier, *Innocent Abroad*, 1.

4. David Stevens, "Dickens in Eden: The Framing of America in *American Notes*," *Nineteenth-Century Prose* 23, no. 2 (Fall 1996): 43–44, 47, 51. See also Harry Stone, "Dickens' Use of His American Experience in *Martin Chuzzlewit*," *PMLA* 72, no. 3 (June 1957): 464–78.

5. See Slater, *Dickens on America*, and John, *Dickens and Mass Culture*.

6. Charles Dickens, *The Pilgrim Edition of the Letters of Charles Dickens*, 12 vols., ed. Madeline House et al. (Oxford: Clarendon Press, 1965–2002), 3:156.

7. Meckier, *Innocent Abroad*, 1.

8. Dickens, *Letters*, 3:156 and note 4; Charles Dickens, *American Notes for General Circulation*, 2 vols. (London: Chapman and Hall, 1842), 1:3.62. Citations to *American Notes* include volume number followed by a colon, and chapter and page number(s) separated by a period.

9. See Dickens, *Letters*, 3:155–56, for the reference to burning his last letter to Macready because of his "desire to be so honest and just to those who have so enthusiastically and earnestly welcomed" him to America.

10. Dickens, *Letters*, 4:11 (3 January 1844).

11. Dickens, *American Notes*, 1:4.64.

12. Meckier, *Innocent Abroad*, 1.

13. Natalie McKnight, "Dickens and Industry," *Dickens Quarterly* 19, no. 3 (2002): 133–40, 138 (quotation).

14. This exhibition won a prestigious juried award competition in September 2013; the American Association for State and Local History gave our work an Award of Merit in the category of Leadership in History, based on "excellence of scholarship" and innovative delivery.

15. Dickens, *Letters*, 3:50n.

16. Ibid., 12:80.

PART I

Exhibition

◆

Dickens and Massachusetts: A Tale of Power and Transformation
Exhibition Narrative with Illustrations

Diana C. Archibald with Joel J. Brattin

✦

What follows is the original master text for the award-winning public exhibition Dickens and Massachusetts: A Tale of Power and Transformation, *30 March 2012 through 20 October 2012 at the Lowell National Historical Park. The material we include below was written for a mixed audience of both experts interested in our claims about Dickens and Massachusetts as well as a general audience who may have had little knowledge about the author. The master script includes information not incorporated into the exhibition due to gallery space constraints, so readers will find a fuller explanation here than appeared in the exhibition at the Lowell National Historical Park in 2012 or than can be accessed through the virtual exhibition currently available online at http://library.uml.edu/dickens/exhibit/virtualtour.html. The following text presents a scholarly argument couched in terms suitable for lay and academic audiences. This essay not only shows what Dickens did, whom he met, and how he felt about the Commonwealth of Massachusetts, but also demonstrates just how important his visits were and how much his experiences shaped his vision and attitudes. The chapters that follow the exhibition text, in part II of this volume, delve even further into this impact and explore the influence of Massachusetts on Dickens's literary career.*

Introduction

In 1842 when Charles Dickens traveled to North America, he had already achieved immense fame. Blockbuster hits such as *The Pickwick Papers, Oliver Twist, Nicholas Nickleby,* and *The Old Curiosity Shop* had established the twenty-nine-year-old Dickens as the most popular writer of the era, and, in a new age of mass media culture,[1] he was the first true celebrity. People lined the docks at Boston Harbor awaiting his disembarkation from the steamship *Britannia,* a process that took almost eight hours. Crowds on the streets tried to catch a glimpse of the visiting superstar and followed him with scissors attempting to snatch a plug of his bearskin coat. The press hounded him, fans burst into his hotel room, and countless bundles of letters arrived at Tremont House within days of his arrival, requiring him to hire a secretary. While Dickens knew before arriving in the New World that he had become a famous literary man, it was the American trip that showed him the full extent of his power. After this transatlantic visit his writing demonstrated a new vigor and complexity and a heightened social consciousness. America changed him. He began to see that his role as a pop culture hero came with great responsibility. It is no coincidence that the year after he returned home, he published his iconic book, *A Christmas Carol* (December 1843), a tale of radical transformation and social responsibility. This man, understood by many as the quintessential English gentleman, was in fact deeply connected to the United States, particularly to the Commonwealth of Massachusetts.

Our exhibition narrative largely focuses on several pivotal moments in 1842, with subsections exploring the cult of celebrity and the source of the young Dickens's power, the interconnectedness of the transatlantic world, and the call for social reform. Dickens came to America to write a book about his visit to the new country, expecting to be pleased. In reality, the United States was "not the Republic of [his] imagination," but his experience in Massachusetts did not disappoint.[2] In fact, his day in Lowell was "the happiest he had passed in America."[3] Massachusetts's institutions, such as the Lowell factories and the Perkins School for the Blind, offered Dickens a view of a different way to effect change and enhanced his already strong social conscience that sought a better path forward for his own country. In Massachusetts he also formed deep and lasting friendships with several Bostonians such as Cornelius Conway Felton, Henry Wadsworth Longfellow, and James and Annie Fields; these relationships continued to exert influence over him in years to come.

Did Dickens and America live up to the great expectations people held for them? The contrast between Dickens's 1842 and 1868 trips to the United States reveals a tale of power and transformation. America had changed a great deal by the time Dickens returned in 1868. Slavery had been abolished, though the scars of the Civil War remained. Industrialization had taken hold and led to monumental economic growth as well as upheaval. America was no longer viewed as an isolated outpost and cultural wasteland. Between his two journeys to the United States, Dickens became even more wildly popular, yet he also left his wife, Catherine—the mother of his ten children—for a nineteen-year-old actress, Ellen Ternan. He lost two children, and he experienced the shock of a terrifying railway disaster. During this period, he became increasingly concerned about money and reputation, achieving tremendous popularity and financial success at the cost of ruining his health through stress and exhaustion. It is widely believed that his death at age fifty-eight, just two years after his grueling 1868 trip to America, might have been postponed if he had not undertaken the journey. The world mourned his passing, and his friends in Massachusetts had only their fond memories of his visits and his brilliant letters and literature to comfort them.

Dickens Finds His Power
The Early Years

Born on 7 February 1812, Charles John Huffam Dickens was the eldest boy of John and Elizabeth Dickens. A small and sickly child who could not play sports or active games, he took great pleasure in observing people and reading. His father was a clerk in the Navy Pay Office in Portsmouth, making a modest living to support his growing family (fig. E.1). Unfortunately, John Dickens was irresponsible with money and often got into trouble with creditors, so the family moved frequently.

When he was about five years old, Charles and his father were walking in their new neighborhood in Chatham when they spied a beautiful house on a hill, Gad's Hill Place. John turned to his son and said, "If you were to be very persevering and were to work hard, you might some day come to live in it."[4] Every time the boy passed the house in the following years, he thought of his father's words. Charles wished to grow up to be a respected and rich gentleman, and he knew that the first step was to become educated. He did well in school, but soon the family moved again, this time to a poor London suburb where Charles lived among those in wretched poverty. His family did not send him to school in London, as there was no free public education at that time in England.

At age twelve, Charles was sent to work at Warren's Blacking Warehouse (fig. E.2) at Hungerford Stairs (fig. E.3), pasting labels on boot polish bottles for six shillings a week. Shortly after this, John Dickens was arrested for unpaid debts and taken to the Marshalsea Prison (fig. E.4) where his family joined him, as was the custom. Charles lived in a

JOHN DICKENS.
(Father of Charles)

MASTER BURNETT.
The Original of Little Paul Dombey.

Figure E.1. John Dickens, ca. 1840. Reproduced by courtesy of
Charles Dickens Museum, London.

CHARLES DICKENS.——THE BOY.

Figure E.2. Charles Dickens pasted labels onto bottles in Warren's Blacking Warehouse. Reproduced by courtesy of Charles Dickens Museum, London.

boardinghouse near his work and visited his family in prison on Sundays. Humiliated and depressed, Charles felt his dream of becoming a gentleman was impossible.

The heart-wrenching legacy of this early trauma is captured in the excerpts below from "The Autobiographical Fragment," first quoted directly in John Forster's 1872 biography of Charles Dickens:

It is wonderful to me how I could have been so easily cast away at such an age. . . . [N]o one had compassion enough on me—a child of singular

Figure E.3. Hungerford Stairs, ca. 1828. Reproduced by courtesy of Charles Dickens Museum, London.

Figure E.4. Second Marshalsea Prison. Reproduced by courtesy of Charles Dickens Museum, London.

abilities, quick, eager, delicate, and soon hurt, bodily or mentally—to suggest that something might have been spared, as certainly it might have been, to place me at any common school. . . . The blacking warehouse . . . was a crazy, tumble-down old house, abutting . . . the river, and literally overrun with rats. Its wainscoted rooms, and its rotten floors and staircase, and the old grey rats swarming down in the cellars, and the sound of their squeaking and scuffling coming up the stairs at all times, and the dirt and decay of the place, rise up visibly before me, as if I were there again.[5]

As Forster notes, this early experience inspired some of Dickens's greatest work, including *David Copperfield*. This degrading experience also likely colored Dickens's feelings about the factories he visited in the Old and New Worlds: "No words can express the secret agony of my soul. . . . The deep remembrance of the sense I had of being utterly neglected and hopeless . . . cannot be written. My whole nature was so penetrated with the grief and humiliation of such considerations, that even now, famous and caressed and happy, I often forget in my dreams that I have a dear wife and children; even that I am a man; and wander desolately back to that time of my life."[6]

The man who was to become an international celebrity beyond anything the world had heretofore known carried deep scars and a realization that he was extremely fortunate to escape: "I know I do not exaggerate . . . the scantiness of my resources and the difficulties of my life. . . . I know that I have lounged about the streets, insufficiently and unsatisfactorily fed. I know that, but for the mercy of God, I might easily have been, for any care that was taken of me, a little robber or a little vagabond."[7] The fragility of his socioeconomic position as a boy surely gave rise to his deep and abiding interest in social welfare as an adult.

LITERARY FAME

After his father inherited a sum of money and was released from debtors' prison, and Charles was rescued from the blacking warehouse, Dickens was able to resume his schooling from 1824 to 1827. The Wellington House Academy and Mr. Dawson's in Henrietta Street, however, offered a poor educational experience. John Dickens once remarked when asked about his son's education, "Why, indeed, Sir—ha! ha!—he may be said to have educated himself!"[8]

At age fifteen, Charles began work as an office boy for an attorney, but he studied shorthand at night in order to become a journalist, first as a freelancer at Doctor's Commons, then as a reporter of parliamentary debates in the House of Commons for the *Mirror of Parliament*, and finally as a reporter for the newspapers the *True Sun* and the *Morning Chronicle* (fig. E.5). His work as a journalist taught him to write quickly to meet deadlines, and his excellent observational skills helped him to succeed in that profession.

His first story, "A Dinner at Poplar Walk," appeared in the *Monthly Magazine* in 1833, and in 1834 he began using the pen name Boz. The first collection of *Sketches by Boz* was published in February 1836 (fig. E.6), and based on its success, he landed his first big break, writing *The Pickwick Papers*, serialized in monthly installments from 1836 to 1837 (fig. E.7). Mr. Pickwick's comic ramblings about the country with his faithful cockney

Figure E.5. Charles Dickens, 1830, by Janet Barrow (an aunt of Charles Dickens).
Reproduced by courtesy of Charles Dickens Museum, London.

Figure E.6. Engraved title page of *Sketches by Boz*. Courtesy of Worcester Polytechnic Institute Curation, Preservation, and Archives, George C. Gordon Library.

Figure E.7. "The Valentine," from the first edition of *The Pickwick Papers*.
Courtesy of Worcester Polytechnic Institute Curation, Preservation, and Archives,
George C. Gordon Library.

servant, Sam Weller, captured the public imagination, and the novel became a huge international hit, launching Dickens's career as a full-time novelist.[9]

Well beloved for his comic portraits of a wide range of characters from the middle and working classes, Dickens was praised for the faithfulness of his representations. Always a keen observer, he had a knack for capturing people in print, a talent that he often put to use in his biting social critiques. He was a tireless advocate for the poor and disadvantaged, and became famous for his relentless attacks on hypocrisy wherever he found it: in schools, churches, social welfare institutions, or government.

MARRIED LIFE

With the success of his first novel, *The Pickwick Papers,* Charles Dickens (fig. E.8) was able to marry and start a family. His wife, Catherine Hogarth (fig. E.9), a cultured and well-read Scotswoman, was the daughter of

Figure E.8. Charles Dickens, 1837, by Samuel Laurence. Reproduced by courtesy of Charles Dickens Museum, London.

Figure E.9. Catherine Dickens, 1837, by Samuel Laurence. Reproduced by
courtesy of Charles Dickens Museum, London.

Georgina Thomson and Edinburgh solicitor George Hogarth, who had
turned from law to journalism in the early 1830s and moved his family to
London. Hogarth, a newspaper editor, introduced Catherine to Dickens,
then an aspiring young journalist, and the two wed in 1836.

By the fall of 1841, Charles had made up his mind to travel to North
America as a tourist, planning to write a travel book about the young
republic on his return to England. He insisted that his wife join him, but
Catherine was reluctant, fearing to leave behind their four small chil-
dren, the youngest not yet one year old. She cried "dismally" every time
Dickens mentioned the subject.[10] After some cajoling and persuasion,

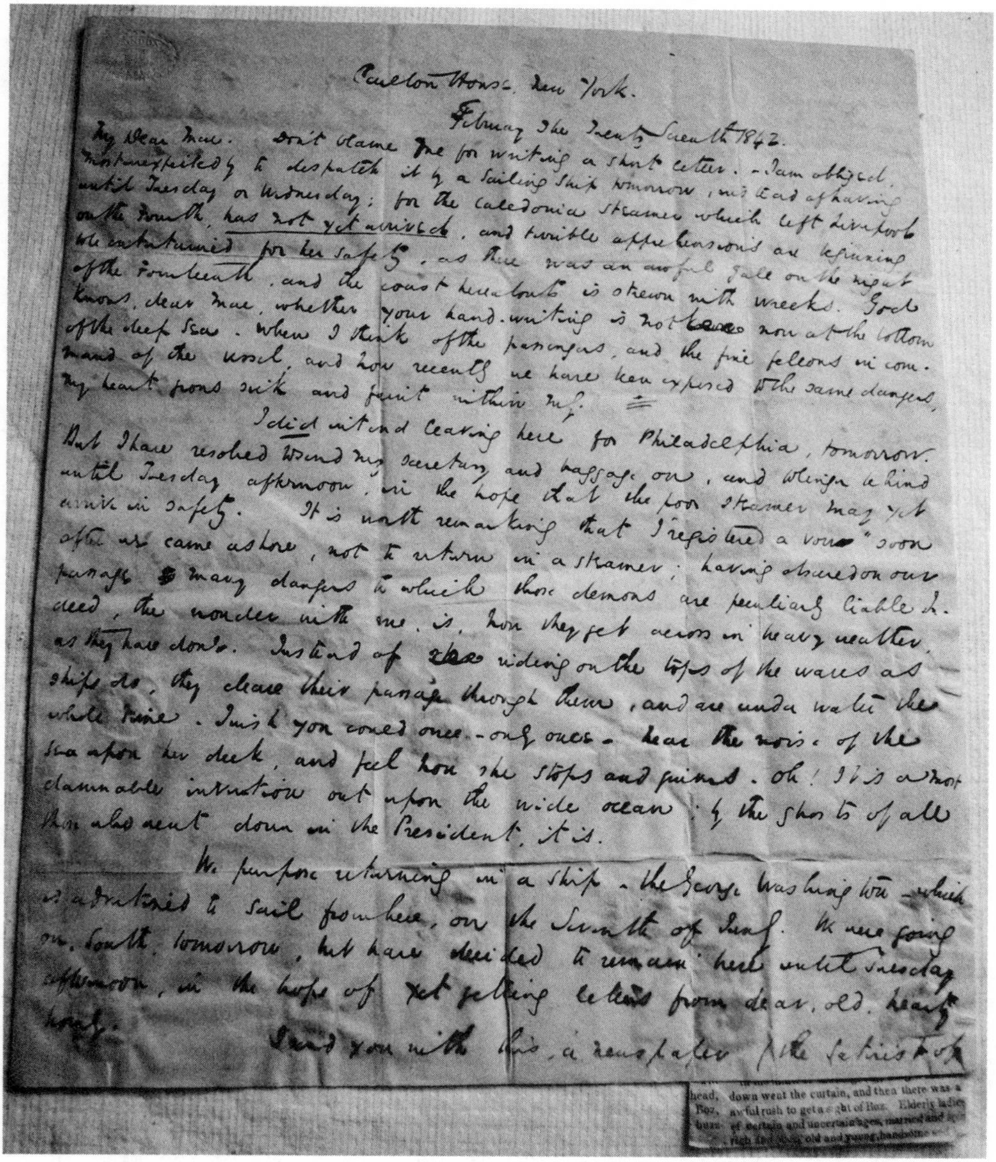

Figure E.10. This letter, written by Dickens on 27 February 1842 to his friend Daniel Maclise, includes a description of their travels and refers to Maclise's portrait of the Dickens children (see fig. E.12). Reproduced by courtesy of Charles Dickens Museum, London.

Figure E.11. This page of the letter includes clippings of American newspaper articles about the Boz Ball and dinner, and a stock image of a lady claimed to be Mrs. Dickens but looking nothing like her. Reproduced by courtesy of Charles Dickens Museum, London.

however, she agreed to do her duty by her husband and go along. She would be troubled by her sense of maternal "truancy" throughout their trip, though. Charles, too, was clearly concerned about the dangers of the voyage. He bought extra life insurance policies before they left to secure his children's future if the worst should happen and their parents should perish on the hazardous journey.

Terrified by the storm that disrupted their Atlantic crossing and longing for home and her children once safely on shore, Catherine nonetheless made the best of her situation as Dickens's companion. Although she was bitten by fleas and hounded by strangers on their travels, and required to attend dozens of balls and dinners and shake hands with thousands of people, she earned her husband's praise for having "always accommodated herself, well and cheerfully, to everything."[11] As Catherine put it to her sister-in-law Fanny Burnett, writing from Boston, "The people are most hospitable, and we shall both be killed with kindness. We are constantly out two or three times in the evening" (figs. E.10, E.11).[12]

American Views of Catherine

Among the Americans who met and scrutinized the wife of the famous English novelist, responses to Catherine Dickens were varied. Some Bostonians found her more genteel than her loudly dressed, "cockney" husband and believed she "showed signs of having been born and bred [his] social superior."[13] In Washington, D.C., Priscilla Cooper Tyler, the president's daughter-in-law, found Catherine "more English looking than Boz himself."[14] John Quincy Adams paid tribute to Catherine in a poem he wrote in her honor, and spoke of his pleasure and "good fortune" in meeting her, while Senator John Calhoun praised the novelist's wife for her feminine domesticity.[15] As Calhoun told his daughter, Catherine was "amiable and sensible, of which . . . she gave proof by continuing at her needle all the time, when I visited them in the morning, except when she took part in the conversation."[16] Bostonian George Putnam, hired to serve as Dickens's secretary throughout the tour, offered this description of Catherine's appearance and manner:

> Mrs. Dickens was a lady of moderate height; with a full, well-developed form, a beautiful face and good figure. I call to mind the high, full fore-head, the brown hair gracefully arranged, the look of English healthful-ness in the warm glow of color in her cheeks, the blue eyes with a tinge of violet, well-arched brows, a well-shaped nose, and a mouth small and of uncommon beauty. She was decidedly a handsome woman, and would have attracted notice as such in any gathering of ladies anywhere. She had a quiet dignity mingled with great sweetness of manner; her calm quiet-ness differing much from the quick, earnest, always cheerful, but keen and nervous temperament of her husband,—a temperament belonging to the existence, and absolutely necessary to the development, of a great genius like that of Charles Dickens.[17]

The Dickens Children

Charles and Catherine Dickens had ten children, many of whom bore the names of famous authors as well as of friends and family of the couple:

Charles Culliford Boz Dickens (6 January 1837–20 July 1896)

Mary "Mamie" Angela Dickens (6 March 1838–23 July 1896)

Catherine "Kate" Elizabeth Macready Dickens Perugini (29 October 1839–9 May 1929)

Walter Savage Landor Dickens (8 February 1841–31 December 1863)

Francis Jeffrey Dickens (15 January 1844–11 June 1886)

Alfred D'Orsay Tennyson Dickens (28 October 1845–2 January 1912)

Sydney Smith Haldimand Dickens (18 April 1847–2 May 1872)

Henry Fielding Dickens (16 January 1849–21 December 1933)

Dora Annie Dickens (16 August 1850–14 April 1851)

Edward "Plorn" Bulwer Lytton Dickens (13 March 1852–23 January 1902)

On their trip to America in 1842, the Dickenses brought a portrait of their four children left at home (fig. E.12). Dickens's secretary, George Putnam, wrote about this portrait in his memoir:

Figure E.12. Charles and Catherine Dickens carried Daniel Maclise's 1841 portrait of Charley, Mamie, Katie, and Walter Dickens, with Grip the raven, to America in 1842. Courtesy of John Dickens and Charles Dickens Museum, London.

Mrs. Dickens felt all a mother's anxiety for the little ones left at home, and seemed impatient to return to them. They brought from England a large pencil-drawing of their four children, "Charles, Walter, Kate, and Mary," made by their friend Maclise, the eminent English artist. The picture was framed, and wherever we afterwards went it was at once taken from its case and placed on the mantel-piece or table. Mr. and Mrs. Dickens talked constantly of their children, and seemed to derive great comfort from the pictured presence of their little ones. The picture possessed also great attraction for the thousands who called, and who were much interested, of course, in the children of their distinguished visitors.[18]

Bridging Two Worlds
CROSSING THE ATLANTIC

In the digital age, it takes less than a minute to send an e-mail to the other side of the Atlantic. The World Wide Web connects people across the globe and provides us with an astounding amount of information, literally at our fingertips. In January 1842, when Charles and Catherine Dickens visited North America, there were only two means of transatlantic communication available: mail a letter or travel in person (fig. E.13). An effective transatlantic cable was not installed until 1865, limiting telegrams to domestic use only. The telephone had not yet been invented, and transatlantic calls via radio signal were not possible until 1927.

Letters were expensive to send, with charges calculated on the basis of both weight and distance traveled. Even the domestic post was pricey, especially prior to the invention of the penny post in 1840. Previous to that time, a letter sent from London to Liverpool might cost the equivalent of nearly eight dollars per ounce in today's terms, and cross-Atlantic letters could be up to fifteen times more than that.[19] Further, before 1840 it was the recipient who paid for receiving a letter. With the reform of 1840, costs were lowered and standardized, helping to foster economic growth by providing a cheaper way to conduct business. Still, even with the penny post, mailing a transatlantic letter from Great Britain would run around nine dollars per ounce in modern-day terms.

To save money, some correspondents "crossed" their letters, writing on the page, rotating the sheet of paper ninety degrees, and then writing directly on top of the other script, crossing over the other text at a right angle (fig. E.14). To our eyes the result looks chaotic and messy, but crossed letters used half the paper of a regular letter and were often

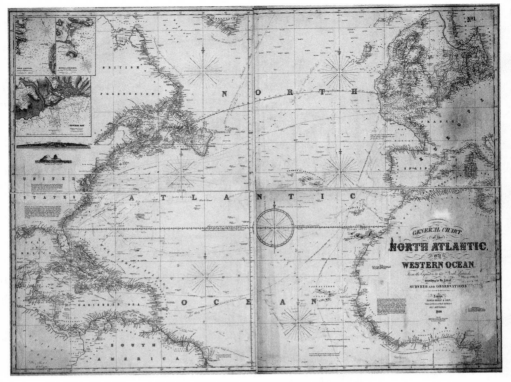

Figure E.13. Navigational chart of the Atlantic Ocean.
Map reproduction courtesy of the Norman B. Leventhal Map Center
at the Boston Public Library.

used for transatlantic correspondence. Catherine Dickens used crossing to write home to her brother-in-law Fred Dickens, who was looking after the children. She had to wait many weeks to hear news of her darling children and was always anxious lest something terrible happen to them in her absence. Exchanging letters was an essential feature of the transatlantic travel experience, and crossed texts were common with female letter writers. Charles did not cross letters; only Catherine used the technique.

The British & North American Royal Mail Steam Packet Company

During the colonial period, the British government operated its own monthly mail brigs from England to New York. These ships carried no cargo and few private passengers. By the early 1800s, clipper ships and sailing packets began running other routes and carrying both mail and passengers. Sailing ships took from three to six weeks, or longer, to make the crossing from England to the United States, depending on weather. Due to the unreliability and the danger of such crossings, delivering the

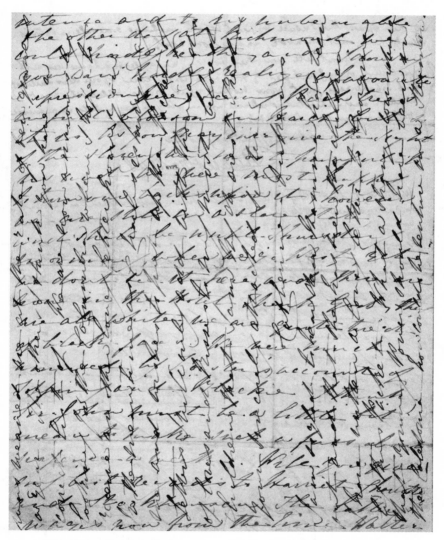

Figure E.14. Catherine Dickens wrote to her brother-in-law Fred Dickens on 22 March 1842, utilizing the crossed style to save space. Courtesy of Mark Dickens and the Berg Collection, New York Public Library.

Figure E.15. The *Britannia* in Boston Harbor. Courtesy of the Boston Museum of Fine Arts.

mail was very expensive. In 1836 Parliament decided that Post Office
ships should be replaced with private contractors, and the newly invented
steamship became an attractive alternative with its twelve-day journey.
In 1839 Samuel Cunard won the first British transatlantic steamship mail
contract, and in 1840 he formed the British and North American Royal
Mail Steam Packet Company to operate four paddle steamers, including
the *Britannia* (fig. E.15).

In the early 1840s steamships carried relatively few passengers, with
only sixty-eight on board the *Britannia* during Dickens's journey. Since
steamship technology was still quite new, the ship builders combined
both steam and sail in one vessel, hedging their bets against problems
with either system. The ship's design was not created with passenger hospitality in mind but rather speed of mail delivery, so it is no wonder that
Dickens found the voyage uncomfortable. His negative portrait of transatlantic travel in the second chapter of *American Notes* proved so powerful
that Cunard strove for generations to overcome the unfavorable image
Boz had bestowed on the company. Even though ships grew in power,

Figure E.16. This sketch of Dickens's cabin on the *Britannia* was used in Cunard advertising materials juxtaposed against a luxurious image of its fleet's modern facilities to combat the unfavorable image of transatlantic travel created by Dickens in *American Notes*. Courtesy of Christie Jackson.

size, and luxury by the dawn of the twentieth century, Dickens's legacy still had to be combated in marketing materials (fig. E.16).

Departure

It was common practice for literary figures to write travel books about America, usually critical of American manners and customs. Such books were familiar enough, in fact, that Dickens could joke about them in his first novel, *The Pickwick Papers.* When Mr. Pickwick is imprisoned, Mr. Weller, Sr., suggests that they smuggle him out of prison in a fake piano and send him to America. Once across the Atlantic, Mr. Pickwick is sure to be safe since "the 'Merrikin gov'ment vill never give him up, ven vunce they finds as he's got money to spend." Of course, upon his return, he would "write a book about the 'Merrikins as'll pay all his expenses and more, if he blows 'em up enough."[20] Dickens copied out this passage the day before his thirtieth birthday, during his first visit to Worcester, Massachusetts (fig. E.17).

The idea of going to America and publishing a travel book had thus been on Dickens's mind for quite some time when he finally determined to go. In September 1841 Dickens received a letter from author Washington Irving with assurances that if Dickens would make the trip, "it would be a triumph . . . from one end of the States to the other, as was never known in any nation." Dickens was "haunted by visions of America, night and day," yearning to see the great experimental democracy across the sea.[21] Despite the usual anti-American stance of most travel books, Dickens expected to love America and to write a positive account.

In the late 1830s and early 1840s, however, tensions between the United States and England were running high. Massive American loan defaults ruined dozens of British financial institutions that had lent money to the United States. Since America could not pay back the money it had borrowed from English banks and investors, those investors could not pay their shareholders and refused to offer additional loans. Many British citizens were ruined by the American economic collapse, and resentment rose on both sides of the Atlantic. To make matters worse, ongoing border disputes about Canada (including raids, arson, and murder) made the political situation extremely volatile. As diplomats struggled to defuse the escalating crisis, Dickens decided to go to America himself—some hoped as an ambassador of good will in his own right. The title of the book that Dickens wrote about his travels, *American Notes for General Circulation,* offers a punning allusion to the financial crisis, "notes" being the British word for "bills" or paper money.

Leaving Liverpool

In 1842 almost all transatlantic passengers still crossed by sailing ship, leaving from docks on the Thames River, east of the capital. Such a port would have been most convenient for the London couple, but after some

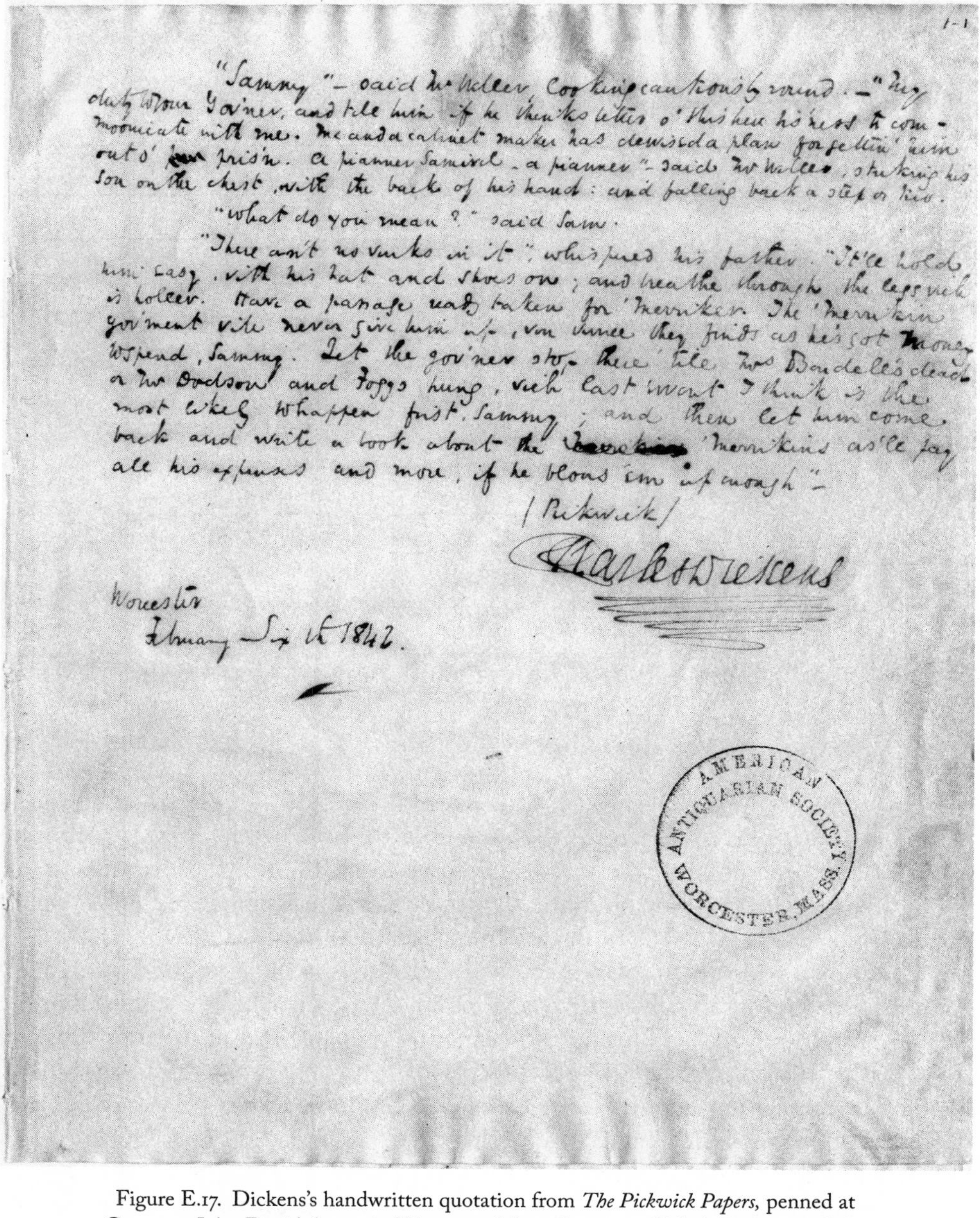

"Sammy"— said Mr Weller, cocking his cautious'ly round.—"My duty to your gov'ner, and tell him if he thinks better o' this here his'ness to communicate with me. Me and a cabinet maker has deviss'd a plan for gettin' him out o' pris'n. A pianner Samivel— a pianner"— said Mr Weller, striking his son on the chest with the back of his hand: and falling back a step or two.

"What do you mean?" said Sam.

"There ain't no vurks in it"; whispered his father. "It'll hold him easy, with his hat and shoes on; and breathe through the legs vich is holler. Have a passage ready taken for 'Merriker. The 'Merriker gov'ment vile never give him up, ven vunce they finds as he's got no money to spend, Sammy. Let the gov'ner stop there tile Mrs Bardell's dead or Mr Dodson and Fogg's hung, vich last event I think is the most likely to happen first, Sammy; and then let him come back and write a book about the ~~Merrikins~~ 'Merrikins as'll pay all his expenses and more, if he blows 'em up enough"—

(Pickwick)

Charles Dickens

Worcester
February Six th 1842.

Figure E.17. Dickens's handwritten quotation from *The Pickwick Papers*, penned at Governor John Davis's house in Worcester, Mass. Courtesy of Mark Dickens and the American Antiquarian Society.

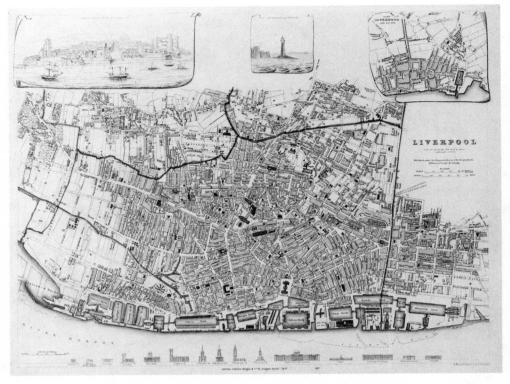

Figure E.18. Map of Liverpool. Map reproduction courtesy of the Norman B. Leventhal Map Center at the Boston Public Library.

intense research, Dickens chose a more distant point of embarkation in order to take advantage of the most technologically advanced mode of transportation available in his day—the steamship. Dickens settled on the British and North American Royal Mail Steam Packet Company's *Britannia*, scheduled to depart from Liverpool on 4 January 1842 (fig. E.18). The largest provincial town in England at the time, with a high population growth rate, Liverpool also had one of the highest mortality rates in Britain.[22] Housing and sanitation problems led to overcrowding and disease, especially near the docks. Despite these problems, Liverpool was an exciting city that appealed to the energetic Dickens. Nearly 40 percent of the world's trade was passing through Liverpool, and many new buildings were being erected in the 1830s and 1840s. Lime Street Railway Station, where they arrived in town, had opened in 1836 (fig. E.19). The Coburg Dock, used by the *Britannia*, was only completed in 1840, and the massive Albert Dock project had just begun in 1841 (fig. E.20).

Figure E.19. Charles and Catherine arrived in Liverpool at the Lime Street Station, built in 1836. Courtesy of the Liverpool Record Office, Liverpool Libraries.

Figure E.20. The Liverpool docks, where Charles and Catherine boarded the *Britannia*, were bustling. Courtesy of the Lowell National Historical Park.

The Passage

Charles Dickens described his cabin aboard the *Britannia* as being an "utterly impracticable, thoroughly hopeless, and profoundly preposterous box," so cramped that his luggage fit as easily into his room as a "giraffe could be persuaded or forced into a flower-pot." His unfavorable descriptions continued with the public spaces onboard ship, noting how the lounge was like "a gigantic hearse with windows in the sides."[23] Seasickness, a common complaint of travelers, struck Catherine and Charles for nearly a week. Vessels of this time were cramped and dark, and lacked anything but the most basic passenger amenities. Adjustable oil lamps, unstable and dirty, were the only light source besides small portholes. Passengers lived out of their trunks, as there were no closets. In-cabin basins offered limited washing facilities. Cabins were unheated, smelly, and drafty.

While some of Dickens's observations may seem harsh, crossing the Atlantic in 1842 was indeed a dangerous and uncomfortable undertaking. At 1,154 tons and 207 feet long, the *Britannia* was a large vessel for its time, but it was barely a match for the treacherous seas and gale-force winds encountered during a typical fourteen-day passage across the Atlantic. During this particular crossing, the ship faced a winter hurricane, making this an exceptionally perilous journey. The steam engine's furnace itself posed a significant risk of fire on board the wooden vessel. If the ship's big red "funnel" chimneystack were to blow over in a storm, the fire could quickly engulf the ship in flames. Still, for all its dangers, the *Britannia* offered the latest in steam-driven, side-paddle propulsion, a big step up from sailing vessels that were solely dependent on the wind for power.

Dickens brings the terrifying voyage to life in *American Notes* with this evocative description of the sounds of the ship during the storm:

> Imagine the ship herself, with every pulse and artery of her huge body swoln and bursting under this mal-treatment, sworn to go on or die. Imagine the wind howling, the sea roaring, the rain beating: all in furious array against her. Picture the sky both dark and wild, and the clouds, in fearful sympathy with the waves, making another ocean in the air. Add to all this, the clattering on deck and down below; the tread of hurried feet; the loud hoarse shouts of seamen; the gurgling in and out of water through the scuppers; with, every now and then, the striking of a heavy sea upon the planks above, with the deep, dead, heavy sound of thunder heard within a vault. . . .

I say nothing of what may be called the domestic noises of the ship: such as the breaking of glass and crockery, the tumbling down of stewards, the gambols, overhead, of loose casks and truant dozens of bottled porter, and the very remarkable and far from exhilarating sounds raised in their various state-rooms by the seventy passengers who were too ill to get up to breakfast.[24]

The Atlantic crossing of the *Britannia* nearly tore the ship to pieces. Dickens's account helps readers to imagine the absolute helplessness of the passengers, at the mercy of the hurricane:

A heavy gale of wind . . . came slowly up at sunset, when we were about ten days out, and raged with gradually increasing fury. . . . But what the agitation of a steam-vessel is, on a bad winter's night in the wild Atlantic, it is impossible for the most vivid imagination to conceive. . . . To say that she is flung down on her side in the waves, with her masts dipping into them, and that, springing up again, she rolls over on the other side, until a heavy sea strikes her with the noise of a hundred great guns, and hurls her back—that she stops, and staggers, and shivers, as though stunned, and then, with a violent throbbing at her heart, darts onward like a monster goaded into madness, to be beaten down, and battered, and crushed, and leaped on by the angry sea—that thunder, lightning, hail, and rain, and wind, are all in fierce contention for the mastery—that every plank has its groan, every nail its shriek, and every drop of water in the great ocean its howling voice—is nothing. To say that all is grand, and all appalling and horrible in the last degree, is nothing. Words cannot express it. Thoughts cannot convey it. Only a dream can call it up again, in all its fury, rage, and passion.[25]

ARRIVAL

With battered lifeboats strapped to the beleaguered ship, the *Britannia* entered the port of Boston eighteen days after leaving Liverpool and docked around 5 p.m. on Saturday, 22 January 1842, just after sunset. For several hours before that, Dickens had been watching the shoreline, harbor islands, and cityscape. As he writes in *American Notes*, "The indescribable interest with which I strained my eyes, as the first patches of American soil peeped like molehills from the green sea, and followed them, as they swelled . . . into a continuous line of coast, can hardly be exaggerated."[26] The *Britannia* aimed for Long Wharf, in the heart of the waterside district, at the foot of one of the main commercial roads

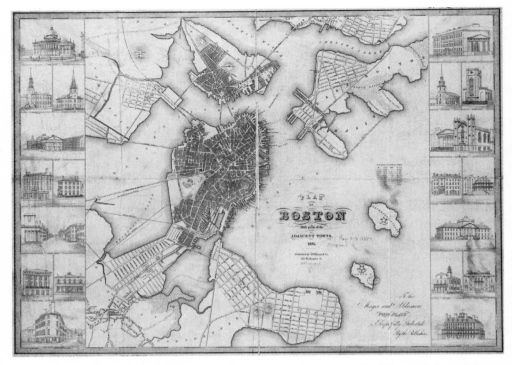

Figure E.21. Map of Boston in 1842. Map reproduction courtesy of the Norman B. Leventhal Map Center at the Boston Public Library.

downtown, State Street, only a few blocks from the Custom House (fig. E.21). As Dickens and Captain John Hewitt watched the ship slowly dock, suddenly, long before they "were moored to the wharf, a dozen men came leaping on board at the peril of their lives."[27] One of these leaping newspaper editors, a Dr. Palmer of the *Boston Transcript*, finding that Dickens had not "engaged" any hotel rooms yet, jumped off the boat and took a cab to Tremont House to secure rooms for the party.[28]

What welcome did Dickens receive beyond the pack of leaping, pushy, hand-pumping newspaper editors? "No sooner was it known that the steamer with Dickens on board was in sight, than the Town was pouring itself out upon the wharf; and when this remarkable man reached the Boston side, the 'hacknies' were all calling out, each anxious to have the honor to carry Boz. . . . For days the streets were a flutter with ribbons & feathers."[29] Once the gangplank was lowered, the painter Francis Alexander, with whom Dickens had corresponded before arriving, came on board and "took charge of the party." He had brought a carriage, which promptly took them to the Tremont, where they found another crowd of admirers had gathered in front of the hotel. Tremont House had achieved

Figure E.22. Tremont House served as Dickens's Boston headquarters.
Courtesy of the Boston Public Library.

an international reputation for luxury and "was the pioneer first-class hotel in America" in 1842, with many hotel innovations such as bellboys, free soap, indoor plumbing, and running water (fig. E.22).[30]

Boston in 1842

Boston was a small city in 1842, with about 95,000 inhabitants in the smallest square acreage of any major city of the time. Like Liverpool, the population of the city had more than doubled in the twenty years before Dickens arrived, but the city fathers had decided early on that if Boston were to maintain its position as the center of arts and literature for the nation, and a leader of commerce and the maritime industry, the city needed to invest in public works.[31] In the first decade after being declared a city (1822), Boston underwent extensive improvements such as the installation of sewers and gaslights under the leadership of mayor Josiah Quincy. Boston boasted eight different railroad stations, two major theaters, and several other places of amusement.[32] The "Athens of America" that Dickens visited in 1842, like Liverpool, was booming.[33] Amid this thriving though by no means perfect city, Boz found a hero's welcome. Writing to John Forster, he said, "It makes my heart quieter, and me a more retiring, sober, tranquil man to watch the effect of . . . [my flights of imagination] in all this noise and hurry." Through all that Dickens subsequently experienced in the New World, Boston would remain his ideal. "Boston is what I would have the whole United States to be," Dickens wrote to his friend, William Macready.[34] But Boston was *not* the rest of America.

Dickens Takes a Walk

Although Dickens writes in *American Notes* that, due to arriving after dark, "I received my first impressions of the city in walking down to the Custom-house on the morning after our arrival," this was not really the case.[35] In fact, Dickens and his shipboard friend, Lord Mulgrave, decided to take a peek at the city in a midnight ramble. Those who know of Boz's habitual night strolls will not be surprised to learn that Dickens braved the streets of Boston on that first winter evening. As fate would have it, a young James T. Fields, who would later become Dickens's dear friend and American publisher, was loitering in the hotel lobby with his friends, hoping to catch another glimpse of the celebrity. Their plan was rewarded when Boz and Mulgrave descended to the lobby once more and left the building. Fields writes:

> It was a stinging night and the moon was at the full. Every object stood out sharp and glittering, and "Boz" muffled up in a shaggy fur coat ran over the shining frozen snow, wisely keeping the middle of the street for the most part. We boys followed cautiously behind, but near enough not to lose any of the fun. Of course the two gentlemen soon lost their way on emerging into Washington from Tremont Street.... Dickens kept up one continual shout of uproarious laughter as he went rapidly forward, reading the signs on the shops and observing the architecture of the new country into which he had dropped as from the clouds.[36]

Dickens Takes a Seat

Early in his visit, Dickens was obliged to sit for a promised portrait by his new friend Francis Alexander (see book cover). Alexander's wife had encouraged her husband to write to Dickens in London and offer to paint his portrait, and, in fact, Alexander was the only American who was able to paint Boz on the 1842 trip. Dickens's American secretary, George Putnam, reported the scene when Dickens arrived for his first sitting at Alexander's Boston studio:

> Mr. Dickens had appointed ten o'clock, on the Tuesday morning succeeding his arrival, for his first sitting to Alexander. The artist's rooms were at No. 41 Tremont Row, not far from the Tremont House. The newspapers

had announced the fact, and, long before the appointed hour, a crowd of people were around the hotel and arranged along the sidewalk to see him pass. The doorway and stairs leading to the painter's studio were thronged with ladies and gentlemen, eagerly awaiting his appearance.... He pleasantly acknowledged the compliment their presence paid him, bowing slightly as he passed, his bright, dark eyes glancing through and through the crowd, searching every face, and reading character with wonderful quickness, while the arch smiles played over his handsome face.

The engravings in his books which had then been issued either in England or America were very little like him. Alexander chose an attitude highly original, but very characteristic.... The pen in his right hand seems to have been stopped for a moment, while he looks up at you as if you had just addressed him. His long brown hair, slightly curling, sweeps his shoulder, the bright eyes glance, and that inexpressible look of kindly mirth plays round his mouth and shows itself in the arched brow. Alexander caught much of that singular lighting up of the face which Dickens had, beyond any one I ever saw, and the picture is very like the original, and will convey to those who wish to know how "Boz" looked at thirty years of age an excellent idea of the man.[37]

A MAN OF POWER

Only a few days after his arrival in Boston, Dickens wrote to a friend back home: "There never was a King or Emperor upon the Earth, so cheered, and followed by crowds, and entertained in Public at splendid balls and dinners, and waited on by public bodies and deputations of all kinds."[38]

In 1842 when Charles Dickens arrived in Massachusetts, he was already world-renowned as the author of *The Pickwick Papers, Oliver Twist, Nicholas Nickleby, The Old Curiosity Shop,* and *Barnaby Rudge;* the literary man was as much a celebrity as any pop star today (fig. E.23). As Dickens's letters show, he was initially overwhelmed and flattered by the interest of his American fans. Writing to his dear friend John Forster, again from Boston, Dickens remarked, "How can I give you the faintest notion of my reception here; of the crowds that pour in and out the whole day; of the people that line the streets when I go out; of the cheering when I went to the theatre; of the copies of verses, letters of congratulation, welcomes of all kinds, balls, dinners, assemblies without end?" (figs. E.24, E.25).[39]

Dickens was not exaggerating. The press pestered him for interviews, and strangers attempted to meet him by entering his hotel room. Once his residence at Tremont House became known, he was also inundated with correspondence—he received requests for countless autographs (all given), invitations for him to edit book manuscripts, a plea for him to write an original epitaph for the tombstone of a dead child, and summonses to hundreds of proposed dinners. He quickly became overwhelmed and asked for advice from Francis Alexander, who recommended that he hire George Putnam for assistance. Clearly Dickens enjoyed the attention at

ARRIVAL OF CHARLES DICKENS.

Among the passengers in the Britannia, came CHARLES DICKENS, Esq., the most popular author living. The whole American people will delight to extend a cordial welcome to one who is, in every respect, a true man—who combines the highest intellectual endowments with those genial feelings which prompt him to use his great endowments for the good of his race. To no living man is the world more indebted, than to Dickens, for putting down that school of misanthropy and false sentimentality, established by Byron—and which has, until lately, numbered too many pupils. We heartily welcome the man who has so often delighted us with his inimitable humor—who is next only to Shakspeare in the truthfulness of his characters—and who has enlarged the circle of our sympathies and made us feel a greater interest in all that concerns humanity.

OUR FOREIGN PAPERS. Besides our regular files of European papers received by the Britannia, which were very ample, we have been favored by others from our friends, among whom, we acknowledge the politeness of Mr T. Motley, Jr., Capt. Hewitt, of the Britannia, and also of the Purser. We were favored, also, with a copy of the European from Mr Snelling Powell.

STEAMSHIPS.—The Caledonia, Capt. Lott, hence, arrived at Liverpool on the 15th ult. and the Acadia, Capt. Ryrie, hence, also arrived at Liverpool on the 31st ult.

No Steamboat mail was received yesterday from New York. The Steamboat Narragansett, on leaving Stonington on Friday night last, ran on a sand bank, which compelled her to put into New London, and to return to Stonington, from whence she steered off yesterday morning for New York, and may be expected on her return this morning.

NAVAL. The U. S. frigate Macedonian, Com. Wilkinson, sailed from St. Thomas on the 4th inst. for St. Jago de Cuba.

Figure E.23. The arrival of the twenty-nine-year-old Dickens and his wife in Boston was widely reported in Boston's newspapers, including this selection from the *Boston Atlas*. Courtesy of the American Antiquarian Society.

Figure E.24. A sumptuous affair at a Boston hall in 1842, the dinner at Papanti's was the social climax of Dickens's stay in Boston. Reproduced by courtesy of Charles Dickens Museum, London.

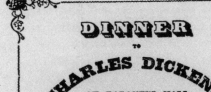

DINNER
TO
CHARLES DICKENS,
AT PAPANTI'S HALL,
February 1, 1842.

BILL OF FARE.

SOUPS.
Consommé.
Purée au Croutons.

FISH.
Cod's Head and Oyster Sauce.
Bass, Sauce Holandaise.
Baked Cod Fish, Sauce au Vin de Madére.
Pickerel — English Soles.

RÉLÉVES.
Turkey, Sauce aux Huitres.
Ham, Sauce au Vin de Champagne.
Filets de Bœuf, garni d'atelettes.

PIÈCES FROIDES.
Salade de Volaille au jardinière.
Des Huitres en aspec.
Pates Foie à la Perigrue.
Perdrix au Choux au Sorbreux.

ENTRÉES.
Tête de Veau en Tortue.
Vol au Vent aux Huitres.
Ris de Veau en Casse.
Suprême de Volaille.
Casserolle au Pommes de Terre, garni d'Oiseau.
Fricandeau de Veau, Sauce au petits Pois.
Anguille a la Tartare.
Timbale de Macaroni à la Milanaise.
Canton de Volaille à la Royale.

HORS D'ŒUVRES.
Salade d'Homard,		Chou Croute,
de Volaille,		Cornichons,
Olives,		Sardines.
	Céleri.	

ROAST.
Beef,		Mongrel Geese,
Saddle Mutton,		Partridges,
Turkey,		Quail,
Chickens,		Brandt,
Ducks,		Canvas Back Ducks.

ENTREMETS DE LÉGUMES.
Petits Pois,		Epinards,
Celeri au jus,		Pommes de Terre au gratin,
Choux fleur au gratin,		Navets au sucre.

ENTREMETS AU SUCRE.
Tartelettes de Pommes.
Charlotte Russe a la Conti.
Charlotte Russe au Marasquin.
Omelettes Soufflée.
Gelée au Rhum.
Blancmanger au Creme d'Amandes.

DESSERT.
Fruits—Ice Creams—Roman Punch—Ice Orange Water, &c.
Café et Liqueur.

DICKINSON, PRINTER.

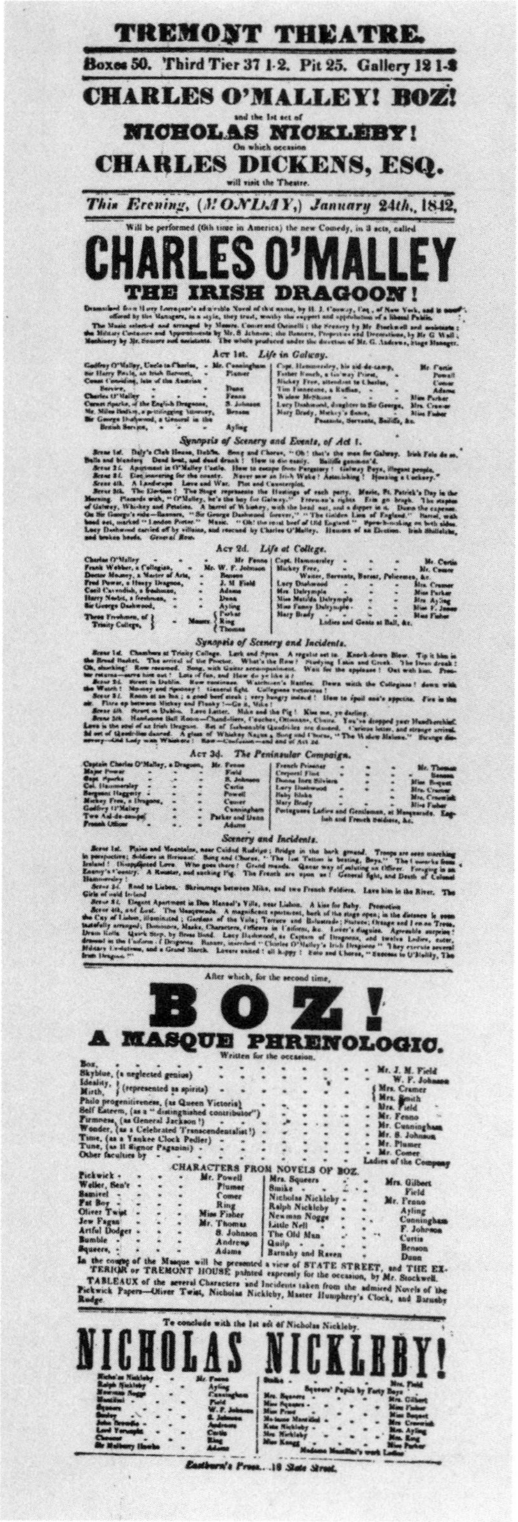

TREMONT THEATRE.

Boxes 50. Third Tier 37 1-2. Pit 25. Gallery 12 1-2

CHARLES O'MALLEY! BOZ!

and the 1st act of

NICHOLAS NICKLEBY!

On which occasion

CHARLES DICKENS, ESQ.

will visit the Theatre.

This Evening, (MONDAY,) January 24th., 1842,

Will be performed (6th time in America) the new Comedy, in 3 acts, called

CHARLES O'MALLEY

THE IRISH DRAGOON!

Act 1st. Life in Galway.

Synopsis of Scenery and Events, of Act 1.

Act 2d. Life at College.

Synopsis of Scenery and Incidents.

Act 3d. The Peninsular Campaign.

Scenery and Incidents.

After which, for the second time,

BOZ!

A MASQUE PHRENOLOGIC.

Written for the occasion.

CHARACTERS FROM NOVELS OF BOZ.

To conclude with the 1st act of Nicholas Nickleby.

NICHOLAS NICKLEBY!

Eastburn's Press...18 State Street.

Figure E.25. The Dickenses were invited to an evening at Boston's Tremont Theatre, where they saw an original work, *Boz: A Masque Phrenologic,* and the first act of an adaptation of *Nicholas Nickleby.* Courtesy of the Lowell Historical Society.

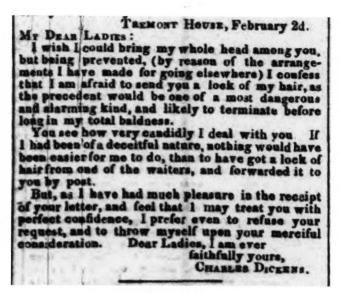

TREMONT HOUSE, February 2d.

MY DEAR LADIES:

I wish I could bring my whole head among you, but being prevented, (by reason of the arrangements I have made for going elsewhere) I confess that I am afraid to send you a lock of my hair, as the precedent would be one of a most dangerous and alarming kind, and likely to terminate before long in my total baldness.

You see how very candidly I deal with you. If I had been of a deceitful nature, nothing would have been easier for me to do, than to have got a lock of hair from one of the waiters, and forwarded it to you by post.

But, as I have had much pleasure in the receipt of your letter, and feel that I may treat you with perfect confidence, I prefer even to refuse your request, and to throw myself upon your merciful consideration. Dear Ladies, I am ever

faithfully yours,
CHARLES DICKENS.

Figure E.26. Dickens responded, in charming style, to a request from "Unknown Ladies of Plymouth" for a lock of his hair. Dickens received hundreds of similar requests throughout the trip. Courtesy of fultonhistory.com.

first and could look on his stardom with a bit of humor—as can be seen in his response to the Ladies of Plymouth in answer to their request for a lock of his hair (fig. E.26). As the trip wore on, however, the invasions of privacy and constant demands of the public began to wear on the Dickenses. Celebrity gave him power, but he paid a price for his popularity and influence.

A Magnetic Personality

Many felt drawn to Dickens, who was often described as a charismatic figure. Catherine Dickens deferred to her husband's powers, literary and otherwise, embracing her subordinate position. "I will not pretend to give you any account, dear Fan, of the manners and customs, and so on," she wrote to Fanny Burnett from Boston, "as my powers of description are not great, and you will have it some day or other so much the better from Charles."[40] In what was perhaps the most striking instance of Catherine's wifely submission on the tour, she twice allowed her husband to mesmerize her in the company of two male observers. Dickens was fascinated by mesmerism, an early form of hypnosis also known as "animal magnetism," having seen it demonstrated repeatedly in London by Dr. John Elliotson (fig. E.27), the leading mesmerist of the day.[41] Elliotson was, in fact, the Dickenses' family doctor and godfather to their second son. It was in America that Dickens decided to "try [his] hand" on his wife. His success at controlling her consciousness was so "sudden and complete" that he was both delighted and alarmed by his ability "to exercise the influence" (fig. E.28).[42] Although Catherine testified to her husband's powers in 1842, she would resist them later in her marriage, when she felt that he misused them in his "influence" over other women.

Figure E.27. Born in 1791, Dr. John Elliotson was a physician in London at the University College Hospital and a passionate advocate for the medical and therapeutic use of mesmerism. Reproduced by courtesy of Charles Dickens Museum, London.

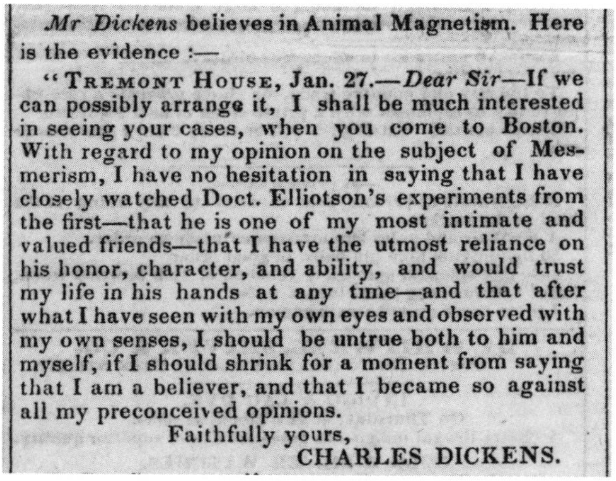

> *Mr Dickens* believes in Animal Magnetism. Here is the evidence :—
>
> "TREMONT HOUSE, Jan. 27.—*Dear Sir*—If we can possibly arrange it, I shall be much interested in seeing your cases, when you come to Boston. With regard to my opinion on the subject of Mesmerism, I have no hesitation in saying that I have closely watched Doct. Elliotson's experiments from the first—that he is one of my most intimate and valued friends—that I have the utmost reliance on his honor, character, and ability, and would trust my life in his hands at any time—and that after what I have seen with my own eyes and observed with my own senses, I should be untrue both to him and myself, if I should shrink for a moment from saying that I am a believer, and that I became so against all my preconceived opinions.
>   Faithfully yours,
>   CHARLES DICKENS.

Figure E.28. A letter from Dickens published in the *Boston Morning Post* states his belief in mesmerism, referred to here as "Animal Magnetism." Dickens proclaimed Elliotson as "one of my most intimate and valued friends." Courtesy of the American Antiquarian Society.

Conscience and Controversy
HARVARD AND THE UNITARIANS

In the 1840s Massachusetts society was dominated by two main groups: the more puritanical and conservative Congregationalists and Presbyterians, and the "liberal Christians" and intellectuals. The former were the majority in towns outside of Boston, and the latter dominated in Boston and Cambridge. Dickens quite naturally fell in with the second crowd, most of whom were Unitarians connected to Harvard (fig. E.29). Regarding that esteemed Massachusetts educational institution, Dickens wrote:

> There is no doubt that much of the intellectual refinement and superiority of Boston, is referable to the quiet influence of [Harvard]. . . . The resident professors at that university are gentlemen of learning and varied attainments; and are, without one exception that I can call to mind, men who would shed a grace upon, and do honour to, any society in the civilised world. . . . Whatever the defects of American universities may be, they disseminate no prejudices; rear no bigots; dig up the buried ashes of no old superstitions; never interpose between the people and their improvement; exclude no man because of his religious opinions; above all, in their whole course of study and instruction, recognise a world, and a broad one too, lying beyond the college walls.[43]

Figure E.29. Harvard Yard, ca. 1840. Courtesy of the Lowell National Historical Park.

Figure E.30. Dr. William Ellery Channing, ca. 1840. Channing's liberal teachings and sermons countered more conservative Congregationalist and Presbyterian views, greatly influencing New England's abolitionists and Transcendentalists. Courtesy of John Hay Library, Brown University Library.

Perhaps the most famous Bostonian that Dickens met was Dr. William Ellery Channing (fig. E.30), a Harvard graduate and renowned Unitarian minister in Boston, courageous opponent of slavery, and champion for a new American national literature. Dickens owned a copy of Channing's collected works and admired him enough to seek a letter of introduction to him from a mutual acquaintance before leaving England. A fellow passenger on board the *Britannia* was a member of Channing's church and invited the Dickenses to hear Channing preach the day after their arrival. With their luggage still being held at customs, they could not appear in public and had to decline. But Mr. and Mrs. Dickens enjoyed breakfast with the cleric a few days later, and they corresponded until Channing's death.

Cornelius Conway Felton (fig. E.31), another Boston Unitarian, was the "heartiest of Greek Professors" when Dickens met him in 1842; he later became president of Harvard University.[44] Dickens described him as "a most delightful fellow—unaffected, hearty, genial, jolly; quite an Englishman of the best sort"; in fact, he was the "best fellow in the

Figure E.31. Cornelius Conway Felton. Felton was president of Harvard University, 1860–62. Courtesy of Mark Dickens and the New York Public Library, Pageant of America Photo Archive.

States."[45] Felton came from a poor family and, like Dickens, had worked his way up to his high position in society through effort and industry.[46] The two self-made men instantly hit it off and maintained a deep and genuine friendship for the rest of their lives (fig. E.32). In Felton, Dickens

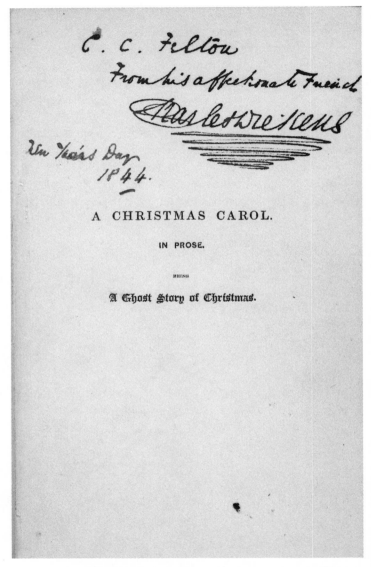

Figure E.32. Dickens inscribed this copy of *A Christmas Carol* to Cornelius Felton in 1844. Courtesy of Mark Dickens and the New York Public Library, Berg Collection.

found an amiable companion and an ardent supporter. Dickens's letters to Felton are among his most engaging, as can be seen by this excerpt from a letter written in Washington, D.C., on 14 March 1842:

My dear Felton,

I was more delighted than I can possibly tell you to receive . . . your welcome letter. We and the oysters missed you terribly in New York. You carried away with you more than half the delight and pleasure of my New World; and I heartily wish you could bring it back again.

There are very interesting men in this place,—highly interesting, of course,—but it's not a comfortable place; is it? If spittle could wait at table we should be nobly attended, but as that property has not been imparted to it in the present state of mechanical science, we are rather lonely and orphan-like, in respect of "being looked arter." . . .

We shall be in Buffalo, please Heaven, on the 30th of April. If I don't find a letter from you in the care of the postmaster at that place, I'll never write to you from England.

But if I *do* find one, my right hand shall forget its cunning, before I forget to be your truthful and constant correspondent; not, dear Felton, because I promised it, nor because I have a natural tendency to correspond (which is far from being the case), nor because I am truly grateful to you for, and have been made truly proud by, that affectionate and elegant tribute which —— sent me, but because you are a man after my own heart, and I love you *well*. And for the love I bear you, and the pleasure with which I shall always think of you, and the glow I shall feel when I see your handwriting in my own home, I hereby enter into a solemn league and covenant to write as many letters to you as you write to me, at least. Amen.

Come to England! Come to England! Our oysters are small I know; they are said by Americans to be coppery, but our hearts are of the largest size. . . .

Affectionately yours,
Charles Dickens[47]

Dickens's Harvard Unitarian friends—William Ellery Channing, Cornelius Conway Felton, and Henry Wadsworth Longfellow, among others—exercised considerable influence over Dickens, who when he returned to England, joined a Unitarian church for several years before returning to his broad church Anglican roots near the end of his life. It was an advertised memorial sermon for Channing, in fact, that brought Dickens to Reverend Edward Tagart's Unitarian chapel in Little Portland Street in London's West End, which Dickens subsequently joined. Channing-style moderate Unitarianism with its commitment to rational

examination of theological and doctrinal claims; its emphasis on bib-
liocentric ideas; its nonsectarian, tolerant openness; and its admiration
for literature and the arts as activities of worth—this was a religion that
Dickens admired in the New World and sought in the Old. He wrote to
Felton that he decided to "join the Unitarians . . . who would do something for human improvement, if they could; and who practice Charity
and Toleration."[48] Indeed, Dickens's American friends continued to be a
source of great pleasure and comfort through the years, prompting one
another to "do something for human improvement."

A CONTROVERSIAL STAND

By the time Dickens arrived in Boston, he had already published *Sketches
by Boz* and five major novels, all of which had been reprinted in pirated
copies in every country of the English-speaking world. Printers waited on
the docks for the latest installments of his novels, rushing to their offices
to set type and sell bootleg copies for pure profit. Considering his immense popularity, Dickens lost a fortune from these "piracies," and on the
occasion of his first official speech in America, at a public banquet given
in the drawing-rooms of Papanti's Hall in Boston, he called for the establishment of an international copyright agreement. Not only would such a
treaty provide authors with their fair reward, he argued, but it would also
promote the national literatures of the colonies and the United States.
Without international copyright protections, it was not just Dickens who
was being cheated out of his earnings but also American authors such as
Washington Irving and William Cullen Bryant.

   At the end of this charming speech in which Dickens praised and
delighted his American audience, he added,

> I hope the time is not far distant when they, in America, will receive of
> right some substantial profit and return in England from their labours; and
> when we, in England, shall receive some substantial profit and return for
> ours. Pray do not misunderstand me. Securing for myself from day to day
> the means of an honourable subsistence, I would rather have the affection-
> ate regard of my fellow men, than I would have heaps and mines of gold.
> But the two things do not seem to me incompatible. They cannot be, for
> nothing good is incompatible with justice.[49]

His remarks irked some of the newspapermen in the crowd, men who had
much to lose if Dickens was successful in his campaign, and they soon
published attacks on Dickens as a vulgar, money-grubbing ingrate. The

gauntlet had been thrown down, and the battle over copyright escalated throughout the rest of the trip, with Dickens refusing to stop speaking on the subject and newspapers becoming increasingly vicious. Even after the trip, he did not let the matter go, satirizing cut-throat and "piratical" American journalists in his next novel, *Martin Chuzzlewit* (1843–44).

Powerful Institutions

PERKINS SCHOOL FOR THE BLIND

As the most popular and well-beloved writer of the nineteenth century, Dickens felt that he had both an opportunity and a responsibility to use his power to help make the world a better place. Throughout his adult life, Dickens toured many social institutions in England, America, and Europe. He visited prisons, hospitals, mental institutions, orphanages, and schools. This was not an unusual practice for British travelers. Harriet Martineau and Frances Trollope had earlier made similar visits during their tours of the United States and had written about them in travel books. Touring such institutions was considered essential to a full understanding of a country, but for Dickens, it was also an essential step in improving practices in his own country.

The Perkins School for the Blind (fig. E.33) was already world-renowned in 1842 as a leading institution for educating the blind and deafblind. Opened in 1832, Perkins soon became famous for its innovative educational techniques and its success in teaching Laura Bridgman, the first known deafblind person in the world to become literate (fig. E.34). Dickens was captivated by Bridgman when he visited the school and wrote extensively about her in *American Notes*. Many years later, Helen Keller's mother read this description with new-found hope for her own deafblind daughter, and in 1887, Perkins sent an instructor, Anne Sullivan, to Alabama to work with Helen Keller.

Laura Bridgman first came to Perkins as an eight-year-old girl, and she lived there the rest of her life, first as a student and then as a needlework teacher (fig. E.35). Dickens met her when she was thirteen and was impressed by her quick intelligence and expressiveness. Quoting extensively from a Perkins annual report, Dickens describes Laura for his readers:

> When left alone, she seems very happy if she have her knitting or sewing, and will busy herself for hours: if she have no occupation, she evidently

Figure E.33. The Perkins School for the Blind was opened in South Boston by Samuel Gridley Howe in 1832. School trustee and vice president Thomas Perkins donated the funds to purchase this building, home to the school when Dickens visited in 1842. Courtesy of Perkins School for the Blind.

amuses herself by imaginary dialogues, or by recalling past impressions; she counts with her fingers, or spells out names of things which she has recently learned, in the manual alphabet of the deaf mutes. In this lonely self-communion she seems to reason, reflect, and argue: if she spell a word wrong with the fingers of her right hand, she instantly strikes it with her left, as her teacher does, in sign of disapprobation; if right, then she pats herself upon the head, and looks pleased. She sometimes purposely spells a word wrong with the left hand, looks rougish for a moment and laughs, and then with the right hand strikes the left, as if to correct it.[50]

In regard to Dickens's own visit, he remarks,

I turned over the leaves of her Diary, and found it written in a fair legible square hand, and expressed in terms which were quite intelligible without any explanation. . . .
She had, until now, been quite unconscious of the presence of visitors. . . .
My hand she rejected at once, as she does that of any man who is a stranger

Figure E.34. To prevent inappropriate stares from the sighted, Perkins School director Samuel Gridley Howe requested that students, such as Laura Bridgman here pictured, wear masks if their eyes were malformed. Courtesy of Perkins School for the Blind.

Figure E.35. Laura Bridgman taught needlework at the Perkins School. Courtesy of Perkins School for the Blind.

to her. But she retained my wife's with evident pleasure, kissed her, and examined her dress with a girl's curiosity and interest.[51]

In some ways, Bridgman was a perfect object of study for Dickens, a young girl whom he could idealize and by whom he could be inspired. The real Laura Bridgman, as scholars have noted, was not much like the portrait her teacher, Dr. Samuel Gridley Howe, painted for his audience, but literary Laura continued to gain fame worldwide through Dickens's lengthy discussion of her in *American Notes.*

"To gladden their hearts": A Book for the Blind

When Dickens returned to America in 1868, Howe, the school's director, requested a special donation from Dickens:

My Dear Sir:
    Lend me your heart for a moment. More than half a century ago the happy device of raised letters promised material relief to that numerous class of every generation who suffer under the infirmity of blindness. That promise has never been fully realized. . . . In this country there are twenty-three institutions, in all of which the blind are taught to read—but, alas, their reading books are as yet very few in number. "Paradise Lost" is really the only book we have of a literary character. . . .
    Now they want something to gladden their hearts. They have had lugubrious food enough; they want happier news of life. They want some books which will give pleasure and joy in their dark chambers. . . .
    Your books do this, and I want the blind to have one of them at their fingers' ends. I want, moreover, for several reasons, that you yourself should place one there. First, for the lasting pleasure it will give them; second, for the effect it would surely have of inducing others to follow your example.
    This is the auspicious moment to do it, because now the blind want books; and the public ear is yours. Your star is at its zenith, and your example will be followed.
    Think of this, my dear Sir; and if possible make the blind of this country happy and grateful by leaving them in close, grateful relations with its author, whether he be in this world or another.

Faithfully
S. G. Howe[52]

Dickens told George Dolby he wanted to "leave some gift of good will in America."[53] Dickens thereafter paid $1,700 to J. S. Amory of Boston to print 250 copies of *The Old Curiosity Shop* in Boston Line Type (fig. E.36), a raised-letter, tactile writing technology used before braille

MASTER HUMPHREY'S CLOCK.

PERSONAL ADVENTURES OF MASTER HUMPHREY.

The Old Curiosity Shop.

IGHT is generally my time for walking. In the summer I often leave home early in the morning, and roam about fields and lanes all day, or even escape for days or weeks together, but saving in the country I seldom go out until after dark, though, Heaven be thanked, I love its light and feel the cheerfulness it sheds upon the earth, as much as any creature living.

I have fallen insensibly into this habit, both because it favours my infirmity and because it affords me greater opportunity of speculating on the characters and occupations of those who fill the streets. The glare and hurry of broad noon are not adapted to idle pursuits like mine; a glimpse of passing faces caught by the light of a street lamp or a shop window is often better for my purpose than their full revelation in the daylight, and, if I must add the truth, night is kinder in this respect than day, which too often destroys an air-built castle at the moment of its completion, without the smallest ceremony or remorse.

4.   E

Figure E.36. When the Perkins director asked Dickens to donate copies of one of his books to be printed in raised letters for the blind, he chose *The Old Curiosity Shop.* Courtesy of Worcester Polytechnic Institute Curation, Preservation, and Archives, George C. Gordon Library.

Figure E.37. Laura Bridgman reading a Boston Line Type book in 1860.
Courtesy of Perkins School for the Blind.

became popular in the states (figs. E.37, E.38).[54] In today's dollars, that generous donation would amount to almost $27,000.

LOWELL MILLS

Dickens visited Lowell in February 1842 because he had heard about the innovative and humane industrial project founded there. Dickens had visited factories in England and called them "great haunts of desperate misery."[55] He was deeply concerned by the poor working conditions he found in English cities such as Manchester and Birmingham, where the infant mortality rate had reached 50 percent and the majority of the working population lived in unspeakable conditions. In visiting Lowell and writing about his positive impressions in his travel narrative *American*

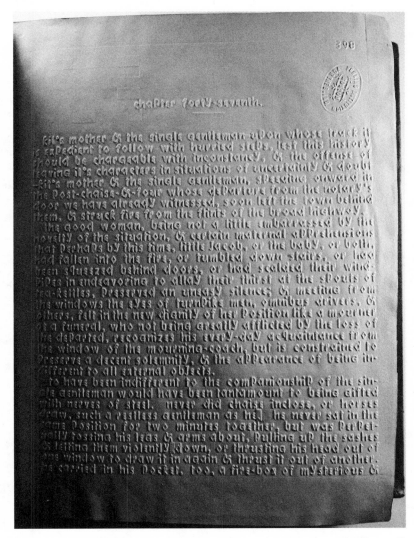

Figure E.38. One of the original 250 copies of *The Old Curiosity Shop* printed in Boston Line Type, a kind of tactile writing that proved difficult for the blind to read and was mostly used for the convenience of sighted instructors. Courtesy of Perkins School for the Blind.

Notes, Dickens hoped to suggest a better system of factory management for his own country.

Dickens and his guides grabbed a quick lunch at the Washington Tavern (fig. E.39) and then toured a woolen mill, a cotton mill, and a carpet factory during his visit to Lowell. Compared to British factories, the Lowell mills struck Dickens as surprisingly clean and organized. They were as "well ordered," Dickens wrote, as the young women who worked there (fig. E.40). There were green plants in some windows, and "there was as much fresh air, cleanliness, and comfort, as the nature of the occupation would possibly admit of."[56]

The contrast between the industrial cities of England and the planned manufacturing town of Lowell was, as Dickens remarked, the difference "between the Good and Evil, the living light and deepest shadow."[57] While the actual conditions in Lowell at the time were not as salubrious as Dickens believed, by comparison with English manufacturing cities Lowell, indeed, offered a superior system. Dickens later wrote that his day in Lowell was "the happiest he had passed in America," in large part because it showed him that it was possible for industry to be successful and humane at the same time.[58]

DICKENS AND THE MILL GIRLS

Dickens was impressed with the well-dressed factory girls who "thronged" him on the stairs as they returned from their dinner hour:

> They were all well-dressed, but not to my thinking above their condition: for I like to see the humbler classes of society careful of their dress and appearance, and even, if they please, decorated with such little trinkets as come within the compass of their means. . . .
>
> These girls, as I have said, were all well dressed: and that phrase necessarily includes extreme cleanliness. They had serviceable bonnets, good warm cloaks, and shawls; and were not above clogs and pattens. . . . They were healthy in appearance, many of them remarkably so, and had the manners and deportment of young women: not of degraded brutes of burden.[59]

He also noted the comparatively well-rounded lives of the factory girls. Some boardinghouses for the factory workers had pianos, and many of the girls subscribed to circulating libraries and used the savings bank (fig. E.41). In addition, the girls produced a periodical called *The Lowell*

Figure E.39. As an honored guest on his day-long visit to Lowell, Dickens lunched at the Washington Tavern. Courtesy of the Lowell Historical Society.

Figure E.40. "The Bobbin Girl," ca. 1870, by Winslow Homer. Courtesy of the Lowell National Historical Park.

Offering, which included articles, stories, and poems written "exclusively by females actively employed in the mills" (fig. E.42). Dickens appreciated that the tales encouraged "habits of self-denial and contentment, [and taught] good doctrines of enlarged benevolence," themes that he emphasized in his own writings.[60]

Figure E.41. Many of the mill girls deposited their earnings at the Lowell Institution for Savings. Dickens proclaimed in *American Notes* that the bank had holdings "estimated at one hundred thousand dollars." Courtesy of the Lowell National Historical Park.

Figure E.42. *The Lowell Offering* title page. Courtesy of the
Lowell Historical Society.

Reading Dickens, Reading America
CAPTURING DICKENS

It seemed that most of America could not get enough of Dickens in
1842. Not only did people follow him everywhere he went and send him
invitations to dine and dance, talk and tour, but many people also sought
to capture some physical memento of "the inimitable Boz." By the end of

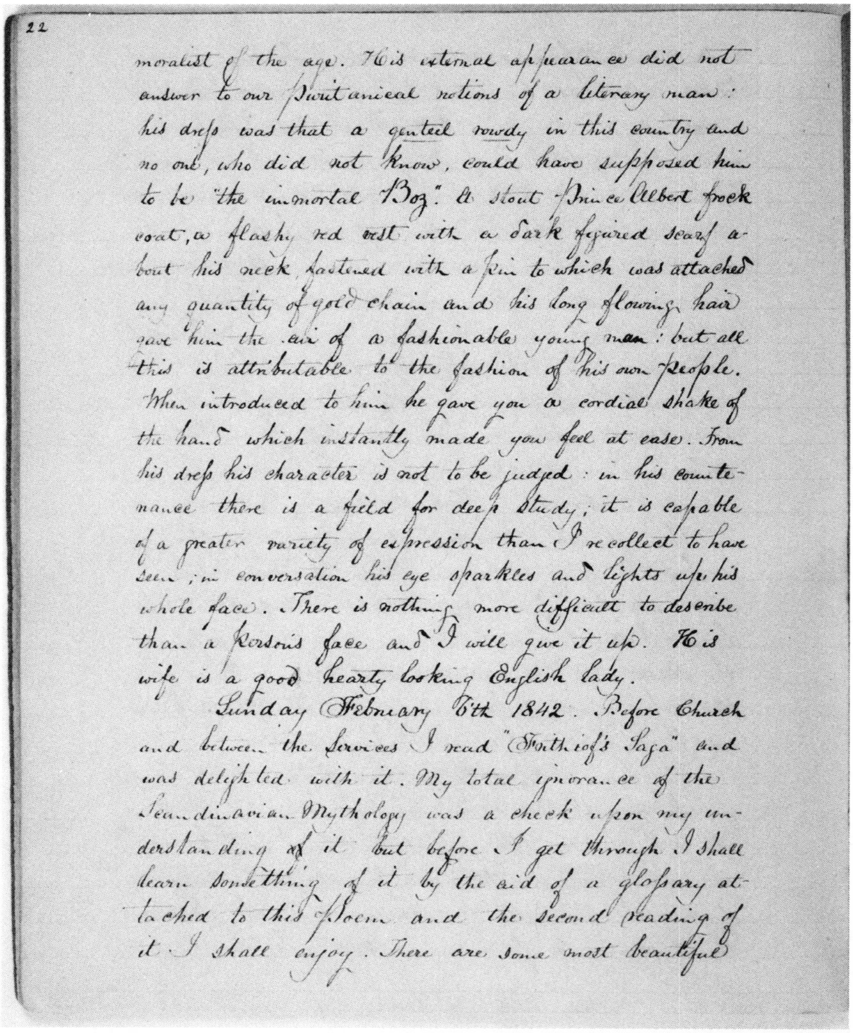

22
moralist of the age. His external appearance did not
answer to our Puritanical notions of a literary man:
his dress was that a genteel rowdy in this country and
no one, who did not know, could have supposed him
to be "the immortal Boz." A stout Prince Albert frock
coat, a flashy red vest with a dark figured scarf a-
bout his neck, fastened with a pin to which was attached
any quantity of gold chain and his long flowing hair
gave him the air of a fashionable young man: but all
this is attributable to the fashion of his own people.
When introduced to him he gave you a cordial shake of
the hand which instantly made you feel at ease. From
his dress his character is not to be judged: in his counte-
nance there is a field for deep study; it is capable
of a greater variety of expression than I recollect to have
seen; in conversation his eye sparkles and lights up his
whole face. There is nothing more difficult to describe
than a person's face and I will give it up. His
wife is a good hearty looking English lady.
Sunday February 6th 1842. Before Church
and between the Services I read "Frithiof's Saga" and
was delighted with it. My total ignorance of the
Scandinavian Mythology was a check upon my understanding of it but before I get through I shall
learn something of it by the aid of a glossary attached to this Poem and the second reading of
it I shall enjoy. There are some most beautiful

Figure E.43. This entry in Levi Lincoln Newton's journal vividly describes Dickens during his visit to Worcester. Courtesy of the American Antiquarian Society.

his trip, his bearskin coat was nearly bald from fans' snipping and plucking tufts of fur, and scores of individuals sought to secure locks of his hair. Diarists, too, attempted to capture Dickens in words, if not materially. On his visit to Worcester, Massachusetts, Dickens stayed with the governor of the state, the honorable John Davis. One of Davis's guests, Levi Lincoln Newton, wrote in his dairy (fig. E.43) that Dickens's "external appearance did not answer to our Puritanical notions of a literary man: his dress was that [of] a *genteel rowdy* in this country. . . . A stout Prince Albert frock coat, a flashy red vest with a dark figured scarf about his neck, fastened with a pin to which was attached any quantity of gold chain and his long flowing hair gave him the air of a fashionable young man."[61]

Artists, amateur and professional, also tried to capture the essence of the man. Sketches and cartoons of Dickens in newspapers were published in all the major newspapers. Only two professional artists were granted access to Dickens during the trip, however, due to time constraints— both Bostonians. Francis Alexander painted the only oil portrait of the author during the trip, and Henry Dexter created the only sculpture of him during his 1842 visit (fig. E.44). Dickens's secretary, George Putnam, described the scene of Dexter at work:

Figure E.44. Although Henry Dexter's original 1842 bust of Dickens is lost, this reproduction captures the youthful confidence of the author. Reproduced by courtesy of Charles Dickens Museum, London.

While Mr. Dickens ate his breakfast, read his letters and dictated the answers, Dexter was watching with the utmost earnestness the play of every feature, and comparing his model with the original. Often during the meal he would come to Dickens with a solemn, business-like air, stoop down and look at him sideways, pass round and take a look at the other side of his face, and then go back to his model and work away for a few minutes; then come again and take another look and go back to his model; soon he would come again with his callipers and measure Dickens's nose, and go and try it on the nose of the model; then come again with the callipers and try the width of the temples, or the distance from the nose to the chin, and back again to his work, eagerly shaping and correcting his model.[62]

QUANTIFYING CHARACTER: DICKENS GETS READ

The poking and prodding of Dickens in order to capture his "features, attitude, and look" continued throughout the 1842 trip, but nowhere perhaps as obviously as during his phrenological examination by Lorenzo Niles Fowler in Worcester, Massachusetts. Developed by Franz Joseph Gall, a Viennese physician, organology or the "physiology of the brain" was the nineteenth-century science of character prediction. In the 1820s, it was dubbed "phrenology" (from the Greek: *phren* = mind, *logos* = study). Gall's system was built on the assumption that the "mind" is composed of "multiple, distinct, innate faculties," each located in a different place in the brain.[63] Since Gall believed that the skull formed around the brain like a mold, he thought that the brain could be "read" by the physical examination of the skull, using one's fingers to feel its shape. Different sections of the skull would thus reveal different aspects of a person's character or personality (fig. E.45). Larger bumps (given high numbers) signaled a well-developed organ in that spot, and dips and indentations (given low numbers) meant the corresponding character trait was underdeveloped.

The Fowler brothers (Orson Squire Fowler and Lorenzo Niles Fowler) popularized the pseudo-science in America, performing readings of many famous people. Lorenzo Fowler's reading of Dickens was predictable, matching exactly what was commonly assumed to be true of Dickens's character and personality. For all of Fowler's claims to scientific accuracy, clearly his perception of the shape of Dickens's skull was deeply influenced by what he *expected* to find there. Furthermore, Fowler used his phrenological "portrait" of Dickens for his own purposes, to help prove the validity of his system. The summary of his findings (fig. E.46) is as follows: "Charles Dickens is a mirthful, philosophical author. He generates original thoughts, and expresses them in a mirthful way; at the same time he has a strong desire to do good, and hence hits off the absurdities and excesses of every-day life in a pleasing manner. The peculiar phrenological developments of Charles Dickens are Casuality, Mirthfulness, Ideality, Approbativeness, Imitation, and Language. I examined his head when he was in America, and found in him the elements of one of the most successful authors of the age."[64]

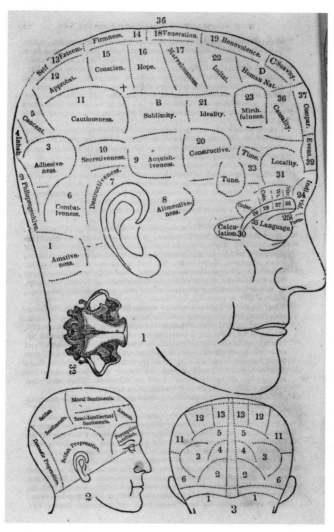

Figure E.45. Fowler phrenology map. Courtesy of the American Antiquarian Society.

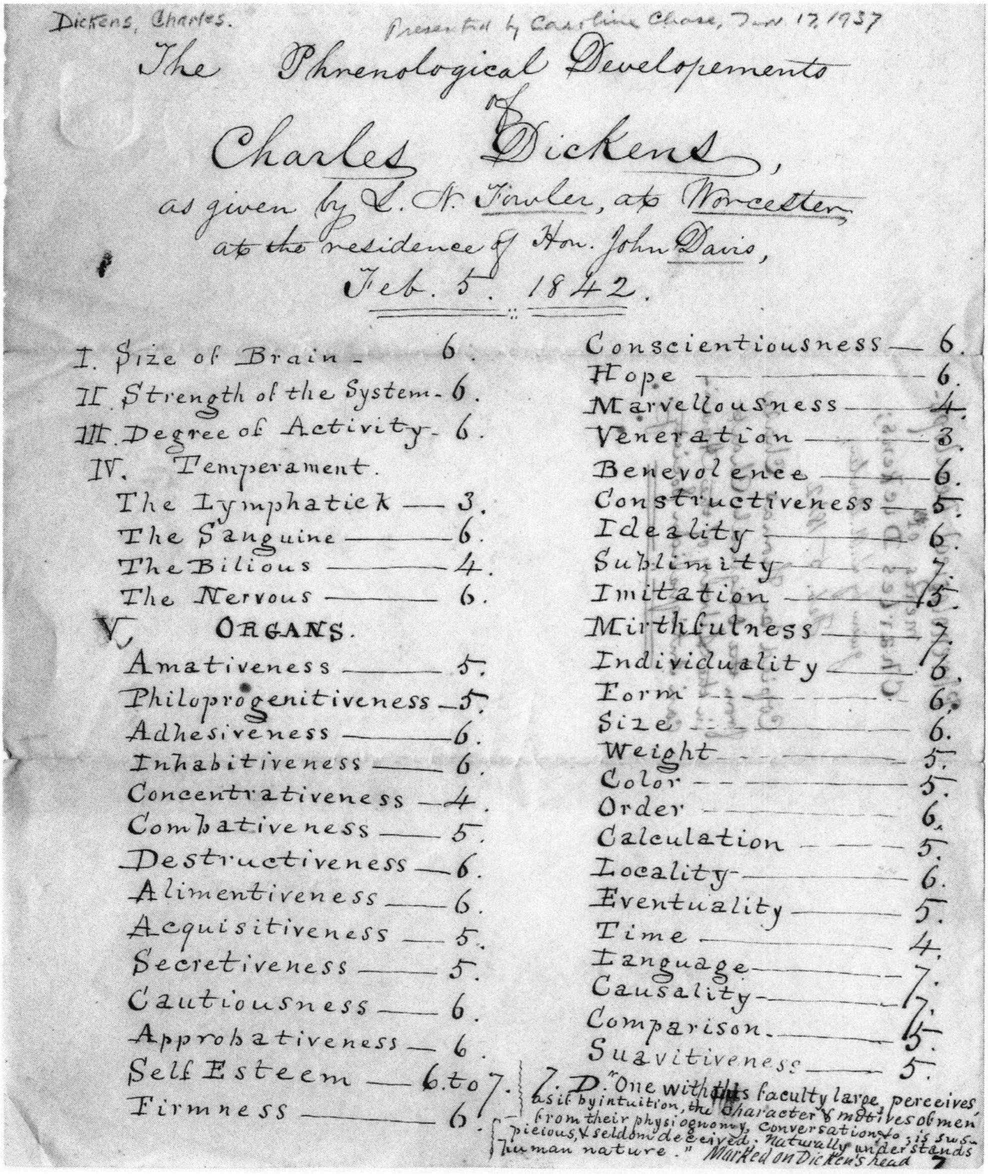

Presented by Caroline Chase, Jan 17, 1937

The Phrenological Developements
of
Charles Dickens,
as given by L. N. Fowler, at Worcester,
at the residence of Hon. John Davis,
Feb. 5. 1842.

I. Size of Brain	6.	Conscientiousness	6.
II. Strength of the System	6.	Hope	6.
III. Degree of Activity	6.	Marvellousness	4.
IV. Temperament.		Veneration	3.
The Lymphatick	3.	Benevolence	6.
The Sanguine	6.	Constructiveness	5.
The Bilious	4.	Ideality	6.
The Nervous	6.	Sublimity	7.
V. ORGANS.		Imitation	5.
Amativeness	5.	Mirthfulness	7.
Philoprogenitiveness	5.	Individuality	6.
Adhesiveness	6.	Form	6.
Inhabitiveness	6.	Size	6.
Concentrativeness	4.	Weight	5.
Combativeness	5.	Color	5.
Destructiveness	6.	Order	6.
Alimentiveness	6.	Calculation	5.
Acquisitiveness	5.	Locality	6.
Secretiveness	5.	Eventuality	5.
Cautiousness	6.	Time	4.
Approbativeness	6.	Language	7.
Self Esteem	6. to 7.	Causality	7.
Firmness	6.	Comparison	5.
		Suavitiveness	5.

N. B. "One with this faculty large, perceives
as if by intuition, the character & motives of men
from their physiognomy, conversation &c, is sus-
picious, & seldom deceived. Naturally understands
human nature." Marked on Dickens's head 7

Figure E.46. Lorenzo Fowler documented his phrenological reading of
Dickens's skull with this report, copied here by Thomas Chase from the original.
Courtesy of the American Antiquarian Society.

Capturing America: "Slavery, Spittoons, and Senators"

Dickens always knew that he would be writing about his visit to North America, and he kept his "eyes open, pretty wide" to observe "subjects for description."[65] His letters home were written, in part, as rough drafts of his travel book. Initially Dickens expected to write a favorable review of the young republic. He liked the idea of democracy in America, and he approved of most of what he found in Massachusetts. In a letter written from Boston, tentatively dated 4 February 1842, an enthusiastic Dickens wrote, "The American poor, the American factories, the institutions of all kinds—I have a book, already. There is no man in this town, or in this State of New England, who has not a blazing fire and a meat dinner every day of his life. A flaming sword in the air would not attract so much attention as a beggar in the streets. . . . A man with seven heads would be no sight at all, compared with one who couldn't read and write."[66] This was an exaggeration, of course, but it was based on what Dickens was shown and how those scenes compared with the urban blight and waking nightmare of industrial England.

The farther he traveled from Massachusetts, however, the more distasteful his experience became. He was nearly mobbed in New York City, and he found invasions of his privacy and personal space inappropriate and irritating. Dickens was also disgusted by the American habit of spitting tobacco juice, noting how the carpeted floors of Congress were covered in tobacco spit, "squirted and dabbled upon it in every direction."[67] Writing from Washington, D.C., to his Bostonian friend Charles Sumner, the abolitionist and future Massachusetts senator, Dickens said, "I have seen no place, yet, that I like so well as Boston. I hope I may be able to return there, but I fear not. We are now in the regions of slavery, spittoons, and senators—all three are evils."[68]

As the trip wore on and Dickens made his way as far south as Richmond, Virginia (fig. E.47), he became increasingly angered by the American institution of slavery. While Massachusetts was certainly complicit in this horrific injustice, profiting from trade based on slave-produced raw materials, most of Dickens's Bostonian friends and acquaintances belonged to the antislavery set. His distress at seeing so many slaves seems to have contributed to a change in his itinerary; the Dickenses decided not to travel on to Charleston, South Carolina, as planned but instead struck out west, going as far as St. Louis, Missouri. America did not improve on further acquaintance, however, and Dickens left the continent with

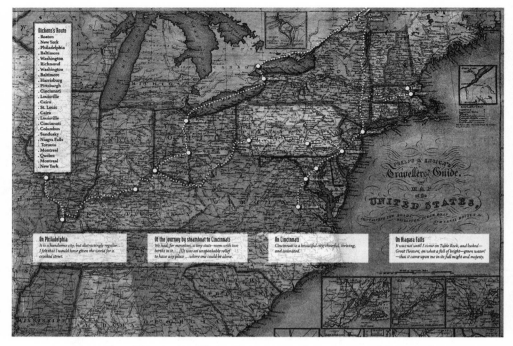

Figure E.47. Map showing Dickens's route across America in 1842. Map reproduction courtesy of the Norman B. Leventhal Map Center at the Boston Public Library.

his great expectations for the prodigal nation disappointed. He would, in fact, write a largely critical account of the young republic.

Backlash

Given the unfavorable picture Dickens painted of most of the United States in his travel narrative *American Notes,* it is not surprising that almost all American reviews panned the book. Notable exceptions include a pleasant review in *The Lowell Offering* and a defense of Dickens written by his dear friend Cornelius Felton. What may seem surprising today is that the book was also attacked in England. One has to look back to the international politics of the time to understand why Dickens was attacked by his own countrymen. Tensions between the two countries had been running so high in those years that the nations were on the verge of war, and Dickens had been seen as an unofficial envoy whom some hoped would help to ease tensions. His book, however, was viewed as an insult to the Americans who had welcomed him enthusiastically, and as an incendiary piece, fanning the flames of conflict between the two nations.

Reviewers on both sides of the Atlantic voiced two main complaints: that the book was an unfair criticism of American manners and values, and that it contained inflammatory remarks about slavery. Emblematic of the first variety of complaint is Christopher North's review in the Scottish magazine *Blackwood's*, which argued that Dickens's portrait of American manners was exaggerated, ungracious, and spiteful—"dwelling . . . with ill-nature on the weak parts of [America's] character," something that would be better left "to the hack travelers and tourists who can see and describe nothing else." The *London Quarterly* called *American Notes* "an entire failure," a work of "general insipidity" and "utter inanity."[69] Many Americans felt that Dickens had come to the United States not on a voyage of goodwill but on a mercenary errand, taking advantage of their hospitality and then stabbing them in the back by accusing them of "love of trade" and worship of the Almighty Dollar.

The Scourge of Slavery: Dickens, Channing, and Longfellow

The response to Dickens's antislavery chapter in *American Notes* was more complicated. Although slavery had been banned in England since 1772 and in Massachusetts since 1783, slavery was still woven into the world economy. Abolitionists in both countries used strong tactics to try to force a ban on slavery, while the less radical opponents of slavery spoke out against the evils of the institution, hoping to use moral persuasion rather than legal or military force to secure change (fig. E.48). Dr. William Ellery Channing's sermon commemorating the emancipation of the slaves in the British West Indies called for "passive resistance to slavery."[70] The sermon was published in a New York journal, the *New World*, on 29 October 1842, just ten days after publication of *American Notes* in London but prior to its arrival in North America. The bookseller in Charleston, South Carolina, who was selling the *New World* was arrested by the censors, and hearings were held about whether to burn the publication. The seller was eventually released on bail and the *New World* copies sold, but he refused to offer *American Notes* before the book had been approved by the censors. According to the *Southern Quarterly Review* in January 1843: "We understand that the South-Carolina Association was . . . disposed to suppress the circulation of the abolition production of the English novelist, but the ultra opinions of its writer were so ultra, so false, and so utterly incredible to the South, that they concluded that its circulation could do no harm,— . . . that [it] would fall to the ground by

SLAVE AUCTION AT RICHMOND, VIRGINIA.

Figure E.48. "Slave Auction, Richmond, 1856." Courtesy of the Lowell National Historical Park.

Figure E.49. Henry Wadsworth Longfellow, 1840, by Cephas Giovanni Thompson. Courtesy National Park Service, Longfellow House–Washington's Headquarters National Historic Site (LONG 4127).

[its] own weight, and would be regarded, by every one, only as evidence of the bitterness and malignity of [its] author."[71]

American Notes, it seems, was deemed too harmless to ban. It is interesting to note, however, the influence that "the grand chapter on slavery" had on Henry Wadsworth Longfellow (fig. E.49), who visited Dickens in England in the fall of 1842 and published *Poems on Slavery* upon returning home from a "very agreeable fortnight" with his friend. The first of the eight poems in the volume was addressed to Channing, urging him to "Go on, until this land revokes/The old and chartered Lie,/The feudal curse, whose whips and yokes/Insult humanity."[72] Dickens, Channing, and Longfellow all took a public stance on an unpopular side of a contentious issue, and they appear to have encouraged one another to act according to conscience.

Dickens Returns

TRANSFORMATIONS

In the twenty-five years following Dickens's first trip to America, both Boz and the United States became more powerful and prosperous. Great financial gains accrued from their boundless energy, innovation, and persistence. The United States added nine more states and three territories, the economy expanded, and the population grew from just over 17 million in 1840 to close to 40 million by 1870, with a large portion of that increase due to immigration. Infrastructure developed and raw materials became more readily accessible, fueling an industrial boom and propelling America into a leading role on the world stage. Dickens, too, continued to be extremely productive, publishing nine more novels and five Christmas books; founding, editing, and writing for two magazines; traveling extensively; and giving public readings. Dickens finally achieved his childhood goal of financial success and bought Gad's Hill Place, his dream home (fig. E.50).

For all of their triumphs, Dickens and America had also faced terrible tragedy, and their experience of loss and deep sadness gave them a hard-won maturity. During the years after Dickens left America, conflict over slavery intensified, eventually erupting in a bloody civil war, the unspeakable horrors of which chastened and humbled the American people. Families torn apart, death, and destruction—these were still fresh just two and a half years after the end of the war when Dickens returned to the continent. One of the first industrial wars of the modern age—

Figure E.50. Around the age of five, Dickens saw Gad's Hill for the first time; at forty-four, he purchased it. Courtesy of Worcester Polytechnic Institute Curation, Preservation, and Archives, George C. Gordon Library.

with its use of railroads, the telegraph, steamships, and mass-produced weapons—the Civil War had resulted in the deaths of 620,000 soldiers and uncounted civilian casualties.[73]

While the great tragedy of the American Civil War cannot really compare to one individual's troubles, Dickens was no stranger to suffering. In 1851, his eight-month-old daughter Dora died of sudden convulsions. When some beautiful flowers arrived a couple of days later, and "he was about to take them upstairs and place them on the little dead baby," he broke down emotionally.[74] In the years preceding his second visit to the United States, Dickens endured the deaths of his brother Alfred (d. 1860); his sister's husband, Henry Austin (d. 1861); and his mother, Elizabeth Barrow Dickens (d. 1863). On his birthday in 1864, Dickens learned that his twenty-two-year-old son Walter had died on New Year's Eve in India. Walter had aspired to be a writer like his father, but Dickens insisted his son pursue a career in the army. While serving in India, Walter fell deeply into debt, lost his health, and died. These deaths combined with the fact that Dickens's marriage of twenty-two years disintegrated when he fell in love with another woman (fig. E.51)

Figure E.51. Ellen Ternan in later years; twenty-seven years her senior, Dickens was captivated by Ellen in her youth. Reproduced by permission from Getty Images.

Figure E.52. Ten passengers were killed and forty injured in the Staplehurst railway accident, England's worst rail disaster to that point. Courtesy of the Lowell National Historical Park.

demonstrate how unhappy his personal life had become. He was also nearly killed in the disastrous Staplehurst railway accident (fig. E.52) and spent hours trying to assist the dying victims of the horrific crash, suffering from what seems, essentially, to have been a form of post-traumatic stress disorder for the rest of his life. When he returned to America in 1867, he was already very ill, and some believe the trip hastened his early death.

Significant Dickens Dates

1856   Buys Gad's Hill Place, near Rochester, England, achieving a life-long dream

1857   Meets the eighteen-year-old actress Ellen Ternan and begins a relationship that lasts the rest of his life

1858   Separates from his wife, Catherine, after twenty-two years of marriage and ten children

1865   Dickens, Ellen Ternan, and her mother, narrowly escape from the Staplehurst railway disaster

1867   Returns to America for a public reading tour, performing in many cities

1870   Dies on 9 June (age 58) after collapsing at Gad's Hill from a stroke

Significant American Dates

1848   Gold discovered in California

1857   Dred Scott decision by Supreme Court declares slaves and their descendants noncitizens

1860   Pony Express mail service begins: fastest means of communication with the West

1861   Confederate States of America forms, and the Battle of Fort Sumter begins the Civil War

1865   Robert E. Lee surrenders to Ulysses S. Grant at Appomattox on 9 April, ending the Civil War

1866   First successful transatlantic telegraph cable operates

DICKENS ON TOUR

Charles Dickens always enjoyed performing. As a small child he was fond of reciting poetry with great "action and attitude," and his father would hoist him up on a table at local inns to sing duets with his sister Fanny.[75] He held many fond memories of visiting the theater at Covent Garden and even started his own dramatic company as a schoolboy. As a young man, he considered a career as an actor and studied the craft while working as a reporter. Although he chose to pursue writing instead, he never lost the theatrical flair and employed it in his novels to great effect. Occasionally, Dickens had a chance to act in amateur theatricals, such as those performed in Montreal on the 1842 North American trip. A few times he also acted on a professional stage, and he wrote several plays that were produced.

Although Dickens had given public readings of his work before, it was in 1858 that he began his first professional reading tour of the British Isles. The readings became a valuable source of income, and Dickens needed the money more than ever, with three separate homes to maintain: his own residence, the house where Catherine lived after their separation, and the home he set up for Ellen Ternan. As early as 1859, Dickens began receiving invitations to read in America, but the Civil War made a transatlantic tour impossible. In 1867, with the war over, Dickens's manager, George Dolby, enthusiastically endorsed a return to America, arguing that Dickens would make around twelve thousand pounds, a fortune in those days (fig. E.53). Further, Dickens's American publisher, Bostonian James Fields, had been asking in every letter for his dear friend to come. John Forster, one of Dickens's oldest confidants, was against the idea, due to the author's increasingly poor health. He was overruled, however, and on 30 September 1867, the word "Yes" was sent via the new transatlantic telegram cable to America. Dickens would return.

The American Readings

The first American readings were held in Boston, and tickets went on sale two days before Dickens's expected arrival. By midnight there were a hundred people waiting in freezing temperatures to buy tickets. The

DOLBY.—" *Well, Mr. Dickens, on the eve of our departure, I present you with $300,000, the result of your Lectures in America.*"
DICKENS.—" *What! only $300,000 ? Is that all I have made out of these penurious Yankees, after all my abuse of them ? Pshaw ! Let us go, Dolby !*"

Figure E.53. During his second American tour, Dickens came under fire again by the press—this time for how much money his reading tour made. Courtesy of the Lowell National Historical Park.

Figure E.54. Audiences in New England and around the United States were enthralled by Dickens's stage presence and readings. Courtesy National Park Service, Longfellow House–Washington's Headquarters National Historic Site (LONG 17314 [HWLD Papers], Box 123, folder 11).

next morning the queue was half a mile long. When Dolby read the waiting fans a telegram that he had just received stating that Dickens's ship had reached Halifax and was now en route to Boston, the crowd went wild. Although hordes of people mobbed the docks waiting for the ship, Dolby arranged a Customs House boat to collect Dickens before the ship reached the harbor and to whisk them away to Long Wharf without detection. The Parker House Hotel arranged for Dickens to use a private staircase during his stay and installed a staff member outside his door to keep out unwelcome visitors. This visit to America would be a quieter one, with none of the pushy and rude behavior of the previous journey to endure. Due to his poor health, Dickens refused many invitations to socialize, but his closest American friends, Longfellow and Fields, were always welcome. The readings were, as expected, a triumph (fig. E.54). His performances of *A Christmas Carol* and excerpts from *Pickwick Papers* and *David Copperfield* set the city on fire with "talk of nothing else" but Dickens's triumphal return.[76]

CHARLES DICKENS.

Figure E.55. This 1867 studio portrait of Dickens was taken in New York City. Courtesy of Mark Dickens and the New York Public Library, Berg Collection.

The tour was supposed to include stops in dozens of American cities, including St. Louis, Cincinnati, and Chicago, but a particularly bad winter, coupled with Dickens's declining health, led to a curtailed schedule. Readings were concentrated in Boston and New York (fig. E.55), with shorter stays in other cities such as Washington, D.C., Philadelphia, Buffalo, New Haven, Worcester, and Portland, Maine. With a grueling travel schedule made even more hectic by heavy snows and high winds, Dickens found it difficult to shake a bad cold and developed such a severe case of gout that he had to be helped onto the stage to perform. Visiting Dickens on his birthday in Washington, D.C., Massachusetts Senator Charles Sumner was astounded to see his old friend in such a painful condition, remarking to Dolby, "Surely, . . . you are not going to allow Mr. Dickens to read tonight." But his manager knew better than to think that the Inimitable Boz would disappoint his audience. "His wonderful power of changing when he gets to the little table" would carry him through the performance.[77]

Joe and Kate Field at Boston's Tremont

In 1842 Joe Field, comedian and playwright with the Tremont Theatre Stock Company, dramatized *Nicholas Nickleby*, wrote an original play called *Boz: A Masque Phrenologic*, and composed a comic song in honor of Dickens's first visit to Boston. The famed celebrity was delighted with the performance and enjoyed "nine rousing cheers" from the crowd inside the Tremont Theatre.[78] In 1868 Kate Field (fig. E.56), the daughter of that performer, sat in the audience every night watching Dickens perform on the same stage. In "Pen Photographs of Mr. Dickens's Readings" she attempted to capture the sound of his voice through writing and graphic elements (fig. E.57).

THE GREAT INTERNATIONAL WALKING MATCH

Charles Dickens, an avid walker, spent many a night walking the streets of London observing his surroundings, a habit he picked up as a neglected child. The author seemed to need these wanderings both for inspiration and to rid himself of the tension that his intense writing process created. Long a sufferer from lumbago (lower back pain), Dickens seemed to find relief through walking, though some of his friends thought that walking was the *cause* of his back problems. Dickens walked at the rapid pace of four and a half miles per hour and would sometimes walk up to thirty miles out of London into the countryside in one afternoon. Even when traveling in North America, he walked seven to nine miles almost every day.

On 29 February 1868, in the midst of a particularly cold and snowy winter, James Osgood, an American publisher, and George Dolby, Dickens's British manager, faced off for the Great International Walking Match (fig. E.58), with Dickens serving as umpire. The match was the brainchild

Figure E.56. Kate Field described watching Dickens perform as a profound experience. Courtesy of the New York Public Library, Division of Art Prints and Photographs.

of Dickens's close friend and Boston walking partner, publisher James Fields (fig. E.59). Dickens had planned to give eight readings in Boston at the end of February and the beginning of March, but the impeachment trial of President Andrew Johnson began on the first day of this set of readings, and Dickens worried that there would be little public interest in his performances during this unsettled time. He decided to take the second week off, and Fields, in order to keep the ever-restless Dickens

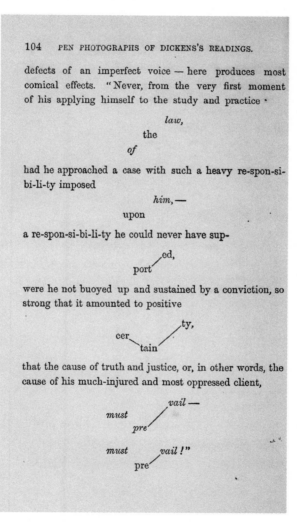

Figure E.57. Page from Kate Field's "Pen Photographs of Mr. Dickens's Readings." Courtesy of the Library of Congress.

Figure E.58. This broadside was printed to commemorate the Great International Walking Match and was distributed to those who participated. Reproduced by courtesy of Charles Dickens Museum, London.

entertained, proposed the walking race between these two representatives of England and the United States.

What started as a sort of joke became a real race, albeit with Dickens providing the comic relief with his ready wit and playful banter (fig. E.60). The route took the men from Boston's Mill Dam Road to Newton's town center and back, just over thirteen miles. By the end of the race, their "hair, beards, eyelashes, [and] eyebrows, were frozen hard, and hung with icicles."[79] James Field's wife, Annie (fig. E.61), drove up in a carriage and distributed oranges and brandy to the walkers, and Dickens raced ahead to spur the men on. Dickens said of Osgood, "The Bantam pegged away with his little drum-sticks as if he saw his wives and a peck of barley waiting for him at the family perch."[80] George Dolby, dubbed "The Man of Ross," lost the race and was very disappointed, feeling that he had "let

Figure E.59. James Fields
was an author, publisher,
and champion and promoter
of contemporary American
writers. He was also Dickens's
authorized American publisher
and close friend. Courtesy of
the Metropolitan Museum
of Art.

Figure E.60. *The Daily
Advertiser* (Boston) published
this caricature of Dickens
after the Great International
Walking Match. Courtesy of
the Lowell National Historical
Park.

Figure E.61. The second wife of publisher James Fields, Annie Fields was a passionate advocate for female writers and a philanthropist. Courtesy of the Metropolitan Museum of Art.

Figure E.62. The Parker House Hotel, opened in 1855, was the Boston residence of Dickens during his 1868 visit. Dickens hosted the postrace banquet at the hotel. Courtesy of the Lowell National Historical Park.

down" Dickens and "his country."[81] Dickens, nicknamed "The Gad's Hill Gasper" due to his lingering cold, wrote a charming account of the event and hosted a sumptuous post-race dinner for all of his American friends at the Parker House Hotel (figs. E.62, E.63).

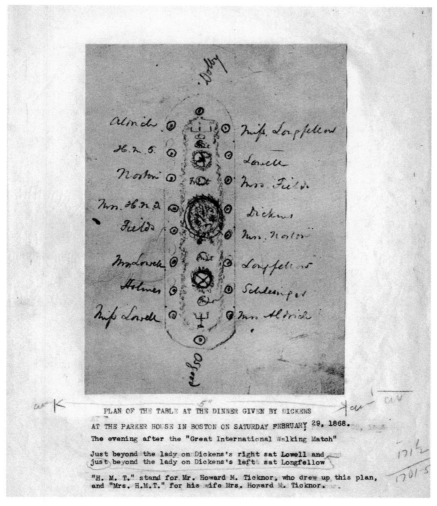

Figure E.63. One of the participants in the Parker Hotel dinner commemorating the Great International Walking Match took note of the seating plan. Attendees at the dinner included Henry Wadsworth Longfellow and his daughter, Dickens's American publishers, and the competitors Dolby and Osgood. Courtesy National Park Service, Longfellow House–Washington's Headquarters National Historic Site (LONG 17314 [HWLD Papers], Photo Box 6, folder 46).

FAREWELL FRIENDS

As a financial enterprise, the American tour was a tremendous success. Dickens earned nearly double what Dolby had estimated as profit. Clearing around twenty thousand pounds, Dickens had made the fortune he desired.[82] But the price he paid was great—two years after returning home Dickens would die of a stroke. Dickens had pushed his body to the breaking point, and the journey left him depleted. Still, almost without exception, he had fulfilled his promise to perform for the American people. As he came to Massachusetts for the last time, he gave a series of "Farewell Readings." His last performance in Boston was on 8 April 1868. A group of ladies had decorated his reading desk with flowers, surprising him as he walked on stage. "I kiss the kind fair hands unknown which have so beautifully decorated my table this evening," he began.[83] After he finished his reading of *Doctor Marigold* and *Mrs. Gamp,* and after the thunderous applause subsided, Dickens began to walk off the stage, hesitated, and came back. In the utter silence of the hall, he began to speak:

> Ladies and Gentlemen, My gracious and generous welcome in America, which can never be obliterated from my remembrance, began here. My departure begins here too; for I assure you that I have never until this moment really felt that I am going away. In this brief life of ours it is sad to do almost anything for the last time, and I cannot conceal from you, although my face will soon be turned towards my native land, and to all that makes it dear, that it is a sad consideration with me that in a very few moments from this time, this brilliant hall and all that it contains, will fade from my view—for evermore. But it is my consolation that the spirit of the bright faces, the quick perception, the ready response, the generous and the cheering sounds that have made this place delightful to me, will remain; and you may rely upon it that that spirit will abide with me as long as I have sense and sentiment.
>
> I do not say this with any limited reference to private friendships that have for years upon years made Boston a memorable and beloved spot to me, for such private references have no business in this public place. I say it purely in remembrance of, and in homage to, the great public heart before me.
>
> Ladies and Gentlemen,—I beg most earnestly, most gratefully, and most affectionately, to bid you, each and all, farewell.[84]

Dickens never returned to America, but all the wonderful memories that "made this place [Massachusetts] delightful" to the Inimitable undoubtedly helped the "spirit" of the commonwealth and its inhabitants to "abide with [him] as long as [he had] sense and sentiment left" (figs. E.64,

Figure E.64. Charles Dickens, 1874, by C. Morris. Courtesy of Worcester Polytechnic Institute Curation, Preservation, and Archives, George C. Gordon Library.

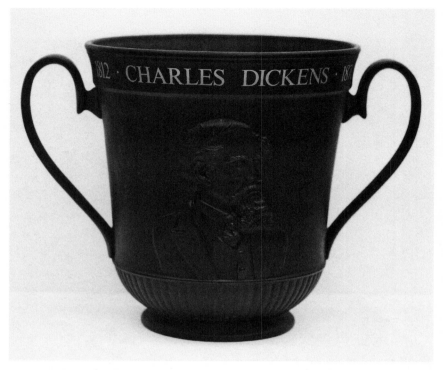

Figure E.65. The centenary of Dickens's death in 1970 led to a host of commemoratives including this Wedgewood urn. Courtesy of Worcester Polytechnic Institute Curation, Preservation, and Archives, George C. Gordon Library.

E.65). Dickens's visits to Massachusetts had a profound influence on the commonwealth, on Dickens, and on the literary creations that constitute his enduring legacy.

NOTES

1. See Juliet John, *Dickens and Mass Culture* (Oxford: Oxford University Press, 2010), especially "Introduction: 'The Most Popular Author in the World'?" 1–35.

2. Charles Dickens, *The Pilgrim Edition of the Letters of Charles Dickens,* 12 vols., ed. Madeline House et al. (Oxford: Clarendon Press, 1965–2002), 3:156.

3. Edgar Johnson, *Charles Dickens: His Tragedy and Triumph,* 2 vols. (New York: Simon and Schuster, 1952), 1:372.

4. John Forster, *The Life of Charles Dickens,* 3 vols. (London: Chapman and Hall, 1872–74), 1:5.

5. Ibid., 1:31.

6. Ibid., 1:33.

7. Ibid., 1:37.

8. Ibid., 1:68.

9. For a list of major works and selected minor works by Dickens, see the appendix.

10. Dickens, *Letters,* 2:381 (13 September 1841).

11. Ibid., 3:204–5 (24, 26 April 1842).

12. Ibid., 3:629 (30 January 1842).

13. Elizabeth Wormeley Latimer, "A Girl's Recollections of Dickens," *Lippincott's Monthly Magazine* 52 (1893): 340, 338.

14. Dickens, *Letters,* 3:121n2.

15. John Quincy Adams, "There Is a Greeting of the Heart" (poem), 16 March 1842, Morgan Library, New York.

16. Dickens, *Letters,* 3:133n7.

17. G. W. Putnam, "Four Months with Charles Dickens," *Atlantic Monthly,* November 1870, 476–82, 591–99.

18. Ibid.

19. Postal information taken from Judith Flanders, *Inside the Victorian Home: A Portrait of Domestic Life in Victorian England* (New York: Norton, 2005), 260; currency equivalencies calculated with the software at www.measuringworth.com and http://coinmill.com.

20. *Pickwick Papers* handwritten excerpt penned by Charles Dickens on 6 February 1842, Aaron Burr Correspondence No. 7, copy in MSS folder (Dickens), American Antiquarian Society, Worcester, Massachusetts.

21. Johnson, *Charles Dickens,* 1:352, 353.

22. John Belchem, ed., *Liverpool 800* (Liverpool: Liverpool University Press, 2006), 173.

23. Charles Dickens, *American Notes for General Circulation,* 2 vols. (London: Chapman and Hall, 1842), 1:1.2, 4. Citations to *American Notes* include volume number followed by a colon, and chapter and page number(s) separated by a period.

24. Ibid., 1:2.27–28.

25. Ibid., 1:2.32–34.

26. Ibid., 1:2.50.

27. Dickens, *Letters,* 3:33 (29 January 1842).

28. Edward F. Payne, *Dickens Days in Boston: A Record of Daily Events* (Boston: Riverside Press, 1927), 13.

29. Dickens, *Letters,* 3:34n1.

30. Payne, *Dickens Days,* 13, 14; A. K. Sandoval-Strausz, *Hotel: An American History* (New Haven, Conn.: Yale University Press, 2007), 54–55.

31. Jane Holtz Kay, *Lost Boston* (Amherst: University of Massachusetts Press, 2006), 139.

32. Payne, *Dickens Days,* 6.

33. Kay, *Lost Boston,* 131.

34. Dickens, *Letters,* 3:35 (29 January 1842); 4:11 (3 January 1844).

35. Dickens, *American Notes,* 1:3.58.

36. See James T. Fields, *Yesterdays with Authors* (Boston: James R. Osgood, 1872), quoted in Payne, *Dickens Days,* 17.

37. Putnam, "Four Months with Charles Dickens."

38. Dickens, *Letters,* 3:43 (31 January 1842).

39. Dickens, *Letters,* 3:34 (29 January 1842).

40. Dickens, *Letters*, 3:629 (30 January 1842).

41. Indeed, Dickens even incorporated mesmerism into his works. For example, Nicholas Nickleby "read the interesting legends in the miscellaneous questions, and all the figures into the bargain, with as much thought or consciousness of what he was doing, as if he had been in a magnetic slumber." Charles Dickens, *Nicholas Nickleby* (London: Chapman and Hall, 1838–39), 7.63. For more on this topic, see Fred Kaplan, *Dickens and Mesmerism: The Hidden Springs of Fiction* (Princeton, N.J.: Princeton University Press, 1975).

42. Dickens, *Letters*, 3:180 (2 April 1842).

43. Dickens, *American Notes*, 1:3.62–63.

44. Ibid., 1:6.209.

45. Dickens, *Letters*, 3:69 (17 February 1842); 3:342 (13 October 1842).

46. Peter Ackroyd, *Dickens* (New York: HarperCollins, 1990), 356.

47. Dickens, *Letters*, 3:129–31 (14 March 1842).

48. Ibid., 3:455–56 (2 March 1843).

49. Charles Dickens, *The Speeches of Charles Dickens*, ed. K. J. Fielding (Oxford: Oxford University Press, 1960), 21.

50. Dickens, *American Notes*, 1:3.85–86.

51. Ibid., 1:3.95–96.

52. Quoted in Payne, *Dickens Days*, 231–32.

53. Ibid., 232.

54. Dickens, *Letters*, 12:113 (18 May 1868).

55. Dickens, *American Notes*, 1:4.164.

56. Ibid., 1:4.159, 1:4.156.

57. Ibid., 1:4.164.

58. Johnson, *Charles Dickens*, 1:372.

59. Dickens, *American Notes*, 1:4.155–56.

60. Ibid., 1:4.159, 162.

61. Levi Lincoln Newton, Diary in MSS Octavo Volumes "N," Newton Family Papers, 1795–1870, octavo volume 9:21–22, American Antiquarian Society.

62. Putnam, "Four Months with Charles Dickens."

63. John van Wyhe, The History of Phrenology on the Web, 1999–2011, www.historyofphrenology.org.uk.

64. L. N. Fowler, *Lectures on Man: Being a Series of Discourses on Phrenology and Physiology* (London: L. N. Fowler, 1886), 137–38.

65. Dickens, *Letters*, 3:43 (31 January 1842).

66. Ibid., 3:50–51 (?4 February 1842).

67. Dickens, *American Notes*, 1:8.294.

68. Dickens, *Letters*, 3:127 (13 March 1842).

69. Sydney P. Moss and Carolyn J. Moss, *American Episodes involving Charles Dickens* (Troy, N.Y.: Whitson Publishing, 1999), 4.

70. Ibid., 20–21.

71. Ibid., 23.

72. Henry Wadsworth Longfellow, *Poems of Henry Wadsworth Longfellow* (Boston: Houghton Mifflin, 1880), 41.

73. According to the Civil War Trust, "approximately 620,000 soldiers died from combat, accident, starvation, and disease," an estimate from an "1889 study of the war performed by William F. Fox and Thomas Leonard Livermore" (www.civilwar.org). Other estimates

vary, with historian J. David Hacker offering a much higher number of 750,000 dead. "Historian Revises Estimate of Civil War Dead," *Discover-e,* 21 September 2011, http:// discovere.binghamton.edu.

74. Mary Dickens, *Cornhill Magazine,* January 1885, quoted in Ackroyd, *Dickens,* 628.

75. Ackroyd, *Dickens,* 40.

76. Raymund Fitzsimons, *Garish Lights: The Public Reading Tours of Charles Dickens* (Philadelphia: J. B. Lippincott, 1970), 116.

77. Ibid., 128.

78. Payne, *Dickens Days,* 5, 30.

79. Dickens, *Letters,* 12:65 (2 March 1868).

80. George Dolby, *Charles Dickens as I Knew Him* (London: T Fisher Unwin, 1885), 268.

81. Fred Kaplan, *Dickens: A Biography* (New York: Morrow, 1988), 524.

82. Fitzsimons, *Garish Lights,* 141.

83. Dickens, *Speeches,* 377.

84. Ibid., 378.

PART II

Essays

◆

CHAPTER 1

Dickens, the Lowell Mill Girls, and the Making of *A Christmas Carol*

NATALIE McKNIGHT AND CHELSEA BRAY

✦

ON 3 FEBRUARY 1842, twenty-nine-year-old Charles Dickens, already a famous novelist, visited Lowell, Massachusetts, and toured several of its factories as part of his first trip to America. There is nothing particularly remarkable about his desire to observe Lowell's factories; it was customary for British writers in the nineteenth century to tour and write about various social institutions when they traveled in other countries. For example, Harriet Martineau visited the Lowell factories with Ralph Waldo Emerson when she toured America in 1834, and while Frances Trollope did not write about the Lowell factories in her *Domestic Manners of the Americans* (1832), she did describe many other public institutions such as markets, museums, schools, theaters, courts, and political and religious organizations, even though her focus was predominantly on "domestic manners." Similarly, when Captain Frederick Marryat toured the United States in 1837, he focused on commerce, transportation, theaters, museums, and educational and religious institutions when commenting on his visit.[1] Since Lowell was the first planned industrial city in the United States, it is natural that Dickens would wish to observe it. So Dickens's decision to visit Lowell is unremarkable; what is remarkable is his reaction to it. He referred to his visit to Lowell as "the happiest day he had passed in the country."[2] Considering that Dickens visited Boston, New York, and the District of Columbia; saw the Great Plains and Niagara Falls; and took a steamship journey on the Mississippi, it might seem odd that Lowell was at the top of his list of favorites. Lowell stood out for Dickens, it seems, because it gave him his first glimpse of how industry could be run humanely and how the life of a factory worker could be something other than degrading. But Dickens's visit to Lowell shaped more than just his image of industry—it also influenced his subsequent fiction, in particular his composition of *A Christmas Carol* the year after his journey through America. Perhaps his day in Lowell was "the happiest day" he spent in America because it had a greater positive impact on his writing than any other place he visited on his tour.

Dickens toured a woolen factory, a carpet factory, and the Merrimack Manufacturing Company textile mill during his day in Lowell. As he writes in *American Notes for General Circulation,* "I happened to arrive at the first factory just as the dinner hour was over, and the girls were returning to their work; indeed the stairs of the mill were thronged with them as I ascended. They were all well-dressed, but not to my thinking above their condition." His account goes on to say that they "were healthy in appearance, many of them remarkably so, and had the manners and deportment of young women: not of degraded brutes of burden" as his tours of factories in England had led him to expect. He notes that there were many "just verging upon womanhood." He also notes their "extreme cleanliness," a factor of great importance to him as he was preoccupied with cleanliness and order.[3] But Dickens was likewise impressed by the attractiveness of the girls' surroundings. As he describes in *American Notes,* "The rooms in which they worked, were as well ordered as themselves. In the windows of some, there were green plants, which were trained to shade the glass; in all, there was as much fresh air, cleanliness, and comfort, as the nature of the occupation would possibly admit of."[4] Compared to what Dickens had seen of factories in Britain, which were run with little or no concern for the comfort or even health of the workers, Lowell was a surprising and hopeful revelation. On 29 December 1838, four years before his first visit to America, Dickens had written to E. M. Fitzgerald, "I went, some weeks ago, to Manchester, and saw the *worst* cotton mill. And then I saw the *best.* . . . There was no great difference between them." He went on to say that what he saw "disgusted and astonished me beyond all measure. I mean to strike the heaviest blow in my power for these unfortunate creatures, but whether I shall do so in the 'Nickleby', or wait some other opportunity, I have not yet determined."[5] The blow he ended up striking was *A Christmas Carol,* although its connection to factory conditions is not immediately obvious.

The boardinghouses for the mill girls also impressed Dickens since they were close to the mills, and their proximity to the factories meant that the women could return to the house for a decent dinner in the middle of the day. They did not have to spend much of their time commuting to work, as was the case for most mill workers in England. For instance, Matthew Crabtree, a British factory worker who was called to testify in Parliament's investigation of child labor in 1831–32, started working in a factory when he was eight years old and regularly worked fourteen hours a day with an hour break at noon, with sixteen-hour days when business was brisk. By contrast, Lowell mill girls worked twelve-hour days. Crabtree lived two miles from the mill, which would add over an hour to his work day, leaving him less than eight hours to sleep when he got home, even if he did nothing else. When asked by the investigator how he managed to get up in the morning, he answered, "I seldom did awake spontaneously; I was most generally awoke or lifted out of bed, sometimes asleep, by my parents." When asked if he was always on time in getting to work, he replied no and said that the consequence was "I was most commonly beaten." "Severely?" the interrogator asked. "Very severely, I thought," he responded. "In those mills is chastisement towards the later part of the day going on perpetually?" he was asked. "Perpetually," he responded. "So that you can hardly be in a mill without hearing constant crying?" "Never an hour, I believe."[6]

Likewise, the testimony of Elizabeth Bentley, who was part of the same investigation, provides a similar example. She began working at a flax mill when she was six years old and regularly worked thirteen-hour days with a forty-minute break in the middle of the day. When they were busy, she worked sixteen-hour days. When they were slow in their work, supervisors would "strap" them, and she says she was severely strapped on occasion. She could not go home for dinner because she lived two miles away, so she had to eat in the mill. "Could you eat your food well in that factory?" she was asked. "No," she responded, "indeed I had not much to eat, and the little I had I could not eat it, my appetite was so poor, and being covered with dust; and it was no use to take it home, I could not eat it, and the overlooker took it and gave it to the pigs."[7]

According to Dickens very few children worked in the Lowell factories, unlike in England, and in Lowell the children were only allowed to work nine months a year, usually twelve hours a day, so that they could be educated during the other three months. Harriet Robinson, who began working in the Lowell mills at age ten, confirmed Dickens's observation in *Loom and Spindle* where she wrote about attending school three months a year until she was thirteen when she began attending Lowell High School on a regular basis for two years. She also noted that in 1842 the work hours for children under twelve were limited to ten per day. She and the other mill girls were conscious of the inferior position of child laborers in England, and would "sing, to a doleful little tune, some verses called, 'The Factory Girl's Last Day,'" which tells of the pathetic life and death of a factory girl who did not have the advantages of the Lowell mill girls. "In contrast with this sad picture," Robinson wrote, "we thought of ourselves as well off, in our cosey corner of the mill, enjoying ourselves in our own way, with our good mothers and our warm suppers awaiting us when the going-out bell should ring."[8] While for us even the Lowell conditions seem harsh for a child, for Dickens they obviously seemed far more humane than those prevailing in England, for both children and women.

It was the general concern for the welfare and quality of life of mill workers that most impressed Dickens in the Lowell operations:

> I am now going to state three facts, which will startle a large class of readers on this side of the Atlantic, very much.
>
> Firstly, there is a joint-stock piano in a great many of the boarding-houses. Secondly, nearly all these young ladies subscribe to circulating libraries. Thirdly, they have got up among themselves a periodical called THE LOWELL OFFERING, "A repository of original articles, written exclusively by females actively employed in the mills,"—which is duly printed, published, and sold; and whereof I brought away from Lowell four hundred good solid pages, which I have read from beginning to end.[9]

For Dickens, who was accustomed to the brutal treatment of mill workers in England, the Lowell mill community's emphasis on cultivating the women's creativity and intellect and fostering their finer sensibilities was a revelation. That they were encouraged to play the piano, produce a literary magazine, and attend lectures testified to the mill owners' concerns for the whole person, not just the labor that could be wrung out of the worker.

Dickens was truly impressed with the publication of the mill women, *The Lowell Offering,* and rightfully so.[10] The quality of writing exhibited there is of a high caliber, and although the tone, themes, and language tend to be more sentimental than most current readers would appreciate, Dickens would have seen much there that would have resonated with his tastes. He would have admired essays like "The Mother's Love," published in the first edition (October 1840, one of the editions he was given during his visit), which describes the devotion of a mother tending a sick child through the night. The piece was written by "M," either Maria Currier or Lucy Larcom.[11] She wrote, "Listen to the prayer which arises from the depths of that mother's heart, that the Giver of life would still spare to her the beautiful flower over which her soul thus yearns,—that He, who above has power, will preserve it amid the rude storms which have stricken down its kindred blossoms." But then the mother thinks of the sorrow the child will experience if it lives, and how in adulthood, "true and lofty spirits [are] sullied by desolating passions." After thinking this, she hears a voice saying, "I am commissioned by Him who lent thee the flower, to gather it back in its brightness, to await thee in a land where neither sin nor sorrow can mar its beauty."[12] While readers today may find this passage treacly, the sentimental description might well have appealed to Dickens, who had already penned the pathos-laden deaths of Smike in *Nicholas Nickleby* and Little Nell in *The Old Curiosity Shop*, and who would subsequently compose moving death scenes for little Paul Dombey in *Dombey and Son* and Jo the crossing sweeper in *Bleak House*. Like the author of "The Mother's Love," Dickens couches child death scenes with the religious consolations of a sorrow-free afterlife that contrasts sharply with the corruptions of earthly life.

But the stories and essays in *The Lowell Offering* did more than resonate with Dickens. Numerous passages in the four hundred pages that he read bear a striking resemblance to *A Christmas Carol*, which he wrote the year after his visit to Lowell. The resemblances include images, narrative structures, themes, and phrasings that suggest that *The Lowell Offering* contributed to a stream of thoughts and feelings that came to fruition in the *Carol*. For instance, in the October 1840 issue of the journal, the essay "The Blessings of Memory" by "Dorothea" (her real name is not identified) shares one of the *Carol*'s central themes as well as key structural elements, and prefigures phrasings Dickens uses at a crucial passage in the novella. "The Blessings of Memory" argues that we need to appreciate the benefits of memory because it sustains and comforts us even more than hope does: "How little do we realize, while passing through this sublunary state of being, how much we are indebted to the ever-constant joys of memory for our present happiness!" The author goes on to say, "It is a lamentable fault of ours, that we allow ourselves so little time for sober retrospection. Unreal phantoms too often supplant the joys of memory. The Hero of yesterday is forgotten, while the Idol of to-day engrosses our attention! To-morrow is destined to become the sepulchre of To-day."[13]

The power of memory is a recurring theme in Dickens's works (more so after 1842 than before), and it plays a key role in *A Christmas Carol*. Scrooge's conversion begins when the Ghost of Christmas Past makes him relive his memories and reconnect to past sorrows and joys. The memories restore his humanity, making him more receptive to the messages of the Ghosts of Christmas Present and Christmas Yet to Come. But it is not only the focus on memory that *A Christmas Carol* shares with this piece from *The Lowell Offering*. The essay also anticipates the *Carol*'s tripartite temporal structure, emphasizing, as does the *Carol*, the importance of keeping past, present, and future integrated. And the essay's reference to "the *Idol* of to-day [which] *engrosses* our attention" is reflected, very closely, in the language Scrooge's fiancée uses when she is breaking off their engagement: "Another *idol* has displaced me. . . . the master-passion, Gain, *engrosses* you."[14] "The Blessings of Memory" also refers to phantoms, the spirit-world, and a sepulcher in relation to the future, all of which, of course, feature prominently in Dickens's first Christmas book. Like Dickens, the author of "The Blessings of Memory" projects ideas about memory against the backdrop of death. In light of what we all must come to, keeping one's memory alive (or "green" as Dickens would put it in *The Haunted Man and the Ghost's Bargain*, his last Christmas book) is essential to being a whole person. In fact, both authors establish a spectrum with memory on one side and death and a sepulcher on the other, suggesting that one is not really fully alive if one has lost touch with one's memories. For both authors, refusing to reignite memories through reflection is tantamount to hurtling headlong and thoughtlessly into the grave.

"The Blessings of Memory" is not alone in sharing similarities with *A Christmas Carol*. Many of the essays and stories in the 1840–41 issues of *The Lowell Offering*, the issues Dickens read, emphasize the themes of the importance of memory and of happiness not resulting from wealth and status, among the main lessons Scrooge learns. Consider the essay "Beauty and Wealth," from the October 1840 *Lowell Offering*, in which the author, "E.S.," muses on the perils that accompany both attributes: "Who would ask for the wealth of a Croesus, if, to obtain it, he must sacrifice 'The soul's calm sunshine, and the heart-felt joy?'"[15] This, of course, is precisely what Scrooge has done—amassed the wealth of a Croesus while sacrificing all heartfelt sources of joy. Similarly, the author of "Contentment" (December 1840) argues that "There is no connecting link between riches and happiness, nor between misery and poverty. . . . happiness is not the offspring of wealth."[16] The author of "The Nature of Man," also in the December 1840 issue, regrets how "man [has] abused that precious gift, intellect! and with how much more ardor does he pursue the things which are merely worldly, and which soon pass away, than the rich treasures . . . which know no decay but grow brighter as earthly pleasures vanish from our sight!"[17] Or again in the February 1841 issue, "Reflections at Home. Written during a Visit to My Kindred and Friends," the author, "Dorothea," writes, "Virtue alone is happiness.

Whether it be found in the obscurity of the cottage, or amidst the dazzle and grandeur of a lordly potentate."[18] Of course the theme of "money can't buy happiness" is hardly original to *The Lowell Offering*, but its preponderance in the issues that Dickens took away and read in 1842 is striking. That greed and selfishness play such central thematic and structural roles in the next two works of fiction Dickens wrote, *Martin Chuzzlewit* and *A Christmas Carol*, seems more than just coincidence. Naturally there are greedy characters in most of his novels, before and after 1842, but in those two, Dickens makes greed a central theme and structural device in a more systematic way than he had ever done before, with each work's plot focused on the redemption of a selfish character.

The thematic similarities between *The Lowell Offering* pieces and the *Carol* become more pronounced when spirits and dream visions enter the mix, as in "A Visit from Hope," "Happiness," "A Vision of Truth," and "Memory and Hope," all from 1841. "A Visit from Hope" (April 1841) opens with a spirit visitation: " 'PAST twelve!' said a sweet, musical voice, as I was seated by the expiring embers of a wood fire. I turned hastily to see who had thus intruded on my presence, when, lo! I beheld an old man. His thin white locks were parted on his forehead, his form was bent, and as he extended his thin, bony hand towards me, it shook like an aspen leaf."[19] The spirit, Hope, comes upon the speaker late at night as she hovers over a dying fire, much as Marley appears to Scrooge late at night as he leans over "a very low fire indeed."[20] The spirit in a "Visit from Hope" starts old but grows younger as he takes the narrator into the haunts of his youth; the Ghost of Christmas Past in *A Christmas Carol* is similarly ambiguous as to age—it looks "like a child: yet not so like a child as like an old man, viewed through some supernatural medium . . . [with its] hair . . . white as if with age."[21] And like Hope, the Ghost of Christmas Past takes its charge back in time to restore the protagonist's "repining spirit." The narrator of "A Visit from Hope" concludes by stating that she will "endeavor to profit by the advice he gave me," much the same as Scrooge promises at the end of his ghostly visits to "honour Christmas in my heart, and try to keep it all the year. I will live in the Past, the Present, and the Future. The Spirits of all Three shall strive within me. I will not shut out the lessons that they teach."[22] "A Visit from Hope" has none of the character development or linguistic richness of *A Christmas Carol*, but the two works share some striking images and structural similarities. In fact, "A Visit from Hope" would be a fitting subtitle to *A Christmas Carol*, since Scrooge's ghostly visitors provide the only hope he has for turning his life around.

"Happiness," published in the May 1841 *Lowell Offering*, presents a dream-vision in which the speaker "traverse[s] the world" observing people who search for happiness and fail to find it in fame, riches, and beauty. The speaker finally finds happiness in a humble country cottage surrounded by "trees and shrubbery" and inhabited by a "venerable man" with "happiness . . . legibly written on his every feature." The man tells the dreamer that one "must cultivate a soil" for the nourishment of happiness, rooting out the "seeds of discontent, pride, [and] envy," and cultivating the "seeds of humility, patience, [and] benevolence, watered by the tears of sympathy."[23] The dream-vision, in addition to its didactic tone, bears visual and structural similarities to the phantoms of misery that Marley reveals to Scrooge at the end of their encounter in stave 1 of *A Christmas Carol*. It also shares similarities with the visions of simple Christmas cheer that the Ghost of Christmas Present reveals to Scrooge in stave 3 at the miners' hut, the lonely lighthouse, and the Cratchit house. In both "Happiness" and the *Carol*, contentment can only be found in the haunts of the humble.

Published in *The Lowell Offering* in May 1841, "A Vision of Truth" by "Tabitha" (her real name was Betsey Chamberlain, an early Native American writer) similarly employs a dream-vision.[24] This vision offers an allegory that involves traveling in a foreign country and encountering a tree composed of interwoven tendrils from seeds "germinated in flower-pots, in the cotton mills." The tree is revealed to be the tree of "*Mental Knowledge*," and its leaves are *The Lowell Offering* itself.[25] While this story's dream-vision of finding worth in humble origins certainly bears similarities to *A Christmas Carol*, a more complex and more relevant vision emerges in "Memory and Hope," written by "Ellen" in the August 1841 *Lowell Offering*. In this vision, the speaker is approached by two spirits, one "a slender, fairy-like form, . . . light and buoyant" and the other "not less fair [but with] the reflection of age." They turn out to be "HOPE and MEMORY" (possibly the positive predecessors of the *Carol*'s disturbing "Ignorance and Want"). They work somewhat at cross purposes, for Hope holds out a garland of fame for which the speaker reaches, but Memory steps in and the laurels fall to the ground. Memory reminds the dreamer that all things cultivated by her own hand have withered, and adds, "think not . . . that the meed of fame will make you happy; but rather seek again the path of science, where you always found a never-failing spring of knowledge; and let the bubble, fame, pass away." The speaker concludes by making a Scrooge-like vow of a better life: "I shall profit by the advice of Memory, and never again covet the garland of fame; but endeavor, by deeds of benevolence, to make myself more useful to my fellow-creatures, and more acceptable to the Giver of every good and perfect gift,'" just as Scrooge makes himself more useful to his fellow-creatures by becoming "as good a friend, as good a master, and as good a man, as the good old city knew, or any other good old city, town, or borough, in the good old world."[26] As with "A Visit from Hope," "Memory and Hope" would serve well as a subtitle to *A Christmas Carol* since it is through the restoration of his memories that Scrooge finds hope for his future.

The essay "Christmas" by "Tabitha" (Betsey Chamberlain), published in the February 1841 *Lowell Offering*, ends with the resolution to lead a life more dedicated to helping her fellow creatures. The author describes a Christmas she spent with Scottish friends, listening to carolers and discussing the Christmas story. At the end of the night they "resolved, that from that time [they] would make it a part of [their] daily employment, to study the life of the Prince of Peace; and endeavor to fashion [their] lives according to the perfect pattern of righteousness which he has furnished."[27] The essay begins with a paean to Christmas as the "best day in the whole year," very similar to Fred's praising of Christmas to Scrooge in stave 1 of the *Carol*: "I am sure I have always thought of Christmas time, when it has come round—apart from the veneration due to its sacred name and origin . . . as a good time: a kind, forgiving, charitable, pleasant time: the only time I know of, in the long calendar of the year, when men and women seem by one consent to open their shut-up hearts freely, and to think of people below them as if they really were fellow-passengers to the grave, and not another race of creatures bound on other journeys."[28] As with Fred's speech, the main theme of the story "Christmas" is that the holiday reminds us to think beyond ourselves and strive to be better human beings, even if we fall short of our resolutions throughout the rest of the year. The essay emphasizes how the Christmas season "brings to remembrance scenes of 'by-gone days,'" scenes which remind us of our better selves, as is clearly the case with Scrooge in the *Carol*.[29]

The preponderance of thematic, imagistic, structural, and phrasing similarities between many of the essays and stories in the first two years of *The Lowell Offering* and Dickens's *A Christmas Carol* is striking. What has become known as "the Carol philosophy" clearly gets voiced earlier and with a similar cast of spirits by the Lowell mill girls in *The Lowell Offering*. This journal was not the only influence on the *Carol*, of course. Dickens's own earlier story, "The Story of the Goblins Who Stole a Sexton," one of the interpolated tales in *The Pickwick Papers* (1836–37), has long been recognized as a predecessor to the *Carol* with its conversion of a curmudgeon through the intervention of supernatural entities. But "The Story of the Goblins Who Stole a Sexton" is less like the *Carol* in tone and emotional effect than many of *The Lowell Offering* pieces, nor does it deal at all with the theme of memory so central to the *Carol* and *The Lowell Offering*. While "The Story of the Goblins Who Stole a Sexton" obviously has a supernatural element, its goblins are an antic, silly cast of characters who do somersaults and play leapfrog in the graveyard, and kick the sexton repeatedly to get their point across about what a miserable man he has been. They lack the mysterious, spiritual appeal shared by both the *Carol*'s ghosts and the supernatural guides of "Memory and Hope" and "A Visit from Hope." And while the sexton, Gabriel Grub, is a changed man after his night with the goblins, there is no emotional catharsis in his conversion nor does he put it to good use as do Scrooge and the narrators of "A Visit from Hope," "Memory and Hope," and "Christmas." Instead, Grub leaves the community for ten years, out of fear that his neighbors will scorn him for his reformation.

Another oft-cited influence on Dickens's composition of *A Christmas Carol* is the Second Report of the Children's Employment Commission, which shocked Dickens seven months before he began writing the *Carol*.[30] On 6 March 1843, Dickens wrote a letter to Dr. Southwood Smith, a physician and health reformer who had sent him the report, stating, "I am so perfectly stricken down by the blue book you have sent me, that I think . . . of writing, and bringing out, a very cheap pamphlet, called 'An appeal to the People of England, on behalf of the Poor Man's Child'—with my name attached, of course. I should be very glad to take counsel with you in the matter, and to receive any suggestions from you, in reference to it."[31] While Dickens never wrote the pamphlet, he wrote to Smith on 10 March 1843 to say that he planned to use the idea later in the year in another project and that Smith would see "that a Sledge hammer has come down with twenty times the force—twenty thousand times the force—I could exert by following out my first idea."[32] The editors of the Pilgrim edition of Dickens's letters suggest that the "Sledge hammer" blow was *A Christmas Carol*, which came out later that year— particularly its portrait of Ignorance and Want. These portraits may also be the "blow" he promised to E. M. Fitzgerald back in 1838 after visiting factories in Manchester: "I mean to strike the heaviest blow in my power for these unfortunate creatures, but whether I shall do so in the 'Nickleby', or wait some other opportunity, I have not yet determined."[33]

But there is a disconnect between the Second Report of the Children's Employment Commission and the *Carol*. The *Carol* does not directly deal with the conditions of working children. Ignorance and Want are terrifying representatives of neglected children, to be sure, but they are not necessarily representatives of factory children, so they are at best an indirect response to the report and to Dickens's visits to factories. Lowell, perhaps, provides the missing link. The report, with its information on children under seven years of age working thirteen-hour days in dangerous conditions, would have naturally reminded Dickens of the superior conditions he had witnessed the year before in Lowell, with its shorter hours, healthier living and working conditions, and limit on the number of months children could work per year so as to insure that they received an education. Lowell had shown Dickens that industry could be conducted more humanely for workers of all ages, so the example of Lowell and all that it had to offer would have been in his mind as he prepared his "Sledge hammer" blow against factory practices in Britain. It is not surprising, then, that images, phrases, themes, and structures from *The Lowell Offering* would come to mind when writing his response. For, in many ways, Lowell was the best possible response to the Second Report since it offered more than an attack—it offered a solution.

In Lowell, Dickens learned that industry could be both efficient and humane; that manufacturing and the arts did not have to be at odds; that a factory worker could work long hours but still cultivate her intellect and imagination. This was an enormously encouraging revelation for Dickens, and it fueled his devotion to social welfare projects for the rest of his life. Dickens indefatigably fought for sanitation reform, education reform, humane treatment for so-called fallen women, and other social projects, to the point that his social welfare work came close to becoming a second full-time job for him. Perhaps his establishment of Urania Cottage for fallen women in 1847, which he conducted with the help of philanthropist Angela Burdett Coutts, was influenced in part by the tidy, well-run boardinghouses he saw in Lowell. Certainly he worked hard to make sure the cottage was attractive and clean, that the women were well-dressed and fed, and that they had opportunities for entertainment, education, and job training that would help them to reclaim their lives. As the Lowell boardinghouses did, Dickens took women in a position that could have been degrading and depressing and gave them dignity and hope.

Lowell also showed Dickens how active and productive women could be—in both industry and the arts—and his subsequent female characters demonstrate his richer appreciation of women's capacities. Before Lowell, Dickens's female characters tended to be stereotypes of femininity—

beautiful and good but also bland and weak (e.g., Rose Maylie, Kate Nickleby, Little Nell). After Lowell, Dickens composed the most active and complex female characters of his career: Sarah Gamp, Edith Dombey, Lady Dedlock, Amy Dorrit, Estella, Miss Havisham, Lizzie Hexam, Jenny Wren.[34] It is almost as if America, and perhaps Lowell in particular, gave Dickens a new appreciation of women's capacity for strength and independence.

Lowell, and America in general, seem to have made Dickens more conscious of his power and responsibility as a writer, and more conscious of his novels as art. In America he came to understand how much power he had to sway people, and what a responsibility that power was. For the first time, he came to realize that he was a celebrity. People surrounded him in the streets and grabbed fistfuls of fur from his coat; they stood in line for hours to meet him and threw elaborate banquets and balls in his honor. Dickens understood that he could wield his celebrity for great good—and should. Of course he had already done so to a certain extent in attacking the New Poor Law in *Oliver Twist* and the Yorkshire schools in *Nicholas Nickleby*, but after his first trip to America, Dickens had a deeper sense of his influence and responsibility, and he engaged more systematically and extensively in social welfare projects for the rest of his career.

Lowell made Dickens aware that art and industry could complement one another and that he should keep both in mind when composing novels. He had certainly already been wildly creative and industrious in his writings, but he had not always composed artfully. His early novels tend to be episodic and show few signs of planning. In Lowell Dickens saw what could be done in a factory city that was well-planned with profits, education, entertainment, and the arts all kept in harmony. He tried to keep all these in balance too in well-planned novels for the rest of his career. After his first visit to America, Dickens became more consciously artful in his novel writing. *Martin Chuzzlewit*, his first novel after his American visit, was his first well-planned novel, with the theme of the dangers of selfishness woven through all the major characters and plot elements. It is not a universal favorite, but Dickens's friend and first biographer, John Forster, called it "the most masterly of his writings hitherto."[35] Numerous other critics agree.[36] From his next novel, *Dombey and Son*, to the end of his career, Dickens made working notes for his novels that reveal the planning he engaged in before starting a new work of fiction. He would sketch out basic plot devices, create brief chapter outlines, and list possible names of characters. He does not appear to have engaged in this kind of planning with his earlier novels. *A Christmas Carol*, written simultaneously with *Martin Chuzzlewit*, was his second well-planned book. Paul Schlicke refers to the *Carol* as "the most perfect work Dickens ever wrote."[37] And since it reflects major themes, images, characters, and phrasings of numerous pieces from the issues of *The Lowell Offering*, the Lowell mill girls deserve some credit for its perfection.

NOTES

1. Frances Trollope, *Domestic Manners of the Americans* (New York: Whittaker, Treacher, 1832); Frederick Marryat, *A Diary in America* (London: Longman, Orme, Brown, Green, and Longmans, 1839).

2. Charles Dickens, *The Pilgrim Edition of the Letters of Charles Dickens*, 12 vols., ed. Madeline House et al. (Oxford: Clarendon Press, 1965–2002), 3:50n.

3. Charles Dickens, *American Notes for General Circulation*, 2 vols. (London: Chapman and Hall, 1842), 1:4.154–55, 156, 157, 155. Citations to *American Notes* include volume number followed by a colon, and chapter and page number(s) separated by a period. Dickens was not the only observer to note the attractiveness of the Lowell mill girls. In *Loom and Spindle; or, Life among the Early Mill Girls*, Harriet H. Robinson, a former mill worker herself, quoted an article by John G. Whittier in which he described the mill girls as "acres of girlhood, beauty reckoned by the square rod,—or miles by long measure! the young, the graceful, the gay,—the flowers gathered from a thousand hillsides and green valleys of New England, fair unveiled Nuns of Industry." Harriet H. Robinson, *Loom and Spindle; or, Life among the Early Mill Girls*, rev. edn. (Kailua, Hawaii: Press Pacifica, 1996), 45.

4. Dickens, *American Notes*, 1:4.156. Dickens was seeing Lowell at its apex; as historian Thomas Dublin points out, the humane conditions Dickens witnessed during his visit deteriorated in the next decades due to growing competition in the textile industry and the increase of immigrants who could be hired more cheaply. See Dublin, *Women at Work: The Transformation of Work and Community in Lowell, Massachusetts, 1826–1860* (New York: Columbia University Press, 1993), 138.

5. Dickens, *Letters*, 1:483–84 (29 December 1838).

6. "Evidence Given before the Sadler Committee," *Parliamentary Papers*, vol. 15, www.victorianweb.org.

7. Ibid.

8. Robinson, *Loom and Spindle*, 27, 19, 22.

9. Dickens, *American Notes*, 1:4.159–60.

10. Dickens was not the only literary figure to write about *The Lowell Offering* with genuine admiration. The editor of the *North American Review*, John G. Palfrey, wrote, "Many of the articles are such as to satisfy the reader at once, that if he has only taken up *The Offering* as a phenomenon, and not as what may bear criticism and reward perusal, he has but to own his error, and dismiss his condescension as soon as may be." Quoted in Robinson, *Loom and Spindle*, 67. As Harriet Robinson noted, "Harriet Martineau prompted a fine review of it in the London *Athenaem*, and a selection from Volumes I

and II was published under her direction as *Mind Amongst the Spindles.*" Ibid., 67. Charles Knight, the editor of *Mind amongst the Spindles,* stated that he began reading the selections as a "duty" but that the reading quickly turned into a "pleasure." See Knight, *Mind amongst the Spindles: A Selection from the Lowell Offering, A Miscellany Wholly Composed by the Factory Girls of an American City* (London: Charles Knight, 1844), ix.

    11. Harriet Robinson, "Names and *Noms de Plume* of the Writers in *The Lowell Offering,*" in Judith Ranta, *Women and Children of the Mills: An Annotated Guide to Nineteenth-Century American Textile Factory Literature* (Westport, Conn.: Greenwood Press, 1999), 299–300.

    12. M, "The Mother's Love," *The Lowell Offering* 1 (October 1840): 2. Issues of *The Lowell Offering* are available at www.cs.arizona.edu/patterns/weaving/lo.html.

    13. Dorothea, "The Blessings of Memory," *The Lowell Offering* 1 (October 1840): 4.

    14. Charles Dickens, *A Christmas Carol,* facsimile edn. (New York: Columbia University Press, 1956), 2.65 (emphasis added). Citations to *A Christmas Carol* are by stave (chapter) and page number.

    15. E.S., "Beauty and Wealth," *The Lowell Offering* 1 (October 1840): 11. E.S. was possibly E. S. Pope. Robinson, *Loom and Spindle,* 300.

    16. Dorothea, "Contentment," *The Lowell Offering* 2 (December 1840): 24–25.

    17. Mariette, "The Nature of Man," *The Lowell Offering* 2 (December 1840): 26.

    18. Dorothea, "Reflections at Home. Written during a Visit to My Kindred and Friends," *The Lowell Offering* 3 (February 1841): 39.

    19. H, "A Visit from Hope," *The Lowell Offering* 1 (April 1841): 13.

    20. Dickens, *A Christmas Carol,* 1.23.

    21. Ibid., 2.43.

    22. "A Visit from Hope," 14; Dickens, *A Christmas Carol,* 4.151.

    23. Caroline, "Happiness," *The Lowell Offering* 2 (May 1841): 41–42.

    24. Ranta, *Women and Children of the Mills,* 48.

    25. Tabitha, "A Vision of Truth," *The Lowell Offering* 2 (May 1841): 44.

    26. Ellen, "Memory and Hope," *The Lowell Offering* 6 (August 1841): 175–76, 177; Dickens, *A Christmas Carol,* 5.165.

    27. Tabitha, "Christmas," *The Lowell Offering* 3 (February 1841): 40–42, 41–42 (quotation).

    28. Dickens, *A Christmas Carol,* 1.8–9.

    29. Tabitha, "Christmas," 40.

    30. Paul Schlicke, ed., *The Oxford Reader's Companion to Dickens* (Oxford: Oxford University Press, 1999), 98.

    31. Dickens, *Letters,* 3:459–60 (6 March 1843).

    32. Ibid., 3:461 (10 March 1843).

    33. Ibid., 1:483–84 (29 December 1838).

    34. See Michael Slater, *Dickens and Women* (Stanford, Calif.: Stanford University Press, 1983).

    35. John Forster, *The Life of Charles Dickens,* 3 vols. (London: Chapman and Hall, 1872–74), 2:41.

    36. Schlicke, ed., *The Oxford Reader's Companion to Dickens,* 377.

    37. Ibid., 98.

CHAPTER 2

Visions of Lowell, Light and Dark, in *Our Mutual Friend*

ANDRÉ DECUIR

✦

IN *American Notes for General Circulation*, Dickens praises the Lowell factory system, having toured the factories in Massachusetts as part of his 1842 visit to North America. He "marveled" at the Lowell mill women, undoubtedly contrasting them in his mind to the English mill workers of Manchester and Birmingham, who lived in "desperate misery."[1] Why, then, did Dickens not incorporate memories of Lowell into his fiction? Perhaps his childhood experience in the blacking factory and his observations of workers in English manufacturing towns may have ingrained in his mind such a sense of hopelessness and disgust that he could not bring himself to create in his novels a depiction of a system like the one he observed in Lowell.

In assessing the impact of the Lowell visit on Dickens's fiction, Natalie McKnight and Jerome Meckier offer opposing viewpoints. McKnight believes that the visit had far-reaching effects on Dickens's portrayal of women in particular. His observation of the Lowell factory girls and his reading of *The Lowell Offering* taught him "just how active, independent, and productive women could be, while still being attractive. After Lowell, Dickens began creating more interesting, active, and independent female characters than he had before."[2] Conversely, Meckier downplays the influence of the Lowell visit as the town's "wholesome advantages ... [were] not the stimulants Dickens's artistry required." Lowell, Meckier contends, did not stir the reformer in Dickens: "Lowell gave him ... no cause to raise the reformer's voice— ... a voice recognized the world over as Dickensian."[3] I believe a middle ground can be reached where we can see the intertwining of Dickens's admiration for Lowell, his social concerns, and even, as Michael Slater writes, his "profound and lifelong interest in the demeanour, behaviour and psychology of murderers" if we turn, as

McKnight suggests, to the later novels.[4] In *The Mystery of Edwin Drood* and in *Our Mutual Friend*, Dickens's primary purpose is to study dark psychological states, culminating in John Jasper but initiated in Bradley Headstone. Dickens seems to draw on his memories of Lowell, recalling images of a simple, picturesque time. He places Bradley Headstone in this context to highlight the character's inner turmoil, which leads to increasingly explosive psychological states.

What struck Dickens even before his visit to the factories was the "newness" of Lowell itself: "Those indications of its youth which first attract the eye, give it a quaintness and oddity of character which, to a visitor from the old country, is amusing enough." Significantly, it is the river, a looming character in *Our Mutual Friend*, which conveys this mood of amusement and wonder: Dickens seems to experience it as one would experience observing a carefree toddler at play. He says the river is "as light-headed, thoughtless, and brisk a young river, in its murmurings and tumblings, as one would desire to see."[5]

Twenty-two years later, in an anachronistic bubble, Dickens situates Lizzie Hexam in a Lowellesque mill of 1842, complete with a youthful, childlike river, but as Dickens was concerned at this point in his literary career with darker themes, he also hints at real-world threats as the river leaves a "protective space": "In those pleasant little towns on Thames, you may hear the fall of the water over the weirs, or even, in still weather, the rustle of the rushes; and from the bridge you may see the young river, dimpled like a young child, playfully gliding away among the trees, unpolluted by the defilements that lie in wait for it on its course."[6]

In such rich, descriptive passages, occurring often in *Our Mutual Friend*, Dickens equals, in prose, early nineteenth-century canvases with their fluffy white clouds reflected in mill ponds, scenes not too removed from his rendering of Lowell. In John Constable's 1820 painting, *Stratford Mill*, for example, while most of the painting is dominated by green trees and white clouds reflected in a pond, one can see on the far left the waterwheel, a feature of Lizzie's pastoral mill, where its sound has a "softening influence," and a feature of the admired Lowell mill as well: "The very river that moves the machinery in the mills (for they are all worked by water power), seems to acquire a new character from the fresh buildings of bright red brick and painted wood among which it takes its course."[7]

In the aforementioned descriptions, the ability of a body of water to reflect its surroundings is an indicator of youth, purity, and safety. Before her death, as Betty Higden approaches Lizzie's mill in the dark, she hears "the sound of a water-wheel at the side." In the pool before her, "the lighted windows were reflected," and as she draws near to what she believes is Heaven, "the lighted windows, both in their reality and their reflection in the water" give her an overwhelming sense of comfort and repose. "'I am safe here,' was her last benumbed thought. 'When I am found dead at the foot of the Cross, it will be by some of my own sort; some of the working people who work among the lights yonder. I cannot see the lighted windows now, but they are there. I am thankful for all!'" After Betty Higden's funeral in the village of Lizzie's mill, Bella Wilfer and John Rokesmith forget their London troubles and become closer on a stroll through a landscape reminiscent of a Constable painting: "The trees were bare of leaves, and the river was bare of water-lilies; but the sky was not bare of its beautiful blue, and the water reflected it, and a delicious wind ran with the stream, touching the surface crisply. . . . But the great serene mirror of the river seemed as if it might have reproduced all it had ever reflected between those placid banks, and brought nothing to the light save what was peaceful, pastoral, and blooming."[8]

Even inside a Lowell factory, Dickens was struck by "pristine" appearances, particularly of the mill women's dress and hygiene, and he describes them as not unlike the fresh "new character" of Lowell itself: "These girls, as I have said, were all well dressed: and that phrase necessarily includes extreme cleanliness. They had serviceable bonnets, good warm cloaks, and shawls; and were not above clogs and pattens. . . . They were healthy in appearance."[9] In *Our Mutual Friend*, river scavenger-turned-mill-girl Lizzie, even after being "up with the night-hands last night" at her Lowellesque mill, has "the earnest face of a woman who is young and handsome." Indeed, a conversation between Bella Wilfer and John Rokesmith after meeting Lizzie at Betty Higden's funeral echoes Dickens's comment on the appearance of the Lowell mill girls:

> "You think well of her, Mr. Rokesmith?" pursued Bella, conscious of making all the advances.
>
>   "I think highly of her."
>
>   "I am so glad of that! Something quite refined in her beauty, is there not?"
>
>   "Her appearance is very striking."[10]

Even Marcus Stone's illustration "The Parting by the River" seems to suggest that in this section of *Our Mutual Friend*, Dickens is recreating his memories of Lowell and its factory girls (fig. 2.1). With her bonnet and outer garment for warmth, factory girl Lizzie wears the "attire" "of a

Figure 2.1. Marcus Stone, "The Parting by the River," from *Our Mutual Friend* (book 4, chapter 6). Courtesy of Worcester Polytechnic Institute Curation, Preservation, and Archives, George C. Gordon Library.

respectable middle-class woman" in a "romantic setting."[11] The blossoming of Lizzie in this setting may indeed reflect a reworking of Dickens's memories of the Lowell girls and their surroundings. According to Dickens, many of the girls "were only then just verging from womanhood, . . . some . . . delicate and fragile" but without painful expressions on their faces. The health of these young women seems to be intertwined with the "green plants" in the windows of some of the factories, "trained to shade the glass." Like tender plants themselves, the girls are given "as much fresh air, cleanliness, and comfort, as the nature of the occupation would possibly admit of."[12]

Turning to living conditions outside the factory, Dickens, in his depiction of Lizzie's life as a factory girl, once again borrows from his memories of Lowell, reworking them to create an even more utopian view of what mill life could be. Dickens was impressed by the girls' living accommodations and seems to have approved of the "protective" regulations set forth by mill owners: the workers "reside in various boarding-houses near at hand. The owners of the mills are particularly careful to allow no persons to enter upon the possession of these houses, whose characters have not undergone the most searching and thorough inquiry."[13] According to historian Thomas Dublin, boardinghouse life served as an "instrument of social control," extending into the private lives of the girls. For example,

"The Suffolk Company regulations noted 'A regular attendance on public worship on the Sabbath is necessary for the preservation of good order,' and stated emphatically 'The Company will not employ any person who is habitually absent [from services].'"[14]

In *Our Mutual Friend*, Dickens writes that Lizzie "had a lodging with an elderly couple employed in the establishment," and while some kind of "parental protection" is implied, it is not so severe as to interfere with religious freedom. Lizzie explains to Mrs. Milvey that the managing partner and his wife "most willingly and cheerfully do their duty to all of us who are employed here, and we try to do ours to them. Indeed they do much more than their duty to us, for they are wonderfully mindful of us in many ways." When Mrs. Milvey fears that the managing partners will convert Lizzie to Judaism, Lizzie calmly explains that they never even asked her about her religion, and they leave "all of us to ours." She continues, "They never talk of theirs to us, and they never talk of ours to us. If I was the last in the mill, it would be just the same."[15] We do not know if there is "a joint-stock piano," as Dickens saw in Lowell boarding-houses, but he does give us a glimpse of Lizzie's room.[16] While it is "very low in the ceiling, and very rugged in the floor," to Bella, Lizzie's visitor, "it was a pleasanter room than that despised chamber once at [Bella's] home."[17]

As to the working hours and working conditions within the factories, Dickens may have been unaware of several failed protests of the 1830s and 1840s, especially the Ten Hour Movement; "women known to be activists, or even those caught reading 'radical' newspapers, were subject to instant dismissal and subsequent blacklisting throughout New England."[18] It is difficult to gauge what Dickens would have thought of the Lowell Mill strikes. From knowledge of his own childhood experiences in the blacking factory and from his novel *Hard Times*, one might expect Dickens to be critical of long working hours. As Slater points out, however, under Dickens's editorship, *The Daily News* "opposed . . . [the] bill seeking to limit factory workers' hours to ten a day." Wages could have been reduced under such an act, so perhaps Dickens's criticism was leveled mainly at the ignorance of those denying the humanity of the factory worker and those without "a more sympathetic *understanding* of the plight of the poor."[19] In *American Notes*, Dickens indicates he is cognizant of the long hours worked in the Lowell mills—"upon an average, twelve hours a day, which is unquestionably work, and pretty tight work too"—but he refrains from being overly critical of the routine. Even child labor seems acceptable as long as education is provided: "There are a few children employed in these factories, but not many. The laws of the State forbid their working more than nine months in the year, and require that they be educated during the other three."[20]

Dickens's enthusiasm over the appearance of the Lowell mills and their workers, and perhaps, as Meckier writes, the brevity of his visit, may have prevented Dickens from looking deeper with the reformer's eye.[21] Still, subtle criticism of the factory workers' conditions may be found in *Our Mutual Friend,* possibly based on actions Dickens observed in the Lowell mills. Despite Lizzie's claims of the magnanimity of her employers, when the mill bell rings, Lizzie, even with out-of-town guests for a funeral, practically disappears, the consequences of tardiness presumably being quite grim. Indeed, as one of the Lowell mill girls writes, "Up before the day, at the clang of the bell—and out of the mill by the clang of the bell— into the mill, and at work, in obedience to that ding-dong of a bell—just as though we were so many living machines."[22] Lizzie's sudden departure to go back to work leaves her guests rather shocked, "the Secretary and Bella standing rather awkwardly in the small street."[23]

Any gentle fault-finding of the Lowell system through his depiction of Lizzie's mill experience wanes when Dickens depicts the evil acts that take place against this innocent setting. In the chapter "Setting Traps," Bradley Headstone's stalking becomes more sinister, and the culminating violence more shocking, when played out against scenes of pastoral beauty: "PLASHWATER Weir-Mill Lock looked tranquil and pretty on an evening in the summer time. A soft air stirred the leaves of the fresh green trees, and passed like a smooth shadow over the river, and like a smoother shadow over the yielding grass. The voice of the falling water, like the voices of the sea and the wind, were as an outer memory to a contemplative listener." Dickens foreshadows the deadly events involving Headstone and Riderhood by pointing out what sometimes comes through the lock when it is opened, despite the green trees, blue skies, and cascading water: "The water rose and rose as the sluice poured in, dispersing the scum which had formed behind the lumbering gates."[24]

The chapter "A Cry for Help" begins very much like "Setting Traps" but contains some of Dickens's richest language, describing a setting with "flushed sky," "the silver river," and "deep green fields of corn." Perhaps recalling the contentment he observed in the Lowell factory girls, Dickens creates a sense of euphoria in the workers as they leave the mill for the day, their already-high spirits infused by and reflected in the expansive beauty of the natural scene: "THE Paper Mill had stopped work for the night, and the paths and roads in its neighbourhood were sprinkled with clusters of people going home from their day's labour in it. There were men, women, and children in the groups. . . . The mingling of various voices and the sound of laughter made a cheerful impression upon the ear. . . . Into the sheet of water reflecting the flushed sky in the foreground of the living picture, a knot of urchins were casting stones, and watching the expansion of the rippling circles." The evening land-scape extends "beyond the hedge-rows and the clumps of trees—beyond the windmills on the ridge—away to where the sky appeared to meet the earth, as if there were no immensity of space between mankind and Heaven."[25] Dickens heightens the drama of the upcoming attack on Eugene Wrayburn by having it take place against such a romantic back-drop, and these lush passages signal the beginning of Dickens's drawing the lines between dark and light more solidly.

Near the end of his impressions of Lowell, a line, often overlooked, demonstrates that Dickens was far from a naive observer. He understood that Lowell's "humane" system might have resulted from its youth and therefore felt that it would be unfair to compare it to the British system, as "many of the circumstances whose strong influence has been at work for years in our manufacturing towns have not arisen here." In the pen-ultimate paragraph of this chapter of *American Notes*, Dickens fails to sound a confident note that the American manufacturing system will bypass the "desperate misery" he observed in English factory towns and will remain "the Good" in a strong contrast "between the Good and Evil, the living light and deepest shadow."[26]

Dickens further explores this evil in *Hard Times* in the story of Stephen Blackpool and in the far-reaching pollution of the natural landscape. In *Hard Times*, the "green landscape . . . over-arched by a bright blue sky" is soiled by debris such as "bricks and beams overgrown with grass, marking the site of deserted works" and made dangerous with "old pits hidden be-neath" the tall grass.[27] By the time Dickens wrote *Our Mutual Friend* and *The Mystery of Edwin Drood*, the evil that most concerned Dickens came from within the human heart of those who found themselves trapped in an iron-clad routine, when self-loathing became twisted and projected on others, eventually resulting in destruction.

Dickens begins to explore this psychological deformation in the character of Tom Gradgrind, whose constraint in a utilitarian system of education causes him to lash out against nature as he picks rosebuds to pieces, even biting "and tearing them away from his teeth with a hand

that tremble[s] like an infirm old man's."[28] This exploration ends with
John Jasper. The choirmaster's frustration at "the cramped monotony of
[his] existence," and his jealousy and obsessive desires, breed a disease
that can infect a garden with a "black mark" on a bright, sunny day.[29]
The transitional figure is Bradley Headstone, whose surname predicts the
fate of those who become trapped by their frustrations. Brian Cheadle
writes that "Bradley, laboriously filling his mind with routine rote
learning, has sacrificed everything to the achievement of a professional
status."[30] When that status is not recognized to the extent he wishes, his
rage, fueled with frustrated sexual desire, leads to his attack on Eugene
Wrayburn, his rival.

Before his attack, even the jaded Wrayburn seems mesmerized by the
reflection of the stars that "kindled deep in the water"—until, "in an instant, with a dreadful crash, the reflected night turned crooked, flames
shot jaggedly across the air, and the moon and stars came bursting from
the sky." The mirror-like reflection in the water, Dickens's symbol of
purity-in-newness, perhaps begun in his descriptions of Lowell in *American Notes,* is shattered. So much blood spills from the assault that even
at nightfall, Lizzie recognizes the grass as "bloody." In his study of the
darkness of human nature, Dickens describes the water as polluted not
by the dye of a factory but by blood spilled by a man in a jealous rage.
Lizzie sees "that the watery margin of the bank was bloody," and as she
pulls the body through the water, it colors "the water all about it with
dark red streaks."[31]

Like the river near Wrayburn's attack, the charming Plashwater Weir
becomes a setting for violence and death. Headstone grabs Rogue Riderhood, his grip like "an iron ring," and plunges both of them from the weir
into the water. The narrator reports that "the two were found, lying under
the ooze and scum behind one of the rotting gates."[32]

Lucinda Hawksley points out that Dickens "experienced several personal tragedies and shocks" while writing *Our Mutual Friend* in 1864–65.
He suffered the deaths of his son Walter and his friend John Leech,
he began "suffering such severe pain in his left foot that he was sometimes left unable to walk," and he was involved in the Staplehurst railway accident, before completing the novel.[33] It may not seem surprising
then, that Dickens would grasp at these memories of newness, fresh-
ness, and innocence, conveyed so long ago in his own impressions of
Lowell, Massachusetts, and incorporate them into scenes in *Our Mutual
Friend.* Dickens's novel throws into stark relief, against the fading back-
drop of romantic art mixed with his memories of Lowell, the polluting

"defilements" that come not from factory runoff but from what haunted Dickens in the latter part of his career—the fragile and potentially dangerous human psyche.

NOTES

1. Charles Dickens, *American Notes for General Circulation*, 2 vols. (London: Chapman and Hall, 1842), 1:4.164. Citations to *American Notes* include volume number followed by a colon, and chapter and page number(s) separated by a period.

2. Natalie McKnight, "Dickens and Industry," *Dickens Quarterly* 19, no. 3 (2002): 138.

3. Jerome Meckier, "Chapter Four of *American Notes:* Self-Discovery in Lowell; or, Why Little Nell Would Have Been Happy There but Dickens Was Not," *Dickens Quarterly* 19, no. 3 (2002): 125, 131.

4. Michael Slater, *Charles Dickens* (New Haven, Conn.: Yale University Press, 2009), 602.

5. Dickens, *American Notes*, 1:4.153, 152.

6. Charles Dickens, *Our Mutual Friend*, 2 vols. (London: Chapman and Hall, 1864–65), 3.8.66. Citations to *Our Mutual Friend* are by book, chapter, and page number(s), with pagination recommencing at the beginning of vol. 2 (book 3).

7. Ibid., 3.9.974; Dickens, *American Notes*, 1:4.155–56.

8. Dickens, *Our Mutual Friend*, 3.8.72, 3.9.79–80.

9. Dickens, *American Notes*, 1:4.155–56.

10. Dickens, *Our Mutual Friend*, 3.8.72, 3.9.76.

11. Philip K. Allingham, "Marcus Stone: An Overview," Victorian Web, http://victorianweb.org.

12. Dickens, *American Notes*, 1:4.156–57.

13. Ibid., 1:4.157.

14. Thomas Dublin, *Women at Work* (New York: Columbia University Press, 1979), 77, 78.

15. Dickens, *Our Mutual Friend*, 3.9.76, 75.

16. Dickens, *American Notes*, 1:4.159.

17. Dickens, *Our Mutual Friend*, 3.9.80.

18. Benita Eisler, "Introduction," in *The Lowell Offering: Writings by New England Mill Women (1840–1845)*, ed. Benita Eisler (Philadelphia: J. B. Lippincott, 1977), 38.

19. Slater, *Charles Dickens*, 244.

20. Dickens, *American Notes*, 1:4.160, 157–58.

21. Meckier, "Chapter Four," 124.

22. Alice K. Flanagan, *The Lowell Mill Girls* (Minneapolis: Compass Point Books, 2005), 20.

23. Dickens, *Our Mutual Friend*, 3.9.76.

24. Ibid., 4.1.161.

25. Ibid., 4.6.206.

26. Dickens, *American Notes*, 1:4.163, 164.

27. Charles Dickens, *Hard Times*, in *Household Words*, vol. 9, nos. 210–29 (1 April–12 August 1854), 34.576. Citations to *Hard Times* are by chapter and page number(s).

28. Ibid., 23.433.

29. Charles Dickens, *The Mystery of Edwin Drood* (London: Chapman and Hall, 1870), 2.10, 19.149. Citations to *The Mystery of Edwin Drood* are by chapter and page number(s).

30. Brian Cheadle, "Work in *Our Mutual Friend*," *Essays in Criticism* 51, no. 3 (July 2001): 323.

31. Dickens, *Our Mutual Friend,* 4.5.213, 4.6.214, 215.

32. Ibid., 4.15.293.

33. Lucinda Dickens Hawksley, *Dickens' Bicentenary 1812–2012: Charles Dickens* (San Rafael, Calif.: Insight, 2011), 106.

CHAPTER 3

Dickens's Visit to the Perkins School and "Doctor Marigold"

DIANA C. ARCHIBALD

✦

DICKENS'S ENORMOUSLY popular Christmas tale "Doctor Marigold's Prescriptions" (1865)[1] has sometimes been dismissed by critics and readers as an overly sentimental and formulaic story.[2] The cheap jack protagonist, a traveling salesman (named "Doctor" after the man who delivered him), recounts his life's story in this dramatic monologue, telling of his failed marriage to an abusive woman who beat their child (Sophy); his daughter's death and his adoption of a deaf-mute girl whom he renames Sophy; and through many years of patient care and sacrifice, Sophy's transformation into a lady.[3] The eventual happy ending features the obligatory family gathered around the Christmas fire. While this lesser-known Dickens holiday story includes some sentimental elements and adheres to some of the Christmas story conventions Dickens established when he invented the genre, in many ways this text is remarkable. Not only is the form of the work exceptionally well-conceived and executed, with an outstanding sense of character development achieved through the monologue technique, but the content of the story is also notably progressive for its day.

Known for his advocacy for the poor and weak, Dickens often stood on the side of the oppressed both in life and literature. His fiction is filled with orphans, widows, beggars, and the sick. Certainly his advocacy for reform stemmed from a commitment to helping the weakest members of society, and his efforts were far-reaching and influential. That said, at times the measures he supported were less enlightened than one would expect from such a vociferous advocate for the oppressed, but he seems to have been influenced by middle-class fears of working-class disorder and disruption. He usually sought measured reform within reasonable bounds, avoiding revolutionary stances. Yet his portrayal of Sophy and her family in "Doctor Marigold" was groundbreaking for its day, taking

the side of the deaf and advocating for sign language education at a time
when oralism was taking hold in English deaf education. Among the
many influences on Dickens's representations of deafness in this work, his
1842 visit to the Perkins School for the Blind in Boston, Massachusetts, is
significant, leading to a more radical vision of deaf education and culture
than most other Victorian authors were able to produce.

At the end of the eighteenth century, schools began to be formed for
the prelingual deaf, that is, children who were born deaf or who were
deafened at an early age. The idea that the deaf could be taught to communicate, even sometimes to speak aloud, was "a revelation to the general
public."[4] Prior to and even persisting into the nineteenth century, most
people believed that the deaf were "automata" without the essential qualities of humanness that speech conferred. In France, education of the deaf
using sign language had already taken hold by the 1760s, and the French
remained influential in deaf education, with Laurent Clerc spreading a
form of French sign language to the United States in the nineteenth century. While it is now understood that sign language ought to be the first
language of the prelingual deaf, as the most natural form of expression
for this group, increasingly throughout the Victorian period, many leading deaf educators (who were themselves hearing) continued to privilege
lip reading and oral expression above what they saw as a more primitive
form of communication: sign language.[5] Efforts to eradicate sign language reached a fever pitch in 1880 at "the second international confer-
ence on the deaf and dumb" held in Milan, where a resolution was passed
to affirm that "oral speech had 'incontestable superiority' over signs, and
that oral speech and only oral speech should be taught to the deaf." Even
in 1865 when "Doctor Marigold" was published, oralism was beginning to
take hold in Britain, with many institutions beginning to require oralist
methods and downplay sign language or even ban it outright.[6]

Dickens's Christmas story, then, must be seen in the context of this
heated debate about language and humanness. While the deaf advo-
cated for sign language as a fully legitimate and deeply expressive form
of human communication, hearing deaf educators sought to humanize
the deaf by forcing them to use an extremely difficult language to acquire,
advocating for a process much akin to the eradication of Native American languages at Indian boarding schools where speaking one's native
tongue was strictly forbidden. Deaf teachers began to be fired for fear that
they would not be suitable teachers for oralist methods, and use of sign
language increasingly became a punishable offense in schools. Where,
then, did Dickens acquire his vision of deaf signers as fully human and

functional, and why did he take this controversial stance in his story, going against the grain not only of the so-called experts but also of almost all literary conventions established for the representation of the deaf?

It was common for Victorian tourists to visit local institutions in the cities on their travel itineraries. Today it may seem strange to include a tour of a mental health facility or a prison as part of a vacation, but interest in such institutions was high for middle-class, reform-minded citizens. The schools, prisons, and hospitals of the young American republic attracted particular attention as potential models for Old Country reform, or as failures that could be held up as evidence of the unfeasibility of democracy. Dickens came to America eager to see the former, expecting to find many examples of new approaches to old problems. In Lowell, Massachusetts, for instance, he observed a well-organized, paternalistic mill system that seemed to obviate many of the terrors of industrialization seen in the factory towns of England. While in Boston, he toured the Perkins School for the Blind, the world's leading institution for the blind and deaf-blind, and met its most famous student, Laura Bridgman, the first deaf-blind person in the world to be taught abstract language.[7] The school had only been open for a decade when Dickens visited, but it had already established itself as a center for innovative education. The school's director, Dr. Samuel Gridley Howe, a shrewd public relations practitioner, wrote extensively about his success with Bridgman, publishing in his annual reports accounts of her education and distributing copies widely to enhance the school's reputation and advance its cause.

During Dickens's visit, he met Bridgman and recorded the scene in his 1842 travel book, *American Notes for General Circulation,* along with several long passages about her quoted directly from Howe's reports. Dickens used quotation marks but failed to acknowledge his source fully. Dickens's visit to the Perkins School strongly impressed the twenty-nine-year-old author, who wholly adopted and replicated the idealized version of the thirteen-year-old girl that Howe had created for public consumption. When Dickens met her, Bridgman had been a Perkins student for five years, and had learned to communicate first through sign language and eventually through writing. Dickens viewed her journal, with its handwriting remarkably legible, considering the difficulty of such production. She also could read texts printed in Boston Line Type, a raised letter font developed in Massachusetts to teach the blind to read.[8] This young girl, who had risen above what the Victorians would dub the severest of "infirmities"—the inability to hear, speak, see, or smell—was clearly intelligent and literate, as well as fully human. Her distinguished guest writes, "Her face was radiant with intelligence and pleasure."[9] Further, in the *American Notes* account Bridgman seems almost angelic in her innocence and transparency, a truly "sentimental heroine."[10] She displays a becoming modesty for a girl, rejecting the touch of the author's hand, as she did with "any man who is a stranger to her," but retaining Catherine Dickens's hand "with evident pleasure." Bridgman "kissed her, and examined her dress with a girl's curiosity and interest."[11] Modest, intelligent, social, and lively, Bridgman had the makings of a Dickensian heroine.

Of special significance for our purposes, Dickens also quotes Howe's description of her speaking in "*finger language*" with her eagerness to "sit close beside [people], hold their hand, and converse with them by signs." Bridgman was capable of producing sounds, but this vocalization is described in *American Notes* as "an uncouth noise which was rather painful to hear," and the girl is gently reminded not to speak when her teacher places a finger to Bridgman's lips.[12] This scene, described first by Howe and reproduced by Dickens, emphasizes the naturalness of sign language and the unnaturalness of speech for the deaf girl. Even though the oralists would not begin to gain ascendancy for another twenty years, the image of the happy and intelligent signing young female student in a community of signers is unusual and powerful. Considering Dickens's popularity and the wide availability of his books, this account of Bridgman continued for generations to attest to the power of signing. The image surfaces again in 1865 in "Doctor Marigold." The visit to the Perkins School, and his encounter with Laura Bridgman, had given Dickens a gift, a vision of the deaf becoming self-actualized through sign language education.

Jennifer Esmail notes that whereas many types of "disability, impairment, and illness [especially blindness] render a character an object of interest in Victorian fiction," by contrast, deafness in a hero or heroine is rare. In fact, the deaf in Victorian literature are usually comic characters who speak but cannot hear. Although Esmail claims that "Collins's novel *Hide and Seek* (1854, revised 1861) and Dickens's Christmas story 'Doctor Marigold' (1865) are the only Victorian fictional texts to feature a deaf character who uses a signed language," there are a few others, for instance, Charlotte Elizabeth's "Jack the Dumb Boy."[13] Esmail's point is well taken, however, since such portraits remain rare in the period and even in contemporary fiction. Edna Edith Sayers argues that one reason the deaf are so rarely portrayed in fiction is that "deaf people are rare in real life," with only "about one-tenth of one percent of the [U.S.] population . . . born deaf." She also notes that portraying deaf communication can be tricky since characters must share a language, and the "technical challenges of creating a deaf character" are significant.[14] Esmail argues that "the efface-ment of deafness from Victorian fiction reveals its investment in a par-ticular and normativized relationship between bodies, spoken language, and textuality: one that understands fiction as a record of what was said and heard," with the deaf thus essentially excluded from the genre be-cause their "constructed signed languages" were seen "as more embodied" and therefore primitive, lacking in the subtlety of the spoken word.[15] Much of the work the novel does is convey oral speech; accordingly, the bias in favor of the hearing is notable. Victorian representations of deaf characters who communicate through signs rarely appear, and when they do, these instances are striking.

What made Dickens choose to portray a signing deaf character in his story, going so much against the grain of Victorian society? Indeed, Dickens usually followed the Victorian norm of including comic deaf characters in his fiction, "deploy[ing] deafness for comic effect." Con-sider, for example, Wemmick's honored "Aged P" from *Great Expectations*, whose only real form of communication is bobbing his head. Likewise, in *The Pickwick Papers*, "the deaf old lady" Mrs. Wardle "must have secrets shouted into her ear."[16] But Sophy in "Doctor Marigold," is no laugh-ing matter. She is a serious character. Sayers argues that the most suc-cessful portraits of deaf characters are "almost always created by authors who either know deaf people firsthand" or have completed extensive re-search.[17] Dickens knew deaf people, having met many on his visits to deaf schools in both the United States and Britain. Shortly after arriving home from his American tour and while writing the Laura Bridgman section of *American Notes*, Dickens also helped a "wretched deaf and dumb boy" that he had found on the beach at Broadstairs, by placing the boy "(for the present) into the union infirmary at Minster" (the Isle of Thanet Union workhouse).[18] He read widely on the subject, most notably John Kitto's autobiography, *Lost Senses* (1845). Kitto's book is particularly interesting since it was written by a deaf person and offers a firsthand account of his experience of deafness. Kitto also cites *American Notes* as a highly influ-ential representation of deafness through its portrait of Bridgman, and the two authors corresponded in 1850. Dickens even recommended the book to his friend Wilkie Collins to use as research for a deaf character that Collins was creating for his novel *Hide and Seek* (1854), a book he subsequently dedicated to Dickens. Beyond the Kitto and Perkins con-nections, Dickens also reportedly became one of the governors of the London Asylum for the Deaf and Dumb in the Old Kent Road, thereby likely gaining additional perspectives on the lives of the deaf.[19]

Dickens thus had the means of creating a realistic portrait of a deaf character, and perhaps some of his motivation for doing so stemmed from his contact with the deaf. But there were artistic reasons for his choice as well. Martha Stoddard Holmes writes that "disability is melodramatic machinery, a simple tool for cranking open feelings."[20] Still, "no matter how close ['imagined women with disabilities'] get to the traditional Victorian heroine's plot of courtship, love, and marriage, disabled women characters almost never become biological parents."[21] Yet after Sophy's marriage to a deaf man whom she meets at school, she bears a child. In this story, as Holmes remarks, "a deaf woman's baby's risk of impairment is invested with pathos and suspense . . . in which the outcome—the birth of a hearing child to two deaf parents—is a good example of narrative fiction palliating the concerns about hereditary 'defect' raised by Victorian medical science."[22] Dickens's Sophy, according to Holmes, is thus used to reassure Victorian audiences about deafness, making this disability less threatening and more sympathetic. The somewhat melodramatic genre conventions of the Christmas story dictate an emotional response for readers, and incorporating a deaf character allowed Dickens to achieve this goal. What is unusual here is the level of Sophy's normalcy achieved throughout the story. Although Dickens may have begun by envisioning melodrama, his faithful adherence to character truths led to a much more radical portrait than Holmes recognizes.

One of the ways in which Dickens accomplished this realism was by focusing much of the text in which Sophy appears on her education. Approximately three-quarters of the story's discussion of Sophy has to do with communication and education. How would a cheap jack educate such a girl? The "gentleman" at the "Deaf and Dumb Establishment in London" asks how it is "possible that [Marigold has] been her only teacher."[23] Indeed, the cheap jack's intense desire for his daughter to become literate, and his ability to make that happen, may be the most unrealistic part of the story. Still, Marigold's methods are accurate, and one can suppose him capable of this kind of instruction. Historically, many poor families of deaf children did manage to create systems of signs for family communication. It is only the extra step that Marigold takes to teach Sophy to read and write that stretches credulity. Impressed with Sophy's ability to read and write as well as to use a manual language that she and her adoptive father have created, the gentleman remarks, "You're a clever fellow, and a good fellow." Note here, though, Marigold's precise response: "I have been her only teacher . . . besides herself."[24] Indeed, Sophy is remarkably intelligent and quick, and she finds many ways to express herself in a complex fashion. Dickens constructs her as an active agent in her own development, not merely a passive object of pity.

It is interesting to recognize that her adoptive father's careful and patient attempts to convey abstract language to Sophy as a young child are mirrored in the descriptions in the Perkins School annual reports of early attempts to teach Laura Bridgman. We know that Dickens was given copies of several of these annual reports, since he transcribed whole sections of them into his account of Laura in *American Notes*. Dickens describes Bridgman as "radiant with intelligence and pleasure," finding her to be a "gentle, tender, guileless, grateful hearted being."[25] Sophy is "wonderful fond" of Marigold, "eager" to please him, and "would clap her hands and laugh for joy" upon communicating effectively with him. Compare this to the first glimpse we have of Sophy when she is described as having "escaped from the Wild Beast Show." The love of her adoptive father leads to his determination that she be "cared for and more kindly used," and she is transformed through his efforts and her own.[26] As a child, locked in her "tomb," Bridgman's condition is also described by Howe as subhuman, for "those who cannot be enlightened by reason, can only be controlled by force; and this, coupled with her great privations, must soon have reduced her to a worse condition than that of the beasts that perish, but for [the] timely and unhoped-for aid" of the Perkins School.[27] She was brought to a place that unlocked language for her and thus gave her the world. Howe taught her language by presenting her with familiar objects labeled with raised-letter type naming the objects. Just as Marigold hangs signs on the objects in his realm, Dr. Howe in his classroom labeled objects with tactile writing.

More notable than these similarities, however, is Dickens's use of a philanthropic school for the deaf in his story. The story's "Deaf and Dumb Establishment in London" has, in the past, been thought to be modeled on the London Asylum for the Deaf and Dumb in the Old Kent Road, where Dickens had reportedly served on the board of governors. But the evidence is unclear on how actively involved Dickens was in the practices of this institution, and the resemblance of the fictional and real institutions appears to be fairly superficial.[28] The real school had already in 1865 begun to adhere to oralist methods by "employing articulation training," but the fictional school offers only a sign-based education for Sophy. In fact, the story's Deaf and Dumb Establishment has more in common with American institutions such as the Perkins School, the world's leading progressive institution at the time for teaching the deaf-blind. As Esmail reminds us, "In *American Notes,* Dickens explicitly supported the establishment of schools" in England modeled "on the American system."[29] For a writer famous for portraying horrendous educational institutions, it is important for us to recognize that *this* fictional school is a model of enlightened instruction.

The fact that Marigold gives up his daughter for two years in order that she "be cut off from the world as little as can be, considering her deprivations," effectively demonstrates the depth of his love.[30] The gift of literacy comes only because of Marigold's sacrifice, but to him it is the key to breaking the deaf girl's sense of isolation. Reading opens up the world to her, but her educational experience does even more—it brings her into close connection with a deaf community. Sayers notes that one of the most common characteristics of deaf characters in literature, even into the 1970s, is that "they are almost invariably solitary figures, isolated in the hearing world."[31] Sophy's father sees her isolation and wants to do everything he can to connect her to the world. This is why he is willing to break his heart in giving her up.

When Marigold returns to London two years later to retrieve his daughter, she is "grown such a woman, so pretty, so intelligent, so expressive!" The unnamed gentleman praises him, saying, "It was you who raised her from misery and degradation, and brought her into communication with her kind," meaning helping her to become human.[32] But it is the *school* that truly connects her to her "kind" by introducing her to a deaf community. This is not a story of a disabled person miraculously cured of her so-called affliction and then subsumed by the dominant culture's values. Neither is it a story of a disabled person meeting a tragic end or being loved but locked away in a safe cottage out of public view. Sophy moves out into the world by moving to the Far East—certainly not the safety net her father had envisioned for his daughter, ensconced in the book cart he devised for her amusement, and venturing forth through books only. Instead, Sophy appears to have become adept enough at navigating the hearing world to function independently and raise a family. By the end, she is no longer an isolated figure.

At the same time that she is moving out into the world, she also becomes more deeply entrenched in deaf culture by marrying a deaf man. And consider how truly remarkable that fact is in some ways. One might think it common to pair disabled characters together, but as Goldie Morgentaler notes, with the rise of eugenics, fear of the spread of undesirable traits through sexual reproduction led to restrictions in life and literature of such intermarrying.[33] What is perhaps the most surprising part of "Doctor Marigold's Prescription" is the positive representation offered of the young man Sophy marries. He is "well dressed and well looking," the son of a merchant. He has enough means "to keep a wife" and has accepted a clerk's position in a business in China.[34] He is fully engaged in the world as a contributing member of society, yet he is deaf and thus in this period would not typically have been portrayed as being so capable. By linking two deaf characters together and making them fully independent, the text actually helps to contest the definition of disability itself.

While Holmes cites the birth of a hearing child to Sophy and her husband as evidence of the text's attempt to palliate "concerns about hereditary 'defect,'" I view this child differently.[35] The child, while hearing, is actually bilingual, easily speaking in both languages without pause. This little girl provides the happy ending the Victorians expect, in that she is without "infirmity"—but she also represents a departure from the expected. She is both hearing and culturally deaf through her participation in her parents' language, and she is beloved by all. This happy ending is silent. Marigold "*saw* the pretty child a talking, pleased and quick and eager and busy, to her mother, in the signs that I had first taught her mother."[36] He does hear his granddaughter speak to him aloud, but thereafter, the text reports the family speaking in sign language alone. The vision offered by the text is truly radical, and even though some of its treatment is stuck in old patterns supporting hearing cultural norms (i.e., the notion that a non-hearing child would be a tragedy), enough of what is offered breaks the old norms that we are left with a fresh approach.

Ultimately, then, this story takes issue with the dominant culture's biases and presents a more nuanced view of deaf people and culture. That such a progressive view was so rare tells us that Dickens had special insight, and it seems likely that his impressions of the remarkable Laura Bridgman, together with his long-term association with the Perkins School for the Blind in Boston, made a lasting impression on him. It is to his credit that he chose to buck contemporary trends and paint a more positive and nuanced picture for our amusement and edification.

NOTES

1. Robert Patten, *Charles Dickens and His Publishers* (Oxford: Clarendon Press, 1978), contrasts the sales of the final serial installments of *Our Mutual Friend* with the sales of "Doctor Marigold," noting, "'Doctor Marigold's Prescriptions' sold a quarter of a million copies where *Our Mutual Friend* sold 19,000" (309–10).

2. Julia Miele Rodas, "Tiny Tim, Blind Bertha, and the Resistance of Miss Mowcher: Charles Dickens and the Uses of Disability," *Dickens Studies Annual* 34 (2004): 51–97,

notes that while Dickens is often blamed for "render[ing] disabled figures as helpless and pathetic victims, as villains, or as objects of fun, . . . [his] representations of disabled bodies . . . appears to be more complex" than has been heretofore recognized (51–52).

3. I use the Victorian term "deaf-mute" here purposefully. This term is not generally employed today since "mute" implies an inability to communicate, and members of the deaf community do clearly communicate through sign language. In the case of Sophy, Marigold's adopted daughter, when he found her, she had no ability even to use signs, so the term seems particularly relevant in this case. Still, I also want to make clear that I recognize the problematic nature of this terminology. For more on this issue, see Jennifer Esmail, "'I Listened with My Eyes': Writing Speech and Reading Deafness in the Fiction of Charles Dickens and Wilkie Collins," *English Literary History* 78, no. 4 (Winter 2011): 991–1020. As Esmail notes, and I follow suit, "The upper-case D 'Deaf' denotes people who use a signed language, belong to a deaf community, and might be considered culturally Deaf whereas the lower-case d 'deaf' refers to the general audiological condition of deafness experienced by many, including non-signers. If we were to apply this distinction retroactively to Victorian fiction, *Deaf* characters are almost entirely absent while *deaf* characters appear rather frequently" (993). My argument in this chapter suggests that Dickens was progressive in portraying what would now be called Deaf culture even though he would not have used this term.

4. Mary Wilson Carpenter, *Health, Medicine, and Society in Victorian England* (Santa Barbara, Calif.: Praeger, 2010), 109.

5. As Elisabeth Gitter notes in "Deaf-Mutes and Heroines in the Victorian Era," *Victorian Literature and Culture* 20 (1992): 179–96, "Like the irrational babble of women, Sign was imagined as disorderly, passionate, and retrogressive" (180–81).

6. Carpenter, *Health, Medicine, and Society,* 109, 117.

7. See Elisabeth Gitter, *The Imprisoned Guest: Samuel Howe and Laura Bridgman, the Original Deaf-Blind Girl* (New York: Farrar Straus Giroux, 2001).

8. See the images of Bridgman and Boston Line Type in figures E.34, E.35, E.37, and E.38, above.

9. Charles Dickens, *American Notes for General Circulation,* 2 vols. (London: Chapman and Hall, 1842), 1:3.73–74. Citations to *American Notes* include volume number followed by a colon, and chapter and page number(s) separated by a period.

10. Mary Klages, *Woeful Afflictions: Disability and Sentimentality in Victorian America* (Philadelphia: University of Pennsylvania Press, 1999), 121.

11. Dickens, *American Notes,* 1:3.96.

12. Ibid., 1:3.93, 94, 97.

13. Esmail, "'I Listened with My Eyes,'" 991. See Edna Edith Sayers, *Outcasts and Angels: The New Anthology of Deaf Characters in Literature* (Washington, D.C.: Gallaudet University Press, 2012), 125. One might also consider baby Turveydrop, Caddy Jellyby's baby, to be another such character since it seems clear that her mother will be communicating with her through sign language when she grows up. (I am indebted to Natalie Cole for this suggestion at the Dickens Symposium in Toronto, Canada, July 2013.) Martha Stoddard Holmes, *Fictions of Affliction: Physical Disability in Victorian Culture* (Ann Arbor: University of Michigan Press, 2007), also mentions Peters in Mary Elizabeth Braddon's *The Trail of the Serpent* (1861), 198, and Carpenter notes *The History of the Life and Adventures of Mr. Duncan Campbell* (1720), 125, attributed by some to Daniel Defoe, as perhaps the earliest realistic representation of a deaf person in English literature.

14. Sayers, *Outcasts and Angels*, 1.

15. Esmail, "'I Listened with My Eyes,'" 992.

16. Ibid., 994.

17. Sayers, *Outcasts and Angels*, 303.

18. I am indebted to a listserv post by Fred Guida to DICKNS-L on 5 August 2013 for first bringing to my attention this information, which originally appeared in a letter dated 30 or 31 August 1842, quoted in John Forster, *The Life of Charles Dickens,* 3 vols. (London: Chapman and Hall, 1872–74), 2:6–7. Unfortunately, further information on this episode is unavailable since the records of the workhouse have been lost. Guida surmises that this "deaf and dumb boy" might have had an "influence on Dickens's creation of the wild, nameless urchin in 'The Haunted Man.'"

19. Jennifer Esmail, *Reading Victorian Deafness: Signs and Sounds in Victorian Literature and Culture* (Athens: Ohio University Press, 2013), discusses how Dickens came to be so well "acquainted with the 'deaf and dumb arts'" (76).

20. Holmes, *Fictions of Affliction,* 3.

21. Ibid., 6. See also Elisabeth Gitter, "The Blind Daughter in Charles Dickens's *Cricket on the Hearth,*" *Studies in English Literature* 39, no. 4 (Autumn 1999): 675–89, for a discussion of Blind Bertha's inability to marry.

22. Holmes, *Fictions of Affliction,* 88.

23. Charles Dickens, "Doctor Marigold's Prescriptions: To Be Taken Immediately," *All the Year Round* 14 (7 December 1865): 7.

24. Ibid.

25. Dickens, *American Notes,* 1:3.74.

26. Dickens, "Doctor Marigold's Prescriptions," 6, 7.

27. Dickens, *American Notes,* 1:3.78.

28. See Esmail, *Reading Victorian Deafness,* 219n, for an explanation of this evidence.

29. Ibid., 77.

30. Dickens, "Doctor Marigold's Prescriptions," 7.

31. Sayers, *Outcasts and Angels,* 323.

32. Dickens, "Doctor Marigold's Prescriptions," 9.

33. Goldie Morgentaler, *Dickens and Heredity: When Like Begets Like* (New York: Palgrave Macmillan, 1999).

34. Dickens, "Doctor Marigold's Prescriptions," 47.

35. See note 22 above.

36. Dickens, "Doctor Marigold's Prescriptions," 48 (emphasis added).

CHAPTER 4

Dickens, Longfellow, and
the Village Blacksmith

LILLIAN NAYDER

✦

SEATED IN Charles Dickens's London study in October 1842, Massachusetts poet Henry Wadsworth Longfellow wrote to his friend Charles
Sumner, praising the newly published *American Notes for General Circulation.* Longfellow was disposed favorably toward the work; not only was
he the guest of Dickens but also the two authors had taken a strong liking
to one another since first meeting in Boston in January. At that time, the
poet and Sumner had gone with Dickens on a ten-mile walk to visit such
sites as Bunker Hill, and Longfellow had hosted the novelist at Craigie
House in Cambridge, Massachusetts, introducing him to several Harvard
professors. Unlike many American reviewers—"generally and predictably
hostile" to *American Notes*[1]—Longfellow described it as "jovial and good-
natured," though "very severe" at times. "You will read it with delight, and
for the most part approbation," Longfellow told Sumner on 16 October
1842. "He has a grand chapter on Slavery. *Spitting* and *politics* at Washington are the other topics of censure. Both you and I would censure them
with equal severity to say the least."[2]

Longfellow knew that Dickens's treatment of slavery would prove
especially interesting to Sumner, who had been encouraging the poet to
address the same subject—to "write some stirring words that shall move
the whole land."[3] Inspired in part by his reading of Dickens's "grand
chapter," Longfellow composed, during his voyage home from London, his *Poems on Slavery* (1842), a collection seen by critics—and by the
poet himself—as uncharacteristically political among his works. While
Dickens depicts the horrors of slavery by reprinting advertisements for
those who had escaped, individuals identified by their scars, brands, and
mutilations, Longfellow portrays the "hunted Negro" in "the Dismal
Swamp," his body mangled and his forehead branded, with "great scars

deform[ing] his face."[4] "Heaven speed your Slavery poems!" Dickens wrote Longfellow on 29 December 1842. "They will be manful, vigorous, and full of Indignant Truth, I know. I am looking for them eagerly."[5]

Dickens seems not to have recorded his response to Longfellow's *Poems on Slavery* once they appeared in print. But he characterized Longfellow as "a fine writer" and "the best of the American Poets," and showed a particular interest in one of Longfellow's earlier *Ballads*—"The Village Blacksmith" (1841)—by repeatedly drawing on it in his own work.[6] He quoted it, for example, when considering titles and epigrams for the periodical that became *Household Words;* he used it in a speech he delivered in Manchester in 1858; and he invoked it in *Great Expectations,* conveying both his debt to and his differences from Longfellow in the process of reworking it. Indeed, Dickens's interest in "The Village Blacksmith" seems ultimately to lie not in Longfellow's ability to express "Indignant Truths" but to suppress them—to foster a nostalgia that questions the value of social change while also acknowledging the resistance to memory triggered by social and personal loss.

As Dickens prepared to launch his new weekly journal in 1850, "The Forge" and "The Anvil of the Time" were among the many titles he considered. He associated these blacksmithing phrases with Longfellow, using the final four lines from "The Village Blacksmith" as a possible epigram for the opening page of each issue:

> Thus at the glowing Forge of life
> Our actions must be wrought;
> Thus on its sounding anvil shaped
> Each burning deed and thought.[7]

Dickens's slight misquotation here ("glowing" for "flaming" and "actions" for "fortunes") may reveal how familiar he was with the poem—that is, knowing it as well as he did, he may have cited Longfellow from memory rather than looking to a printed text. Dickens's substitution of "actions" for "fortunes," however, could well also be intentional, a change meant to emphasize the energy, the purposefulness, and the agency of Victorians as champions of Progress, an ideal celebrated in dozens of *Household Words* articles over the course of its nine-year run. Dickens's second blacksmithing title—"The Anvil of the Time"—points in a similar direction, by emphasizing the topicality of the journal and its interests. Yet the "anvil" that Longfellow celebrates in his poem is not "of the time" but of an earlier age. Although his village blacksmith is sometimes identified as a Brattle Street figure well known in Cambridge, Massachusetts, in the poet's day,

Longfellow himself identified his prototype as a seventeenth-century ancestor, Stephen Longfellow, with a forge in Newbury.[8] Dickens's decision not to draw from Longfellow's poem in devising his new title and epigram points to his recognition that, in 1850, the blacksmith and his forge were more closely allied with the past than the present and future, and hence unsuitable for the purposes of what became *Household Words.*

Although Dickens abandoned his idea of using Longfellow to name his new journal and set its tone, he drew on "The Village Blacksmith" when he spoke in Manchester toward the end of 1858, addressing those gathered to see prizes given to working-class men by the Institutional Association of Lancashire and Cheshire. The association brought together dozens of Mechanics' Institutes and Mutual Improvement Societies, which promoted the education of working-class men in the north of England. The association sponsored periodic exams in "branches of useful knowledge" to its most "eager and enterprising" pupils, awarding "prizes and certificates of merit" to successful competitors. Dickens's 1858 audience had gathered for this purpose, with the novelist himself giving out the "marks of recognition and encouragement."[9]

In his speech, Dickens idealized the working-class members of the association. They were "honest men" engaged in "a continual fight for bread," Dickens claimed, yet eager to improve themselves. They attended evening classes after long days of labor and relished the knowledge that they gained. Whether they were coal miners, factory or foundry workers, wagon- or chain-makers, their "whole existence has been a constant wrestle with 'Those twin gaolers of the daring heart—low birth and iron fortune.'"[10] Yet some had proven successful enough to become teachers themselves. In fact, Dickens observed, those about to receive the highest honors at his hand were the pupils of a working blacksmith from Stockport, England, who taught drawing in his spare time.

Having made this point, Dickens went on to quote from Longfellow, using the poet's idealization of the working man in "The Village Blacksmith" to reinforce his own. "Well may it be said of that good blacksmith," Dickens told his audience, referring to the Stockport drawing teacher, "as it was written of another of his trade, by the American poet":

> Toiling—rejoicing—sorrowing,
> Onward through life he goes;
> Each morning sees some task begun,
> Each evening sees its close;
> Something attempted, something done,
> Has earned a night's repose.[11]

Like Longfellow's blacksmith, the workers represented by Dickens in his 1858 speech combined physical with moral strengths, earning a "higher" reward than their pay. Longfellow envisions the blacksmith's labors as largely spiritual in nature, despite the man's "brawny arms . . . strong as iron bands." Swinging his sledge, the smith resembles a sexton ringing the village bell and calling parishioners to church; working his bellows and sending the sparks flying, he recalls a winnower separating wheat from chaff, a familiar image for judgment and salvation. The workers whom Dickens commended in his speech labored from morning until night yet gained their reward—and the audience's admiration—by virtue of their virtues—earnestness, industry, and resolve—by sweating "honest sweat," as Longfellow's blacksmith does, and by finishing what they started.[12]

Yet the men celebrated by Dickens here also differed from Longfellow's smith in one telling way. Their ambitions, though modest, set them apart from Longfellow's figure, who is satisfied simply to "earn . . . whate'er he can"—to remain self-reliant and imagine the heavenly Paradise where he will join his wife someday.[13] In Longfellow's poem, as one critic puts it, "the virtues of labour" are not "means to social ends."[14] Among the more entrepreneurial workers praised by Dickens in his speech, however, labor's virtues brought social rewards. "Honest sweat," combined with education, helped the men to rise, if modestly, in the class system. The blacksmith described in Dickens's speech learned drawing and became a teacher, while a handloom weaver studied botany and became a mill foreman. Not until Dickens imagined his own blacksmith figure two years later, in *Great Expectations,* did he more clearly incorporate, in the admirable Joe Gargery, what Longfellow commends in his poem—an idealized *absence* of social ambition.

To Pip before his fall into class consciousness, Joe's forge seems "the glowing road to manhood and independence," and Dickens defines the smith according to the integrity of his labor and the clarity of his moral vision. By contrast with Mr. Jaggers, a man morally compromised by the practice of criminal law and the use of false witnesses, Joe warns Pip that "lies is lies" after the boy has told some. "Howsever they come, they didn't ought to come, and they come from the father of lies, and work round to the same. Don't you tell no more of 'em." Joe is kind and forgiving—a "gentle Christian man," as Pip describes him—yet his labors also help to police and punish transgression. The first time we see the blacksmith at work in the novel, in fact, he is repairing handcuffs at his forge for use in apprehending the two escaped prisoners later identified as Magwitch and

Compeyson. "The bellows seemed to roar for the fugitives," Pip observes, "the fire to flare for them, the smoke to hurry away in pursuit of them, Joe to hammer and clink for them, and all the murky shadows on the wall to shake at them in menace as the blaze rose and sank and the red-hot sparks dropped and died."[15]

In *Great Expectations,* Joe's sense of right and wrong converges with his faith in the social order—his support for the social status quo. The blacksmith uses the same sentence structure to express—and to convey as indisputable—his social and moral creeds. Just as he tells Pip that "lies is lies," so he tells his apprentice that "a gridiron IS a gridiron"—that is, we are and remain what we are born—and had best remember our proper place: "You may haim at what you like," Joe goes on, "but a gridiron it will come out, either by your leave or again[st] your leave, and you can't help yourself." Joe is troubled by Pip's intimacy with Miss Havisham, the wealthy gentlewoman uptown; by Pip's newborn sense of class consciousness; and by Pip's growing sense of discontent at the forge. Hence Joe suggests to his apprentice that he keep to his own kind. As the blacksmith puts it, "common ones as to callings and earnings" would "be the better of continuing for to keep company with common ones, instead of going out to play with oncommon ones."[16] But Joe's advice is dismissed once Jaggers arrives with the news that Pip *is* "oncommon"—that he has great expectations and will be a gentleman rather than a blacksmith after all.

In Dickens's novel, as in Longfellow's poem, blacksmithing seems (or becomes) a thing of the past, more mythic than real. Both writers were familiar with the cultural history of the blacksmith figure, a tradition dating back to a time before ancient Greece and the god Hephaestus, in which the smith was renowned for his artistry—hence Dickens's recurring self-references as the "village blacksmith" at his anvil and as a writer with his "iron . . . in the fire," needing to "beat it out."[17] But in their respective works, the poet and the novelist engage in a specifically Victorian form of myth-making, with the blacksmith gaining significance in the context of nineteenth-century industrialization. The village blacksmith, whether in Longfellow's poem or in Dickens's novel, is not only larger than life but also represents a form of labor that had largely passed or that was passing; he can be seen as the "archetypal pre-industrial craftsman."[18] He is mythic not only because he is idealized—and possesses, in Joe's case, the strength of a Hercules—but also because he is imbued with nostalgia.[19] He is both admirable and lost to us, or soon to be. The disagreement over whether Longfellow's prototype was the poet's acquaintance on Brattle Street or his own seventeenth-century forebear reinforces the point: the blacksmith could just as easily date from the seventeenth century as the nineteenth.

In Longfellow's poem, the nostalgia associated with the smith is implicit. We understand what has been lost because of the context in which the poem was written. As critics note, Longfellow wrote "The Village Blacksmith" at a time when the specialization of American labor and demands for efficiency in industry threatened the autonomy and inventiveness of skilled workers—when the growth of industry was replacing workshops with factories and transforming skilled mechanics into hands or operatives, eroding their self-respect. Although the anxieties produced by this change go unexpressed in Longfellow's poem, they inform it nonetheless, particularly its portrait of the smith, autonomous and dignified in labor. In his dignity and his autonomy—as an artist of sorts—Longfellow's blacksmith responds to new working-class realities that go unacknowledged in the poem.[20]

By the time *Great Expectations* began to appear in 1860, Dickens had already portrayed the horrors of industrialization in such works as *The Old Curiosity Shop* (1840–41) and *Hard Times* (1854). Believing that factory workers were being dehumanized, Dickens found, in the labor of the village blacksmith, a preindustrial antidote of sorts. When we see Stephen Blackpool working at his mechanized loom in Mr. Bounderby's factory, he sits amid "the jarring of the machinery," a blighted figure.[21] When Pip looks in at the window of the forge, he sees Joe "at work with a glow of health and strength upon his face that made it show as if the bright sun of the life in store for him were shining on it."[22] Joe is his own master, and the forge is both his workplace and home; with industrialization, the mastery and integrity that Joe enjoys become impossible.

In Dickens's novel, the nostalgia we associate with the blacksmith figure is more pointed than in Longfellow's poem because Joe is, quite literally, left behind by Pip, and with Joe, the older, Edenic world Joe represents. Thus Dickens draws not only on Longfellow's poem but also on Milton's *Paradise Lost* as Pip separates himself from Joe and the forge to pursue his social ambitions in London, gaining the moral and social complexity that defines him against the blacksmith. The ambiguities of London life, and Pip's idleness as a gentleman, as well as his knowledge of Jaggers and the criminal world, divide him from Joe, the integrity and satisfaction of Joe's labor, and the simple moral codes for which the smith speaks. Pip's fall seems unfortunate; we regret his rejection of the village blacksmith and the forge, which, with Pip, we see disappear on the horizon at the end of volume 1, as Dickens echoes Milton's epic: "We changed [horses] again, and yet again, and it was now too late and too far to go back, and I went on. And the mists had all solemnly risen now, and the world lay spread before me."[23] Yet even as Dickens encourages us to feel nostalgic as we look back over Pip's shoulder, he suggests that Pip's loss of Joe and Joe's world is necessary for Pip to develop as the hero of a novel should.

Insofar as loss or nostalgia becomes a theme in Longfellow's poem, it does so in relation to the blacksmith's loss of love—not because the smith himself is left behind in ever more modern times by those eager for social change or upward mobility, but because of his identity as a widower rather than as a worker. In the sixth stanza of "The Village Blacksmith," the smith weeps at the thought of his dead wife, who is brought to his mind when he hears his daughter's voice in the church choir:

> It sounds to him like her mother's voice,
> Singing in Paradise!
> He needs must think of her once more,
> How in the grave she lies;
> And with his hard, rough hand he wipes
> A tear out of his eyes.

In a poem characterized by its celebration of simple virtues and duties— tasks begun and finished, the world looked "in the face"—the smith's simple expression of grief is quite complex.[24] He imagines his dead wife in Paradise; there is no doubt or equivocation in his faith or his view of his wife's salvation. Yet Longfellow complicates matters, not only by pairing strength with weakness here—the smith's hard, rough hand with his soft or tender feeling—but also by describing the smith's nostalgia as he does: the smith "needs must think of her once more." The line is intriguing be- cause of the reluctance that it implies—"needs must"—as if the widower were acting against his will in remembering, or according to some neces- sity that lies beyond his control. The reluctance, Longfellow implies, is due to the pain of his loss (and its recollection). Grief may be tempered over time and softened with sentimentality, yet the blacksmith would avoid rekindling it if he could. The thought of his wife that he "needs must think" is this: "How in the grave she lies." This idea counters the image of his wife singing in Paradise earlier in the stanza and serves as a reminder of the corporeal, of death itself, even in the face of immortality, a realization of loss that brings the tear to the smith's eyes. His daughter's voice sounds like his wife's, but they are not the same after all.

In *Great Expectations*, Dickens's blacksmith, like Longfellow's, is a widower; that is, he becomes one in the course of the novel. Mrs. Joe—

the wife of Joe and the sister of Pip—dies toward the end of volume 2. As Longfellow does in "The Village Blacksmith," Dickens dramatizes the widower's grief. When Pip returns to the forge from London for the funeral, Joe eulogizes his wife before he sheds *his* tear: "Pip, old chap, you knowed her when she were a fine figure of a—," and here, Joe breaks off, unable to finish his sentence by adding the word "woman," mutely clasping Pip's hand instead.[25]

Judging from the grief Joe expresses in this scene, we might expect him to share the village blacksmith's reluctance to remember; we expect that he too might "needs must think" of his dead wife, as if recalling her against his will. Indeed, Mrs. Joe's survivors prove reluctant mourners— but not for the reasons Longfellow provides. "Whatever my fortunes might have been," Pip tells us as he prepares for the funeral,

> I could scarcely have recalled my sister with much tenderness. But I suppose there is a shock of regret which may exist without much tenderness.... [A]s I walked along, the time[s] when I was a little helpless creature, and my sister did not spare me, vividly returned. But they returned with a gentle tone upon them that softened even the edge of Tickler. For now, the very breath of the beans and clover whispered to my heart that the day must come when it would be well for my memory that others walking in the sunshine should be softened as they thought of me.[26]

Joe never expresses the resentment toward Mrs. Joe that Pip voices toward her in this passage, and his grief seems unalloyed. "The dear old fellow was sadly cut up by the constant contemplation of the wreck of his wife," Pip tells us after his sister has entered her decline, noting that Joe "had been accustomed, while attending on her of an evening, to turn to me every now and then and say, with his blue eyes moistened, 'Such a fine figure of a women as she once were, Pip!'" Yet when Mrs. Joe first suffers the attack that ultimately kills her—a violent assault by an unknown assailant that leaves her suffering from a traumatic brain injury—Joe is a prime suspect in the crime. Pip treats such suspicions as absurd, remarking that "it was characteristic of the police people that they had all more or less suspected poor Joe (though he never knew it), and that they had to a man concurred in regarding him as one of the deepest spirits they had ever encountered." But even as we dismiss the idea of Joe's guilt, we must concede that he benefits from the assault and its consequences. Married to a woman "given to government," Joe finds his newly disabled wife anxious to please. "Her temper was greatly improved, and she was patient." As Pip puts it, "Joe became able in some sort to appreciate the greater quiet of his life, and to get down to the Jolly Bargemen now and then for a change that did him good."[27] "Greater quiet" for a husband—"a change that did him good"—if these are the results of a wife's beating, it is no wonder that Joe is a prime suspect.[28]

In *Great Expectations,* as in "The Village Blacksmith," the widowed blacksmith proves to be a reluctant mourner, yet his resistance to memory means something quite different in the two works, as it did to the two writers. From nearly the start of their friendship, Longfellow and Dickens discussed the women that each loved and lost. When Dickens first met Longfellow in Boston in 1842, the poet (a widower since the death of his first wife, Mary Potter, in 1835) was courting Fanny Appleton, unsuccessfully it seemed. When Longfellow traveled to Europe later that year to take the water cure in Germany, staying with the novelist at Devonshire Terrace for two weeks, Dickens understood that the poet was being treated, in part, for the frustrations he had endured in his unsuccessful courtship. On learning that Fanny had finally accepted Longfellow's proposal and that, as the poet told the novelist on 15 June 1843, his heart had "turned [his] brains out of doors,"[29] Dickens joked with their mutual friend Cornelius Felton about the groom's desire for oysters (thought to be an aphrodisiac) rather than cold water, which was only "essential to . . . single life."[30] Dickens's comments showcase his power to recall the woman Longfellow had nearly lost, and suggest the pride he took in that power: "And so Longfellow is married. I remember her well; and could draw her portrait—in words—to the life. A very beautiful and gentle creature—and a proper love for a poet. My cordial remembrances and congratulations."[31]

Longfellow's confidences with Dickens about Fanny Appleton, shared at a time when it seemed that he had lost her, were most likely what spurred Dickens to disclose to the poet his own memory of a beloved woman lost. When Dickens wrote to Longfellow at the end of 1842, glad to know that the poet had arrived in Boston safely, he conveyed his wife Kate's love and went on to describe Kate's sisters, both living and dead: "I wish you had seen her sister who is usually with us, as she is now; but was with her mother when you were here. There *was* another when we were first married, but She has been my better Angel six long years."[32]

In this passage, Dickens refers to Georgina and Mary Hogarth, two of Catherine Dickens's three sisters. Georgina was fifteen years old when she moved in with her sister and brother-in-law around the time of Longfellow's visit in 1842. There in part to help care for the Dickenses' four young children—by 1852, ten in all and nine surviving—she remained with the novelist until his death in 1870, despite his separation from her older sister in 1858. Mary Hogarth, four years younger than Kate and eight years older than Georgina, had spent much of her time with Catherine and Charles during their courtship and first year of marriage. She died at their home on Doughty Street in 1837, at the age of seventeen, of some type of heart failure. Dickens did not love Mary romantically, but he idealized her from the time of her death until his own, sometimes dreaming of her at night and making a "better Angel" out of her, as he told Longfellow. "So perfect a creature never breathed," Dickens wrote of Mary; "she had not a fault."[33]

Eager to remember Mary and to contemplate her loss, Dickens indulged in his grief—invoking her angelic image in such places as Niagara Falls, where he felt her presence, and welcoming her when she came to him unbidden, a spirit in his dreams. The same cannot be said of his attitude toward the wife he "lost"—from 1858 onward—by insisting on a separation and pressuring her to move into her own home near Regent's Park. When the wealthy philanthropist Angela Burdett Coutts wrote to Dickens in 1860, urging a meeting between husband and wife and a possible reconciliation, the novelist refused—and in terms that make painfully clear his reluctance to think of his wife, whom he willfully forced from his memory: "That figure is out of my life for evermore (except to darken it), and my desire is, Never to see it again."[34] As he put it bluntly in 1864, when Burdett Coutts asked Dickens to contact Catherine after the death of their son Walter in India, "a page in my life which once had writing on it, has become absolutely blank, and . . . it is not in my power to pretend that it has a solitary word upon it."[35]

In his desire to forget Catherine—to render blank the "page in [his] life" on which she figured—Dickens more closely resembled the widower portrayed in "The Lazy Tour of Two Idle Apprentices" than he did either Joe Gargery or the village blacksmith. In a story he wrote as he was separating from his wife, three years before he began *Great Expectations,* Dickens portrays a husband who manages literally to wish his wife dead. "She was not worth hating," his narrative reads; "he felt nothing but contempt for her. But, she had long been in the way, and he had long been weary."[36] The reluctance to remember a lost wife may measure the pain of loss but can also mark the desire to escape from marriage or the guilt over having done so.

Although Dickens took pride in his mnemonic powers when writing in 1843 of the woman Longfellow nearly lost, Longfellow rather than Dickens helps us to remember accurately the wife whom Dickens sent away. From 1858 onward, Dickens's recorded memories of Catherine prove unreliable, as he revised the history of his marriage and the character of his wife, forgetting that he had long loved and admired her. Longfellow helps us to see that Dickens's recollections of Catherine as an incompetent wife and neglectful mother are willful constructions, images designed to justify his own unjust behavior toward her. "[Dickens's] wife is a good natured—mild, rosy young woman—not beautiful, but amiable," Longfellow wrote of Catherine on 30 January 1842 after meeting her in Boston. And, after being her guest in London later that year, he described her as "a most kind, amiable person," her household "delightful."[37] These comments stand in sharp contrast to Dickens's later assertions, to American friends such as James Fields and others, that Catherine was unloving and unlovable, she and he "totally uncongenial."[38]

It is possible that in later years Longfellow came under the novelist's spell in regard to Catherine, as many Dickens critics and biographers have done—that he was influenced by Dickens to *mis*remember her. Whether or not this is the case, Longfellow clearly knew about the breakdown of the marriage. In February 1870, more than a year after visiting Dickens at Gad's Hill with his family, Longfellow referred to Dickens's "terrible sadness" at a gathering hosted in Boston by James and Annie Fields.[39] Having read John Forster's *Life of Charles Dickens*, Longfellow characterized the novelist as "the most restless of mortals," a man with "no repose in anything," and he regretted Forster's willingness to write about the marriage and its breakdown, even as tactfully as the biographer did.[40] In fact, Longfellow was reticent even to *explain* the cause of his distress over Forster's work, as if unwilling to call attention to the subject in any way, as his comments to George Washington Greene make clear. Forster's book "is very interesting, but it made me profoundly melancholy; perhaps I can tell you why, but I hardly care to write it."[41] Recalling the village blacksmith, Longfellow "needs must think" of what pains him; he was forced to consider the sad story of the Dickens marriage, evidently reluctant to contemplate the novelist's treatment of his wife—that injustice one mark of the difference between novelist and poet, despite their mutual regard. For while Dickens strove to erase his still-living wife from his memory— to un-write their long history together—a grief-stricken Longfellow memorialized Fanny long after her death in his "strong . . . sense of her presence upon [him]," his expectation that he "should . . . meet her in [their] favorite walk," and in such works as "The Cross of Snow" (1879).[42] "Through all the changing scenes / And seasons," he recalled her "gentle face" in "the long, sleepless watches of the night," his memories of her— and his sense of loss—"changeless since the day she died."[43]

NOTES

1. Michael Slater, *Charles Dickens* (New Haven, Conn.: Yale University Press, 2009), 205.

2. Henry Wadsworth Longfellow, *The Letters of Henry Wadsworth Longfellow*, 6 vols., ed. Andrew Hilen (Cambridge, Mass.: Harvard University Press, 1966–1982), 2:473.

3. Charles Sumner to Henry Wadsworth Longfellow, 14–15 May 1842, quoted in Iván Jaksić, *The Hispanic World and American Intellectual Life, 1820–1880* (New York: Palgrave Macmillan, 2007), 85.

4. Henry Wadsworth Longfellow, *Poetical Works of Henry Wadsworth Longfellow*, 6 vols. (Boston: Houghton Mifflin, 1901), 1:91.

5. Charles Dickens, *The Pilgrim Edition of the Letters of Charles Dickens*, 12 vols., ed. Madeline House et al. (Oxford: Clarendon Press, 1965–2002), 3:407–8 (29 December 1842).

6. Ibid., 3:96 (28 February 1842); 3:340 (?13 October 1842).

7. R. C. Lehmann, ed., *Charles Dickens as Editor: Being Letters Written by Him to William Henry Wills, His Sub-Editor* (New York: Sturgis and Walton, 1912), 21.

8. Longfellow, *Poetical Works*, 1:64.

9. Charles Dickens, *The Speeches of Charles Dickens*, ed. K. J. Fielding (Oxford: Clarendon Press, 1960), 280.

10. Ibid., 280, 281.

11. Ibid., 282.

12. Longfellow, *Poetical Works*, 1:64, 65.

13. Ibid., 1:65.

14. John Stephen Martin, "Longfellow's 'The Village Blacksmith' and the Changing Image of Labour," in *Essays in Honour of Erwin Sturzl on His Sixtieth Birthday*, ed. James Hogg (Salzburg: University of Salzburg, 1980), 412–23, 422.

15. Charles Dickens, *Great Expectations*, first appeared in *All the Year Round* 4 (169–558) and 5 (1–437): 4:14.361, 4:9.291, 5:57.410, 4:5.218. Citations to *Great Expectations* include the volume number of *All the Year Round* followed by a colon, and chapter and page number(s) separated by a period.

16. Ibid., 4:15.362, 363; 4:9.291.

17. Dickens, *Letters*, 12:61 (27 February 1868); 9:403 (?mid-April 1861). Focusing on *Great Expectations*, Naomi Lightman provides an insightful analysis of Dickens's association between the blacksmith and the writer in "The 'Vulcanic Dialect' of *Great Expectations*," *Dickensian* 82, no. 1 (1986): 33–38. For a discussion of Longfellow's vexed identification with the blacksmith and his use of the cultural history surrounding that figure, particularly in regard to the American anxiety of influence and the quest for originality, see Joseph Masheck, "Professor Longfellow and the Blacksmith," *Annals of Scholarship* 10 (1993): 345–61.

18. Robin Gilmour, *The Idea of the Gentleman in the Victorian Novel* (London: George Allen and Unwin, 1981), 127.

19. Dickens, *Great Expectations*, 4:2.171.

20. Martin develops this argument at length, discussing Longfellow in the context of nineteenth-century American labor history and "the impact of mechanization upon the skilled workman" as opposed to the factory operative. "Longfellow's 'The Village Blacksmith,'" 419.

21. Charles Dickens, *Hard Times,* in *Household Words* 9, nos. 210–29 (1 April–12 August 1854): 12.265. Citation to *Hard Times* is by chapter and page number.

22. Dickens, *Great Expectations,* 5:35.78.

23. Ibid., 4:19.438.

24. Longfellow, *Poetical Works,* 1:65.

25. Dickens, *Great Expectations,* 5:35.76.

26. Ibid., 5:35.75.

27. Ibid., 4:16.386, 4:7.244, 4:16.386.

28. The assault on Mrs. Joe and the problem of agency in the attack are subjects of critical scrutiny and debate. For an alternative view of their meaning, see Michal Peled Ginsburg, "Dickens and the Uncanny: Repression and Displacement in *Great Expectations,*" *Dickens Studies Annual* 13 (1984): 115–24.

29. Longfellow, *Letters,* 2:542 (15 June 1843).

30. Dickens, *Letters,* 3:550 (1 September 1843).

31. Ibid.

32. Ibid., 3:409 (29 December 1842).

33. Ibid., 1:259 (?17 May 1837). For a detailed discussion of the marriage of Charles and Catherine Dickens, the roles played by the Hogarth sisters in the Dickenses' home, and the novelist's misrepresentations of his wife after they separated in 1858, see Lillian Nayder, *The Other Dickens: A Life of Catherine Hogarth* (Ithaca, N.Y.: Cornell University Press, 2011).

34. Dickens, *Letters,* 9:230 (5 April 1860).

35. Ibid., 10:356 (12 February 1864).

36. Charles Dickens, "The Lazy Tour of Two Idle Apprentices," *Household Words* 16 (3–31 October 1857): 313–416; the quoted passage is at 16 (24 October 1857): 388. "The Lazy Tour" was coauthored with Wilkie Collins; the passage in question appears in chapter 4, written by Dickens.

37. Longfellow, *Letters,* 2:381 (30 January 1842); 2:495 (6 January 1843).

38. George Curry, *Charles Dickens and Annie Fields* (San Marino, Calif.: Henry E. Huntington Library and Art Gallery, 1988), quoted in Slater, *Charles Dickens,* 579.

39. M. A. DeWolfe Howe, *Memories of a Hostess: A Chronicle of Eminent Friendships Drawn Chiefly from the Diaries of Mrs. James Fields* (Boston: Atlantic Monthly Press, 1922), 211.

40. Samuel Longfellow, ed., *Life of Henry Wadsworth Longfellow,* 3 vols. (Boston: Houghton, Mifflin, 1891), 3:212.

41. Longfellow to George Washington Greene, 23 December 1871, quoted in Robert L. Gale, *A Henry Wadsworth Longfellow Companion* (Westport, Conn.: Greenwood Press, 2003), 62. "What bothered Longfellow," Gale writes, "was Forster's . . . treatment of Dickens's unhappy marriage" (ibid.). Yet Forster's depiction of "the young couple" honeymooning "at the quiet little village of Chalk," and Dickens's praise of Catherine as "a *most admirable* traveller in every respect" during the 1842 American tour, which Forster foregrounds, may have proved at least as distressing to the nostalgic poet. See John Forster, *The Life of Charles Dickens,* 3 vols. (London: Chapman and Hall, 1872–74), 1:87, 378.

42. Longfellow, *Letters,* 4:242 (18 August 1861).

43. Longfellow, *Poetical Works,* 3:220–21.

CHAPTER 5

Slavery in Dickens's Manuscript of *American Notes for General Circulation*

Joel J. Brattin

✦

CHARLES DICKENS returned to England after his first trip to America in 1842 with several criticisms of what he had seen in the New World, which he expressed clearly in his travel book *American Notes for General Circulation*, published in October of that same year. He found the American penchant for chewing tobacco repellant, and he was even more disgusted with the American obsession with money and sharp dealing. But it was American slavery that most appalled Dickens. He returned to slavery repeatedly in his book, and devoted an entire chapter (the penultimate one) to the topic. At key times in the book, Dickens refers to Massachusetts—often as a way to highlight the contrast with what he found elsewhere in the United States. And despite Dickens's decision to avoid naming individual citizens in *American Notes,* he alludes to abolitionist figures from Boston like Dr. William Ellery Channing and William Lloyd Garrison, and was profoundly influenced by the abolitionist work of Theodore Dwight Weld, a New Englander with strong ties to Massachusetts.

Dickens's manuscript of *American Notes for General Circulation* survives, complete, in the Forster Collection at the Victoria and Albert Museum in South Kensington, London. This manuscript, like those for Dickens's novels, is enormously useful to the scholar interested in Dickens's craftsmanship and literary achievement. Unpublished passages, crossed out passages, passages added in proof, extensively revised passages, passages not actually by Dickens, and even passages in someone else's handwriting—all play their part in revealing Dickens's abhorrence of slavery and his methods of communicating the depth of his feelings.

Dickens began the manuscript of his book with an introduction, which he labeled "Chapter the First / Introductory / And necessary to be read." Despite Dickens's clearly stated idea that this chapter was "necessary," it did not, finally, appear in any edition of the book published in Dickens's lifetime. John Forster was the first to print the chapter, in his biography of Dickens.[1] Near the end of this introduction, Dickens noted that he had "no intention of softening down, or glozing over" the abuses he had observed abroad. He wrote, "Of the probable accuracy of my observations, my readers will form their own opinion, from such evidence," then deleted this phrase before finishing the sentence.[2] Dickens wanted to assert the truth of his observations—particularly his comments about slavery—but was evidently unwilling to call those observations into question here. In the final sentence of this unpublished introduction, Dickens wrote that he felt himself bound to do justice "to what, according to my best means of judgment, I found to be the truth."[3] Forster evidently wanted to avoid calling attention to Dickens's judgment, and substituted the far simpler phrase "bound to do justice to the Truth" when he published the chapter in his biography of Dickens.

Dickens's first direct reference to slavery appears in the fourth paragraph of chapter 3, "Boston," as part of his praise for the Massachusetts clergyman Dr. William Ellery Channing, who had settled in Boston in 1803.[4] Channing "first expressed his views on the slavery question comprehensively in 1835 in a work entitled *Slavery*"; in the mid-1830s he could rightly be considered "one of the most outspoken of the Unitarian clergy on the matter of slavery."[5] In the published text of *American Notes,* Dickens extols Channing by name (rare, in this book) for his steadfast opposition to "that most hideous blot and foul disgrace—Slavery."[6] This is strong language, powerful and effective partly through its very brevity. But the manuscript reveals the depth of Dickens's passion: he goes on at some length, borrowing language from the Declaration of Independence. In the manuscript (fig. 5.1), he characterizes slavery as

> that hideous blot and foul disgrace, which makes "the Unanimous Declaration of the Thirteen United States of America" an unanimous lie; and their solemn assertions that all men are created equal; that they are endowed by their creator with certain inalienable rights; that among these are Life, Liberty, and the Pursuit of Happiness; and that to secure these rights Governments are instituted among men, deriving their just power from the consent of the governed; a mockery so gross and monstrous: before which common honor and common sense do so sicken and fall down; that even these noble sentiments, with such alloy, inspire but loathing and disgust.[7]

In the manuscript of *American Notes,* Dickens goes on to give more detail about slavery in the north, noting the progressive views about

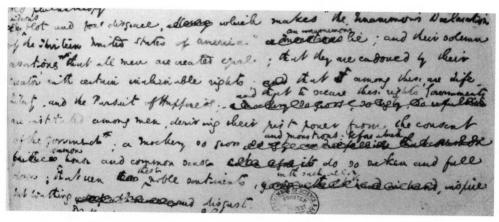

Figure 5.1. Dickens describes slavery as a "hideous blot and foul disgrace." All images of the manuscript in this chapter published by kind permission of Mark Dickens and the Board of Trustees of the Victoria and Albert Museum.

slavery held in Boston but also pointing out that those views were far from universally held. He tells of a passage in the life of America's most prominent abolitionist, William Lloyd Garrison, born in Newburyport, Massachusetts, who began publishing his newspaper, *The Liberator*, in Boston in 1831.[8] In a passage that extends onto two manuscript pages, Dickens writes the following: "Boston, to its honor be it written, is never slow to express its hatred of slavery: and yet it is not many years since a conspicuous advocate of emancipation was dragged through the streets even of this, the most enlightened city in the Union, in broad day, with a rope about his middle, by a fierce mob—advocates, no doubt, and loud ones too, of the inalienable rights of all mankind."[9]

The event to which Dickens alludes took place in October 1835 and is described in various histories: William Lloyd Garrison was "dragged through the streets at a rope's end," "seized by a mob and paraded through the streets of Boston in ropes," and "nearly lynched by a mob."[10] Dickens continues: "But there are many kinds of Hunters engaged in the Pursuit of Happiness; and they go variously armed. It is the inalienable right of some among them, to take the field after *their* happiness, equipped with cat and cart whip, stocks and iron collar, and to shout their view halloo! (always in praise of Liberty) to the musical accompaniment of clanking chains and bloody stripes." Then Dickens begins a new paragraph with the transitional phrase "To return to Boston."[11] The only bit of this passage to appear in the published text is the transition; the material

about the advocate of emancipation being dragged through the streets of
Boston by a fierce mob is gone. But Dickens's passage about the "many
kinds of Hunters engaged in the Pursuit of Happiness" who go "variously
armed" was not lost permanently; Dickens recycled many of these details
later, using them in chapter 8, treating Baltimore (where Dickens first
saw slaves) and Washington, D.C.

Near the conclusion of chapter 3, Dickens writes about the possibilities
he sees for America. Dickens has just described his gratification in sur-
veying some of the enlightened institutions in Massachusetts, including
the State Hospital for the insane, the House of Industry, the hospital, and
the House of Correction. He then adds the following sentence: "If the
time should ever come when some infusion of this good spirit may shine
out from among the degraded polities and public life of the republic—
may weigh in the scale, seen as the lightest straw against the Dollar and
the cotton bole—may illumine the printed broadsheet that directs and
speaks (Heaven save the mark!) the public mind, with scraps of Honesty,
or Honor, or even of common Sense, America will be a model country
yet."[12] Although this sentence, cut from the text before publication, is not
directly about slavery, it is easy to see, through phrases like "the Dollar
and the cotton bole," that slavery is part of what is on his mind.

Chapter 4, treating Dickens's visit to Lowell, Massachusetts, contains
another brief passage regarding race relations in the North before the
Civil War. Discussing trains, Dickens noted that there were separate cars
for ladies and gentlemen; in his manuscript, he added, "There is also a
negro car." Recognizing the opportunity to make a political and moral
point, he crossed out that sentence and substituted, "It not being among
the inalienable rights of all mankind that a black man should ever travel
with a white one, there is also a negro car." But when he moved the initial
passage treating "inalienable rights" to chapter 8, he needed to modify this
passage too; it eventually appeared in print in simpler and less satiric form:
"As a black man never travels with a white one, there is also a negro car."[13]

Chapter 6 treats Dickens's visit to New York City. While there, he
visited the Manhattan House of Detention for Men—that is, the Tombs
Prison. In the manuscript, he asks the keeper about the cells; the keeper
admits, "they're pretty nigh full, and that's a fact, and no two ways about
it." Dickens asks, "Those at the bottom are unwholesome, surely?" and reports the keeper's answer: "Why, we *do* only put niggers in 'em. That's the
truth." Dickens is quoting the keeper's language, presumably accurately.
But Dickens, sensitive to the offensiveness of the word "niggers," crossed
it out, substituting "colored people" in between the lines.[14]

In chapter 8, Dickens enters Maryland, where he says he was "waited on, for the first time, by Slaves." In the manuscript, Dickens wrote, "I felt a kind of shame in the first approach to this," but deleted the phrase, offering greater elaboration about the moral complicity of all those who benefit from slave labor. Dickens wrote, "The sensation of exacting any service from human creatures who are bought and sold, and being, for the time, a party as it were to their condition, is not an enviable one." Dickens says that the presence of the institution of slavery filled him "with a kind of shame." Struggling to express the precise nature of that feeling, he substituted "a sense of" for "a kind of," deleted it, and added it again; he then added to the end of the sentence "and vague distaste." Finding this expression too weak, he finally substituted "self-reproach."[15]

Later in chapter 8, Dickens expresses admiration for a man who "dared to assert the infamy of that traffic, which has for its accursed merchandize men and women, and their unborn children." Here, he introduces the theme of hypocrisy: slaveholders claiming that "All Men are created Equal; and are endowed by their Creator with the Inalienable Rights of Life, Liberty, and the Pursuit of Happiness." This allows him to import the passage he had originally drafted in chapter 3 about the "many kinds of hunters engaged in the Pursuit of Happiness," "equipped with cat and cartwhip, stocks, and iron collar," "to the music of clanking chains and bloody stripes."[16]

In the final pages of the first volume, Dickens says he had originally considered venturing further in the American South but decided against it, partly because of "the pain of contemplating slavery." He expanded this phrase through revision into "the pain of living in the constant pain of contemplation of slavery." Perhaps Dickens caught the redundancy of this expression when reading proofs; the phrase finally appeared in print as "the pain of living in the constant contemplation of slavery."[17]

Several of Dickens's chapter titles in *American Notes for General Circulation* are quite lengthy but none is as long as the one for chapter 9, which appears as chapter 1 in the second volume of the first edition: "A Night Steamer on the Potomac River. A Virginia Road, and a Black Driver. Richmond. Baltimore. The Harrisburgh Mail, and a Glimpse of the City. A Canal Boat." But a false start, preserved on the back of the manuscript page, provides a much more succinct title, perhaps indicating the center of Dickens's interest. Dickens's original title was "An 'old Virginny' road, and a black Driver."[18]

In this chapter, Dickens writes of "the curses of this horrible and hideous Institution" of slavery. It is interesting to see him toning down his expression of outrage; he crossed out the modifiers "horrible and hideous,"

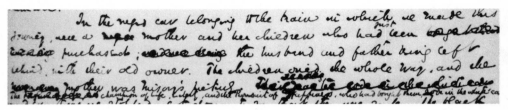

Figure 5.2. Dickens writes of a mother and her children "who had just been purchased."

leaving simply "the curses of this Institution," and then reinstated "hor-rible" through an interlinear addition to the manuscript.[19] Perhaps he was willing to omit "hideous" because he felt the anecdote he was about to relate would communicate his judgment more powerfully than any mere adjective could. He tells of "a negro mother and her children who had just been purchased; the husband and father being left behind, with their old owner. The children cried the whole way, and the woman was Misery's picture. Their master rode in the white car" (fig. 5.2).[20]

The revisions to this passage affect both the mother and the master, and reveal Dickens's attitude quite clearly. First, he deleted "negro," letting "a mother and her children" stand unmodified by any racial marker. In the next sentence, he substituted the capitalized word "Mother" for "woman," emphasizing again the "Misery" slavery brings to the entire family. His revisions to "Their master rode in the white car" are particularly tell-ing. Crossing out the entire phrase, Dickens added in between the lines "The champion of Life, Liberty, and the Pursuit of Happiness, who had bought them, rode in the white car." Dickens retained his heavy irony about "Life, Liberty, and the Pursuit of Happiness" but substituted "the same train" for "the white car" in the published text. Dickens continued to treat this slave owner with irony; at the end of the paragraph, he says that a black cannibal from the *Arabian Nights* is "nature's aristocrat compared with this fellow." Deleting "fellow," Dickens substituted the ironic "gen-tleman." By the time the phrase appeared in print, Dickens had height-ened the contrast even further, substituting "this white gentleman."[21]

Dickens described his trip to Baltimore, via Washington, from Rich-mond, noting parenthetically that "there were two constables on board the steamboat, in pursuit of runaway slaves."[22] The phrase, an interlinear addition to the manuscript, adds little to our understanding of Dickens's travels but speaks to the conditions of life for African Americans in America in 1842.

After Dickens returned north, he had little to say about slavery—until, that is, the final chapter before his conclusion. Dickens narrates his travels in the United States and Canada, and even his journey back to England, before offering the most powerful and memorable chapter in the book, entitled, simply, "Slavery."

Dickens's revisions to the first sentence of this chapter are telling. Dickens originally began the chapter by writing "The upholders of slavery in America, may be divided into two great classes." But through revision, this opening statement becomes much more powerful. First, Dickens added "the frightful system of" before slavery (subsequently deleting it). But more importantly, he added "of the atrocities of which system I shall not write one word for which I have not ample proof and warrant." He also substituted "three" for "two" classes at this point, so the final version reads, "The upholders of slavery in America, of the atrocities of which system I shall not write one word for which I have not ample proof and warrant, may be divided into three great classes."[23]

The first class is of "those more moderate and rational owners of human cattle"; the second, of the cruel slaveholders who "doggedly deny the horrors of the system."[24] The third class, Dickens writes, is of "that Miserable Gentility" which cannot bear a superior. Capitalizing both "Miserable" and "Gentility" in the manuscript to underline his criticism, the phrase appeared in print without capitals, as "delicate gentility." Dickens used capitals in the rest of the passage, as well: he speaks of that class of "Miserable Gentility" whose "Inalienable Rights can only have their growth in Negro Wrongs," underscoring his irony by capitalizing "Inalienable," "Rights," "Negro," and "Wrongs." Unfortunately, all these words were regularized by the time the book was in print.[25]

In 1943 Dickens scholar Louise Johnson revealed the author's unacknowledged debt to American abolitionist Theodore Dwight Weld's 1839 pamphlet *American Slavery as It Is*.[26] Weld, born in Connecticut, "spent the last twenty-five years of his life . . . in greater Boston" where many members of his family resided; *American Slavery as It Is* "became the most widely distributed and most influential of all American antislavery tracts."[27] Ralph Waldo Emerson may have used this "acclaimed compendium" in preparing his "first major antislavery address," and it provided essential background information for Harriet Beecher Stowe's novel *Uncle Tom's Cabin*.[28] In all likelihood, early feminist abolitionists Angelina Emily Grimké, who wed Theodore D. Weld in 1838, and her oldest sister, Sarah Moore Grimké, also helped to compile the book, largely from southern newspapers.[29]

Dickens's chapter in *American Notes* on "Slavery" includes forty-four advertisements for runaway slaves, indirectly exposing the horrible privations, tortures, and maimings resulting from the institution. Although Dickens presented these advertisements as taken directly from southern newspapers, Dickens actually copied them (without acknowledgment) from Weld's pamphlet. Dickens owes more to Weld than just the borrowed advertisements, however: the arguments Dickens offers before and after the quoted advertisements were strongly influenced by Weld's pamphlet as well. Johnson rightly points out that Dickens's argument in 2:9.251–53 is closely based on a paraphrase of Weld's "OBJECTION V. 'IT IS FOR THE INTEREST OF THE MASTERS TO TREAT THEIR SLAVES WELL.'"[30] She shows that Dickens borrowed not only Weld's ideas but also his rhetoric and even wording.[31]

Dickens's argument in 2:9.253–57 focuses on public opinion and its ineffectiveness in controlling abuse of slaves by their owners. In this relatively short eight-paragraph passage, introducing the selection of advertisements for runaway slaves, Dickens uses the phrase "public opinion" more than twenty times—ten times in the first paragraph alone. Although Johnson does not comment on it, Dickens certainly borrowed this key phrase, and this argument, from Weld, who titled his last and most lengthy chapter "OBJECTION VIII. 'PUBLIC OPINION IS A PROTECTION TO THE SLAVE.'"[32]

It is unfortunate that Dickens did not acknowledge the influence of Weld's pamphlet—it would be considered plagiarism today—but it is important to consider his possible motivations. Dickens wanted to make the strongest case against slavery he could. Perhaps he feared that admitting he was reprinting advertisements Weld had collected, or presenting arguments Weld had offered, would diminish their power and effectiveness in changing the minds of his readers.

On the sixth page of Dickens's manuscript for this chapter, toward the end of his consideration of public opinion, Dickens penned a couple of sentences that have not hitherto seen print. Evidently displeased with his start, he deleted his words, turned the paper over, and began again (fig. 5.3). But the false start may be of some interest in communicating Dickens's powerful feelings. In the second sentence, abandoned before completion, Dickens wrote, "Public opinion has enacted a code of laws for the coercion and oppression of the slave, which will one of these days if they be handed down. . . ."[33] Here, Dickens abandons irony, speaking of the appalling true effects of public opinion in America.

Dickens continued to think about his argument in this section on public opinion, making changes after the time of initial inscription. Two paragraphs of text in the published book, running from "Public opinion is

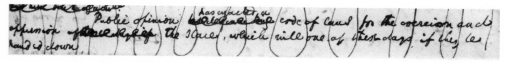

Figure 5.3. Dickens considered (and deleted) a passage about the power of public opinion and "laws for the coercion and oppression of the slave."

deferred" through "*them to Maryland,*" are not in the manuscript; Dickens must have added them later in an attempt to bolster his argument with additional evidence.[34]

After this introductory section on public opinion, Dickens offers what he calls "a few specimens of the advertisements in the public papers," noting that it is "only four years since the oldest among them appeared."[35] (This last claim is not, strictly speaking, true: the item concerning the slave "Pompey," a possible source for "Cicero" in *Martin Chuzzlewit,* was originally published in 1832, ten years before the publication of *American Notes.*[36])

On four pages of his manuscript, Dickens copied out all of the quoted advertisements in longhand, with no revisions except minor corrections of pen slips.[37] The first nine all derive from Weld's subsection on punishments, "II. TORTURES, BY IRON COLLARS, CHAINS, FETTERS, HANDCUFFS, &c."[38] Although Dickens quotes the items in his source in their original order, he omits most of the twenty-eight items in Weld's pages and never selects more than two consecutive items. Dickens copied out the 4th and 5th, the 11th, the 13th, the 19th, the 21st and 22nd, and the 26th and 27th items. Dickens got almost all of the words right but in some cases made minor alterations in the punctuation, italics, and capitalization. Dickens correctly recorded the rather odd name "De Yampert" in one item; the typographical error "De Lampert" appears in the first edition without Dickens's manuscript authority.[39]

The final thirty-five items in Dickens's selection derive from the next of Weld's subsections, "III. BRANDINGS, MAIMINGS, GUN-SHOT WOUNDS, &c."[40] Again, Dickens quotes the items in their original order as given in Weld, and again he omits about three-quarters of Weld's materials. Dickens generally avoided selecting more than two consecutive items (though he twice gives groups of three, and once gives a group of five).[41] Reading Dickens's selection is appalling, in part because of the plenitude of abuses; Weld's list is all the more so, because it is so much more extensive. It is interesting that Dickens would be willing to copy out page after page of these items, yet constantly select from among them. Dickens did not seem to select the most horrific material; in fact, no principal of selection at all is manifest, beyond the fact that Dickens avoided consecutive advertisements. Perhaps his selection (even if based largely on chance or random factors) was Dickens's way of putting his own impress on the advertisements or concealing (slightly) the fact that he was lifting a great deal of material from Weld. Similarly, one wonders why he bothered to copy out these passages by hand, rather than simply cutting and pasting. Elsewhere in *American Notes,* as in the substantial portions of chapter 3 treating Laura Bridgman and Oliver Caswell, Dickens pasted parts of another printed publication into his manuscript, rather than rewriting it in longhand.[42] Again, however, he may have handwritten the advertisements as a way of making them—at least in his own mind—his own.

Two thirds of the way through his excerpts from Weld, Dickens interrupts them to offer a paragraph commenting on a description of a runaway slave with missing teeth: he writes that, "among the other benefits which public opinion secures to the negroes, is the common practice of violently punching out their teeth." Dickens sharpens his irony still more by altering "benefits" to "blessings." The following sentence, "To make them wear iron collars by day and night, and to worry them with dogs, are practices almost too ordinary to deserve mention," does not appear in Dickens's manuscript; he must have added it in the proof stages.[43]

Dickens added meaningful emphasis to two of the last advertisements he quotes. To the advertisement given in Weld as "Ranaway, a negro named Washington—has *lost a part of his middle finger and the end of his little finger,*"[44] Dickens omitted the italics in Weld but lent emphasis to "named Washington" by underscoring these words with broken double-underlining, indicating that the compositor should set them in small capitals (fig. 5.4).[45] By doing so, Dickens highlights the irony of the abused slave being named after the first U.S. president. Dickens also added emphasis to the advertisement Weld gave as "Twenty-five dollars reward for the negro slave Sally—walks as though *crippled* in the back."[46] Dickens took away the italics for "crippled" and added them to "as though"—again highlighting the irony. (It is all too easy for any reader to guess why Sally walks "as though" crippled.) Dickens did not indicate this added emphasis when copying the passage in the manuscript; it was evidently the result of later thought in the proof stages.[47]

Most of the remainder of the "Slavery" chapter is taken up with extracts from newspapers exposing how slaveholders treat not their slaves but each other; Dickens's purpose is to show how the institution of slavery debases an entire culture. These excerpts are similar to the kinds of

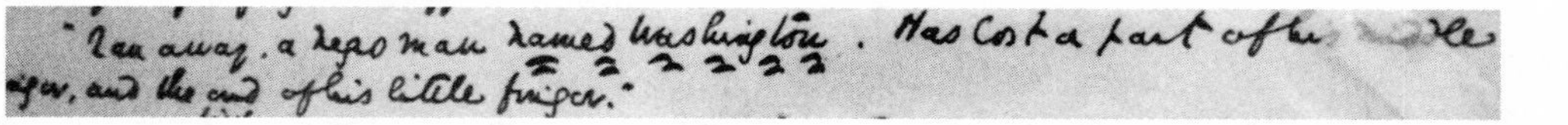

Figure 5.4. Dickens gave new emphasis to one of the advertisements quoted by Theodore Dwight Weld in *American Slavery as It Is.*

things Weld printed in his pamphlet and were almost certainly inspired by Weld's work, but they are not actually from *American Slavery as It Is:* Dickens says he drew these particular examples from newspapers "which appeared from day to day, during my visit to America, and which refer to occurrences happening while I was there." In his final paragraph before the newspaper excerpts, Dickens notes that not every one of the cases occurred "in territory actually belonging to legalized Slave States," but that "the character of the parties concerned was formed in slave districts, and brutalised by slave customs."[48] This paragraph does not appear in Dickens's manuscript; its later addition indicates Dickens's continuing interest in this matter. In part, the added caveat seems a defense against an imagined objection, but it also extends the range of Dickens's criticism: it is not only the slave states but the country as a whole that is debased, disgraced, and demoralized by slavery.

Although these newspaper extracts, twelve in number, are handwritten, most of them are *not* in Dickens's handwriting. They may have been copied by the secretary he employed on his American tour, George Washington Putnam. Again, Dickens seems to have wished to put his impress on the material in some way. Even though he (obviously) did not write the excerpts nor even copy most of them, he did rearrange them before publication: not one of the first ten extracts appears in the same position in the printed book as in the manuscript.

The first extract to appear in the manuscript, "Murder in Arkansas," is pasted onto page 9 of the manuscript after two lines of Dickens's handwriting. Although none of the extracts is identified in the published text, there is a source for this first one provided in the manuscript: the "Van Buren Intelligencer, April 1."[49] (This source was deleted, probably by Dickens, though it is difficult to be certain about the authorship of a simple deletion.) The next item, "Foul Deed," is similarly identified (and deleted): it derives from the "St. Louis New Era."[50] No source is given for any of the subsequent items.[51]

After these twelve extracts, Dickens had very little left to do: there are but four more paragraphs in the chapter. But Dickens needed to set the excerpts in context; more importantly, he needed to show what they mean. In the manuscript, he explicitly appeals to "every human mind, imbued with the commonest of common sense," and asks, "with these revolting evidences of the state of society which exists in the slave districts of America," can they "have a doubt of the real condition of the slave, or can they for a moment make a compromise between the institution or any of its flagrant, fearful features, and their own just consciences?" Before this paragraph was published, Dickens altered "the state of society which exists in the slave districts" to "the state of society which exists in and about the slave districts."[52] The difference is subtle but significant: just as Dickens added the paragraph noting that not all the newspaper excerpts treated slave states, this added phrase serves as a warning. Dickens's indictment of America is not limited to the slave states; he means to demonstrate that all of America is tainted by this hideous and loathsome institution.

Much of the argument in Dickens's closing paragraphs closely parallels Theodore Weld's. In a subsection entitled "FINALLY, THAT SLAVES MUST HABITUALLY SUFFER GREAT CRUELTIES, FOLLOWS INEVITABLY FROM THE BRUTAL OUTRAGES WHICH THEIR MASTERS INFLICT ON EACH OTHER," Weld argues that "Slaveholders, exercising from their childhood irresponsible power over human beings, . . . become in a great measure unfitted for self control in their intercourse with each other. . . . When slaveholders are in the habit of caning, stabbing, and shooting *each other* at every supposed insult, the unspeakable enormities perpetrated by such men, with such passions, upon their defenseless slaves, must be beyond computation."[53]

Dickens closes his chapter with a powerful image of the "brutal savage" that is the American slaveholder, creating this image partly through careful revision. He pictures this man, "a coward in his domestic life, stalking among his shrinking cowering bondsmen," but then deleted "shrinking cowering bondsmen," adding "shrinking men and women slaves" in between the lines. He went on to write "with his whips and rods of steel" but deleted that phrase also, substituting "armed with his heavy whip," noting that he is thus a "coward out of doors" and a "merciless and unrelenting tyrant" as well.[54]

The final chapter of the book, "Concluding Remarks," makes no explicit mention of slavery. But a final deleted paragraph, just before Dickens penned the words "The End," has some relevance to Dickens's outspoken judgments about slavery. Dickens writes, "Neither in these pages, nor in any others I have written, or shall ever write, have I been swayed by any political or party considerations, for I know no politics in the cause of Human Happiness."[55]

American Notes for General Circulation was the first of Dickens's books to be issued without illustration, predating *Hard Times* by over a decade. But the illustrated Library edition of *American Notes* included the provocatively titled "Black and White" by Marcus Stone (fig. 5.5). This

BLACK AND WHITE.

Figure 5.5. Marcus Stone's "Black and White," as published in the Library edition (and, later, the Charles Dickens edition) of *American Notes.* Courtesy of Worcester Polytechnic Institute Curation, Preservation, and Archives, George C. Gordon Library.

image, of a white man leering at a black mother and her children, was subsequently included as the frontispiece for the 1868 Charles Dickens edition. Although it does not clearly illustrate any one specific scene in Dickens's book, it was probably inspired by the scene of the "champion of Life, Liberty, and the Pursuit of Happiness" checking his new property, the "mother and her children," in the first chapter of the second volume. In any case, the image of the uncaring white slaveholder smiling malevolently at the black family is disturbing, and quite in keeping with Dickens's tone in *American Notes for General Circulation*. Dickens wanted his readers, in England and America, to consider closely the effects of an institution he found an abomination—a disgrace making a gross and monstrous mockery of the high values and noble sentiments espoused by the Declaration of Independence.

NOTES

1. John Forster, *The Life of Charles Dickens,* 3 vols. (London: Chapman and Hall, 1872–4), 2:13–17. The interested reader can also consult this omitted chapter as an appendix in Charles Dickens, *American Notes for General Circulation,* ed. and with an introduction by John S. Whitley and Arnold Goldman (Harmondsworth, Eng.: Penguin, 1972, 1985), 297–300, or in Charles Dickens, *American Notes and Pictures from Italy,* ed. F. S. Schwarzbach (London: J. M. Dent, 1997), 274–76.

2. Charles Dickens, *American Notes for General Circulation,* original manuscript in the Victoria and Albert Museum, South Kensington, London, F.47.A.13–14, 3. In citing the manuscript, I first give the number Dickens assigned his manuscript page, and then the volume number followed by a colon, and chapter and page number(s) separated by a period of the corresponding passage in the first edition of *American Notes for General Circulation,* 2 vols. (London: Chapman and Hall, 1842). Dickens failed to number the pages of his manuscript corresponding to the second volume of the first edition; for such pages, I give the penciled number at the top of the manuscript page, assigned by the Victoria and Albert Museum.

3. Dickens, *American Notes* manuscript, 3.

4. David Walker Howe, "Channing, William Ellery," in *American National Biography,* 24 vols., ed. John A. Garraty and Mark C. Carnes (New York: Oxford University Press, 1999).

5. Len Gougeon, *Virtue's Hero: Emerson, Antislavery, and Reform* (Athens: University of Georgia Press, 1990), 42–43.

6. Dickens, *American Notes,* 1:3.59.

7. Dickens, *American Notes* manuscript, 31/1:3.59.

8. James Brewer Stewart, "Garrison, William Lloyd," in *American National Biography;* Seymour Drescher, *Abolition: A History of Slavery and Antislavery* (Cambridge: Cambridge University Press, 2009), 295.

9. Dickens, *American Notes* manuscript, 31–32/1:3.59.

10. Stanley M. Elkins, *Slavery: A Problem in American Institutional and Intellectual Life,* 2nd edn. (Chicago: University of Chicago Press, 1968), 186; Gougeon, *Virtue's Hero,* 35; Sandra Harbert Petrulionis, *To Set This World Right: The Antislavery Movement in Thoreau's Concord* (Ithaca, N.Y.: Cornell University Press, 2006), 16.

11. Dickens, *American Notes* manuscript, 31–32/1:3.59.

12. Ibid., 60.

13. Ibid., 69/1:4.146.

14. Ibid., 93/1:6.200.

15. Ibid., 128/1:8.276.

16. Dickens, *American Notes,* 1:8.288, 289–90.

17. Dickens, *American Notes* manuscript, 142/1:8.306.

18. Ibid., [1] verso/2:1.3.

19. Ibid., 7/2:1.16.

20. Ibid., 7/2:1.17.

21. Ibid.

22. Ibid., 11/2:1.24.

23. Ibid., 1/2:9.249.

24. Dickens, *American Notes,* 2:9.249–50.

25. Dickens, *American Notes* manuscript, 1/2:9.250, 251.

26. Louise H. Johnson, "The Source of the Chapter on Slavery in Dickens's *American Notes,*" *American Literature* 14, no. 4 (January 1943): 427–30; [Theodore Dwight Weld], *American Slavery as It Is,* facsimile edn. of the 1839 pamphlet with a new preface by William Lorenz Katz (New York: Arno Press, 1969).

27. Robert H. Abzug, "Weld, Theodore Dwight," in *American National Biography.*

28. Petrulionis, *To Set This World Right,* 45; James Brewer Stewart, *Holy Warriors: The Abolitionists and American Slavery* (New York: Hill and Wang, 1976), 161.

29. Dennis Wepman, "Grimké, Angelina Emily," in *American National Biography;* Sandra F. VanBurkleo and Mary Jo Miles, "Grimké, Sarah Moore," in *American National Biography.*

30. Weld, *American Slavery as It Is,* 132–38.

31. Johnson, "The Source," 427–30.

32. Weld, *American Slavery as It Is,* 143–210.

33. Dickens, *American Notes* manuscript, 6 verso.

34. Dickens, *American Notes,* 2:9.257–58.

35. Ibid., 2:9.259.

36. Weld, *American Slavery as It Is,* 77.

37. Dickens, *American Notes* manuscript, 5–8/2:9.259–65.

38. Weld, *American Slavery as It Is,* 73–74.

39. Dickens, *American Notes* manuscript, 5/2:9.259.

40. Weld, *American Slavery as It Is,* 77–81.

41. The item numbers Dickens selects are as follows: 1, 3–4, 6, 8–12, 14–16, 18–19, 28–30, 33–34, 41–42, 44, 46, 51–52, 55, 57, 62, 68–69, 74, 80, 83, 87, 99.

42. Dickens, *American Notes* manuscript, 42–45/1:3.75–94, 48–49/1:3.98–102.

43. Ibid., 7/2:9.264.

44. Weld, *American Slavery as It Is,* 80.

45. Dickens, *American Notes* manuscript, 8/2:9.265.

46. Weld, *American Slavery as It Is,* 81.

47. Dickens, *American Notes* manuscript, 8/2:9.265.
48. Dickens, *American Notes,* 2:9.267–68.
49. Dickens, *American Notes* manuscript, 9/2:9.272.
50. Ibid., 10–10 verso/2:9.273–74.
51. "Horrible Tragedy" (11/2:9.268–69) and "The Wisconsin Tragedy" (12/2:9.269–70)
follow. The next excerpt, titled "Recontre" in the manuscript but published as "Rencon-
tre," is written on both the front and back of a manuscript page; though this excerpt, like
the previous ones, is not in Dickens's hand, Dickens did write the word "over" at the bottom of the front of the page (13–13 verso/2:9.274–76). The next page, with the four shortest
excerpts, is entirely in Dickens's handwriting: the excerpts are entitled "Affray in Mississippi" (14/2:9.276), "Personal Encounter" (14/2:9.277), "Duel" (14/2:9.277), and "Murder"
(14/2:9.270). But the next two excerpts, "Terrible Death of Robert Potter" (15/2:9.271)
and "Affray in Clarke County" (16/2:9.278) are once again in a hand that is certainly not
Dickens's. The final excerpt, "Affair of Honor," treating thirteen-year-old duelists, is pre-
ceded by a single short paragraph; this paragraph, along with the title and first sentence
of the excerpt, are in Dickens's handwriting (16–17/2:9.278–79).
52. Dickens, *American Notes* manuscript, 17/2:9.280.
53. Weld, *American Slavery as It Is,* 187–88.
54. Dickens, *American Notes* manuscript, 18/2:9.281–82.
55. Ibid., 28/2:10.306.

CHAPTER 6

Dickens's Visits to Springfield, Massachusetts, in 1842 and 1868

KIT POLGA

✦

IN *The Mystery of Edwin Drood,* Mr. Grewgious wants to see the Cloister-ham Cathedral but is told there is a service in progress, so he peeks in at the door and exclaims, "Dear me, . . . it's like looking down the throat of Old Time."[1] This sense of history and wonder could not be more beautifully conveyed. This deep connection with the past resonates when readers or observers are confronted with a vision or idea to which they immediately feel connected. Looking "down the throat of Old Time" opens the door to vibrant images of Dickens's visits to Springfield in 1842 and 1868. Dickens's first visit was emblematic of his eagerness to experience America, while his second visit reflected the genius and vulnerability of the mature writer who had transformed himself into a performer, bringing his characters alive to his American readers.

Dickens's visits to Springfield have been almost universally ignored. Peter Ackroyd, for instance, writes 1,080 pages about Dickens but loses Dickens's visits to Springfield between Worcester and Hartford in 1842, and between Albany and New Haven in 1868.[2] A more careful look at these trips helps us to understand more fully the young man who traveled across the Atlantic to America in 1842 to meet its people, and to experience their democratic government. Massachusetts came nearest to meeting his great expectations for the young republic. Dickens arrived as an enthusiastic, fresh-faced young man, bringing his young wife and leaving their four very young children at home. The youngest child, Walter Savage Landor Dickens, was nine months old when he was baptized on 4 December 1841, shortly before his parents left for America in January 1842. When Dickens returned to Massachusetts in 1867, he was a single man with eight children, having lost baby Dora in 1851, separated from his wife in 1858, and lost young Lieutenant Walter Savage Landor Dickens in 1863.

When Dickens was contemplating his first trip to the United States, he wrote to William Hall on 14 September 1841, asking his advice about whether to run "over to America about the end of February, and [come] back, after four or five months, with a One Volume book." Dickens mentioned that Washington Irving "writes me that if I went, it would be such a triumph from one end of the States to the other, as was never known in any Nation."[3] Little did Dickens know that both triumph and tribulation would welcome him on that first visit. Juliet John explains that "the extent of his fame was unrivalled and unprecedented; his visit to America exposed his celebrity and his international popularity, to himself as well as to onlookers, and complicated the way he saw America as well as the way America saw him."[4] She notes Dickens's initial euphoria and his eventual claustrophobia in reaction to his reception. Early on, Dickens sent John Forster copies of newspaper accounts of his enthusiastic welcome, and Forster shared these with a number of Dickens's friends, including Sydney Smith. Juliet John notes Smith's mention of Dickens's "American Deification" in a letter Smith apparently wrote to Thomas Carlyle asking him to "Pray tell Dickens for me to remember that he is still but a man."[5] Dickens was to be sorely disappointed, not in the numbers of his admirers but in their assumption that he would welcome any and all intrusions on his privacy. On 22 March 1842, Dickens wrote to his friend William Macready bemoaning the fact that America was "not the Republic I came to see. This is not the Republic of my imagination."[6] Perhaps his imagination had prepared him for something akin to deification, and, as Patrick McCarthy notes, he expected "nothing less than a renewed version of the Old World with its best features retained, others improved, and its corruptions eradicated."[7] When Dickens returned in 1867, he acknowledged America's growth into a more admirable society.

When Dickens, Catherine, and Catherine's maid, Anne Brown, disembarked in Boston on 22 January 1842, they were delighted at their reception. When they embarked on the steamboat *Massachusetts* on 7 February 1842 to travel down the Connecticut River to Hartford, Dickens was unaware that from thence he would be overwhelmed by public attention and disenchanted both by the manners and morals of many of the Americans he encountered. In the seventeen days Dickens first spent in Massachusetts, he felt a warm connection with many of the people he encountered and made many friends: he enjoyed the conviviality of its people and admired its institutions. He continued lifelong friendships with Cornelius Felton, Henry Wadsworth Longfellow, Charles Sumner, and James T. Fields. Dickens became friends with Jonathan Chapman, the energetic, charismatic mayor of Boston in whom Dickens had found a "kindred spirit."[8] Just before Dickens left Boston, Chapman gave a speech in his honor in which Chapman imagined a discussion between Mr. Pickwick and Sam Weller. He explained that they had come from England to help their editor. In their conversation, Mr. Pickwick opines that those "whom the Americans love they utterly kill with kindness," to which Mr. Weller replies, "It is currently reported, in our circles, that, when the Americans fancies a stranger, they makes him into weal-pie and devours him."[9] Chapman could not have realized the prescience of his remarks. Dickens might indeed have felt like "weal-pie" as he continued his travels, but his public did not begin to devour him until after his visit to Springfield. Chapman and Dickens continued to correspond after Dickens's return to England, and Chapman expressed his concern about the reaction to the forthcoming publication of *American Notes for General Circulation*.[10] It seems that their friendship suffered because there is no extant correspondence between Dickens and Chapman after October 1842. Chapman died in 1848 at the age of forty-one.

Dickens traveled through Springfield on 7 February 1842, his thirtieth birthday, very near the beginning of his tour, while he was still full of optimism about what he would find in America. By all accounts, it was a pleasant visit with a warm but small welcome, and none of the public hysteria he was to encounter elsewhere. He hardly spent enough time in Springfield on that first occasion to make any connections in the town. The most notable part of his trip was the travel down the Connecticut River to Hartford. At the time, there were four weekly newspapers in Springfield—*The Republican, The Gazette, The Post,* and *The Independent Democrat*—all of which focused on subjects such as legislative matters rather than on breaking news. The only local paper to take note of Dickens's visit was the *Republican* of 5 February 1842, which remarked that:

> This popular English author who arrived out in the *Britannia,* is now in Boston experiencing the kindness of the inhabitants of that hospitable City. A dinner was given to him in that City on Tuesday evening, by a number of young gentlemen. On Monday he passes through this town on his way to Hartford, where he partakes of a dinner on Wednesday. From thence he goes southward. A ball is getting up in New York in honor of him.
>
> We like to see distinguished strangers treated with respect and courtesy, but when it comes to that obsequious flattery which characterises the manners of some towards the author of Boz, it is decidedly sickening, and certainly must be anything but agreeable to himself, providing he is such a man one would suppose him to be.

Figure 6.1. Court Square, Springfield. Courtesy of the Lyman and Merrie Wood Museum of Springfield History, Springfield, Massachusetts.

This seems like a particularly perceptive view of what was to come. Toward the end of Dickens's stay in America, he wrote to Thomas Beard from Niagara Falls on 1 May 1842, telling Beard that he had been "so beset, waylaid, hustled, set upon, beaten about, trampled down, mashed, bruised, and pounded, by crowds, that I never knew less of myself in all my life, or had less time for those confidential Interviews with myself whereby I earn my bread, than in these United States of America."[11] Dickens had become increasingly disturbed by the unrelenting attention of his admirers.

Dickens made his journey through Springfield when the town had a population of about ten thousand, and was developing rapidly from the community that earlier had "had its church, its school, its town meeting, shops, merchants, artisans, farmers, and paupers, and it was, in sum, nothing more and nothing less than a typical New England town" (fig. 6.1).[12] The first train depot, a wooden building on the west side of Main Street, was built in 1839, and horses and carts awaited the arrival of the trains (fig. 6.2). The delegation from Hartford that was to accompany Dickens back to their city was waiting for him and his wife at the depot, and took them for the short ride up the hill to visit the Springfield Armory (fig. 6.3). According to the arsenal's archives, Dickens and his group were conducted on a tour of the arsenal by Colonel J. W. Ripley and the quartermaster, a Major Ingersoll.[13] Dickens must have seen the rows of muskets that inspired Longfellow (who visited the arsenal on his wedding trip a year later) to compare them to the pipes of an organ in his poem "The Arsenal at Springfield." The group likely admired the ingenuity of Thomas Blanchard's engineering in the workshops where weapons were being made.

The Dickens party saw the arsenal workshops on the Mill River and then traveled back downhill toward the Connecticut River. As was the custom, they must have had a meal at the local tavern before embarking on

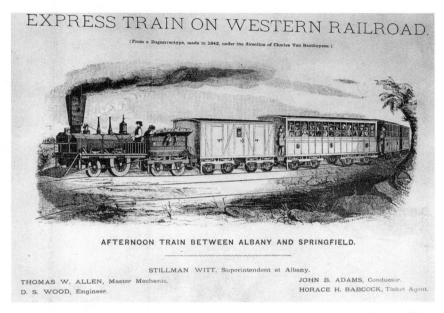

Figure 6.2. Express train on western railroad, 1842. Courtesy of the Lyman and Merrie Wood Museum of Springfield History, Springfield, Massachusetts.

Figure 6.3. Western view of Springfield Armory buildings. Courtesy of the Lyman and Merrie Wood Museum of Springfield History, Springfield, Massachusetts.

the Blanchard steamboat *Massachusetts* for their trip downriver to Hartford (fig. 6.4). In addition to working engineering wonders at the arsenal, Thomas Blanchard had set about solving the problem of navigating the Enfield Falls on the Connecticut River below Springfield, and in 1829 had designed a flat-bottomed, stern-wheel steamboat small enough to navigate through the river's canals and strong enough to ride the rapids:

> This extraordinary man [Blanchard] was a common artisan in the United States' Armory at Springfield, and . . . he had added improvement to improvement in the machinery there, until it would seem to be as perfect as the art and wit of man could make it—the principal of which, however, is the machine for *turning* gun stocks, and any irregular figure. But the improvement for which, perhaps, his country will be most indebted to him is his steam-boat for shoal water—it might be more appropriate to call it an invention—for it is built on a new principle.

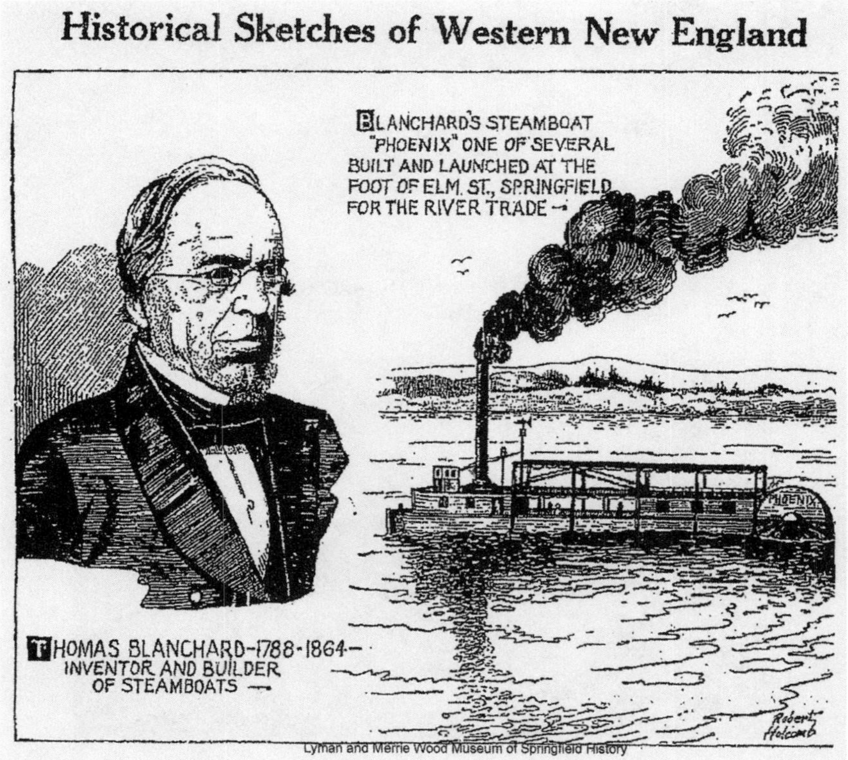

Figure 6.4. Thomas Blanchard and steamboat. Courtesy of *The Republican*.

A contingent from Roanoke, Virginia, had come to Springfield to see Blanchard's work, and when they "saw the steamer *Massachusetts,* ascending the Enfield falls, and what he had done in the United States' Armory at Springfield, we too, had no doubt of Mr. B's ability to put steam-boats on the Roanoke, if mortal man could."[14]

The description in *American Notes* of Dickens's journey states that the steamboat was "about half a pony power," and that the cabin "looked like the parlour of a Lilliputian public-house." The trip was made by boat because the river "was 'open,' or, in other words, not frozen." The trip to Hartford by coach would have taken about ten or twelve hours, so it was an easy choice to take the two-and-a-half hour boat trip to Hartford, roughly twenty-five miles south of Springfield. The steamboat had a crew of five, including the skipper, "Kit" Stebbins, and the pilot, Adin Allen. Dickens was "afraid to tell how many feet short this vessel was, or how many feet narrow: to apply the words length and width to such measurement would be a contradiction in terms. But I may state that we all kept the middle of the deck, lest the boat should unexpectedly tip over." The real length of the boat was 97 feet long, including the stern wheel, and 13½ feet wide. It could carry seventy-five passengers. The *Massachusetts* drew twenty-two inches of water when laden, so Dickens was not exaggerating very much when he estimated that the depth of the river "did not exceed a few inches" in the course they took to avoid the blocks of ice.[15] Rather than having "half a pony power," the *Massachusetts* actually had "two engines of 17½ horse power, each."[16]

A young woman on the boat told Dickens that the Connecticut River was beautiful in the summer time, but it must have looked desolate in February 1842, just as it does in winter every year. Dickens noted that the young woman "should be a judge of beauty, if the possession of a quality include the appreciation of it, for a more beautiful creature I never looked upon."[17] The beautiful young woman was later identified in an 18 June 1905 *Springfield Republican* article as Anna B. Dwight, a member of a prominent Springfield family. She was described as the daughter of Jonathan Dwight, and research shows that she was the niece of Lucinda Dwight of Springfield, who was the wife of Dickens's friend Jonathan Chapman, mayor of Boston. Dickens declared their "alliance ... complete" in a letter to Chapman on 22 February 1842.[18] It is very likely that Dickens knew that young Anna Dwight was Chapman's niece, and it is easy to see his delight in obliquely referring to and complimenting the common connection to a personal friend. Chapman was among those who saw Dickens off at New York, before he set sail for England.[19]

When Dickens returned to America in 1867 for his reading tour, his impressions of America changed dramatically. The country had matured and survived the Civil War. Slavery had been abolished. Dickens was no longer "deified" but treated with dignity. He was in failing health but determined to make the journey for the satisfaction of building a unique connection with his readers, meeting with old friends, and earning the substantial remuneration he expected.

His transition from writer to reader/performer has often been viewed as a curious if successful one. His books have something of performance about them, and people have often described them as cinematic. As John Irving wrote about reading *Great Expectations* as a boy, "It was very visual—I saw everything, exactly—and the characters were more vivid than any I had heretofore met on the page. I had only met characters like that onstage, and not just in any play—mainly in Shakespeare."[20] We know that Dickens acted scenes in the mirror in the course of his composition, and in his performances he shared the dramatic immediacy of his creations. In a way, the readings were a gift to his public and an acknowledgment of the connection between author and reader. Eventually, of course, they also became an enormously successful money-making venture.

Dickens gave his first public readings in December 1853 to raise funds for the Birmingham and Midland Institute. At his 30 December reading of *A Christmas Carol,* Dickens addressed an audience of two thousand, telling them that it had been his "particular wish that . . . the main body of my audience should be composed of working men and their families." He told them that he was animated "by the wish to have the great pleasure of meeting you face to face at this Christmas time, and accompany you myself through one of my little Christmas books."[21] He wrote to Mrs. Richard Watson on 13 January 1854, telling her that the audience "lost nothing, misinterpreted nothing, followed everything closely, laughed and cried . . . and animated me to that extent that I felt as if we were all bodily going up into the clouds together."[22] Dickens sought this same connection with his audiences in the United States. The accounts of Dickens's reading in Springfield would imply that he was able to go "up into the clouds" with them. Malcolm Andrews notes a letter Dickens wrote to Robert Lytton on 17 April 1867 in which Dickens stated, "When I first entered on this interpretation of myself (then quite strange in the public ear), I was sustained by the hope that I could drop into some hearts, some new expression of the meaning of my books, that would touch them in a new way." Andrews also quotes a response by T. C. De Leon to Dickens's readings in America: "There is something indescribable; a subtle essence of sympathy that can only be felt, not described, that puts him *en rapport* with the most antagonistic spirits and makes them his, while the spell is upon them."[23]

Dickens wanted to start his American reading tour in Boston, "inasmuch as all his literary friends lived there."[24] He arrived back in Boston in November 1867 and reached western Massachusetts to perform on 20 March 1868. During the years since his last visit, Springfield had been transformed from a sleepy town to a bustling industrial and residential metropolis. Horse-drawn trolley cars had replaced horses and buggies; "the quaint decade [when] the Connecticut River was Springfield's most colorful connection to the rest of the world" was over, and steamboats had been superseded by railway lines in all directions.[25] The steamboat *Massachusetts* had burned at its dock in Hartford a year after Dickens's 1842 trip.[26] The Springfield Armory had helped to create the rise in Springfield's development, and was of utmost importance to the Union during the Civil War. In 1864, the Springfield Armory employed 2,600 men, and businesses that sprang up during the war continued after 1865. Springfield was a thriving city, and the centers of activity downtown were on Main and Pynchon Streets.

Dickens left Boston on 6 March 1868 and passed through Springfield on his way to Syracuse, Buffalo, and Rochester, New York. He and his party left a day earlier than originally planned because a storm had made trains "some hours, and some of them a day, late in their arrival."[27] *The Republican* of Saturday, 7 March, reported that "Charles Dickens took supper at the Massasoit house last night, and engaged rooms for himself, Mr Dolby and three servants, preparatory to his reading in this city, March 20." The Massasoit House always had meals in readiness for passengers arriving at the train depot, which was next door (fig. 6.5). Trains were held while the passengers ate, and after supper, Dickens and his group traveled to Albany, where they broke their journey overnight before continuing to Syracuse for a 9 March reading there. On 19 March Dickens wrote to Annie Fields asking whether she and her husband might join him in Springfield because "by remaining there next Saturday and Sunday, instead of coming on to Boston, we shall save several hours' travel, and much wear and tear of our baggage and camp followers. Ticknor reports the Springfield hotel excellent."[28] Dickens enjoyed the close friendship of James and Annie Fields, and was comforted by their generous hospitality in Massachusetts, but the trip from Springfield to Boston for a visit of two days must have seemed too daunting to Dickens. James and Annie Fields were unable to make the journey to Springfield, but Dickens dined

Figure 6.5. Massasoit House business card. Courtesy of the Lyman and Merrie Wood
Museum of Springfield History, Springfield, Massachusetts.

with them in Boston on 31 March, writing to his daughter that "they are
the most devoted of friends, and never in the way and never out of it."[29]

It was snowing when Dickens arrived in Springfield on Friday, 20
March, for his reading that night of *A Christmas Carol* and the "Trial"
(from *The Pickwick Papers*). On their way back to Albany from readings
in Buffalo and Rochester, Dickens, his manager, George Dolby, and their
"men" had traveled through historic floods caused by thawing snow. They
were stranded in Utica over a sleepless Tuesday night before they were
able to complete the harrowing journey to Albany, arriving just in time
to get ready for an 8:00 p.m. reading. Dolby wrote that Dickens "gave
the 'Carol' and 'Trial' in his happiest mood, to the great delight of his
crowded audience."[30]

Dickens was in desperate need of a rest after his grueling schedule
and travel to Springfield. Dolby noted that they "determined on staying
in Springfield, which was our next reading town, and by so doing saving some unnecessary traveling," adding that, "as Springfield is a pleasant
city, with an excellent hotel (the Massasoit House), we had no reason
to regret our change of plan; for three most agreeable days were passed
here."[31] Ethan and Marvin Chapin had built the Massasoit House on
Main Street, and their foresight in building a first class hotel near the
railroad greatly enhanced the development of the city. The Chapins had
also been involved in the Underground Railroad, and John Brown had

VIEWS IN

OPERA
HOUSE

SPRINGFIELD,
MASS.

HAYNES'
HOTEL

Figure 6.6. Haynes Hotel and Opera House. Courtesy of the Lyman and Merrie Wood
Museum of Springfield History, Springfield, Massachusetts.

stayed at their hotel in the late 1840s.[32] The Chapins had "fed and hid
slaves in a crawl space beneath the hotel's main stairway."[33]

Tilly Haynes was the owner of the spacious Haynes Music Hall, referred to as the Music Hall block, on Main Street near the Massasoit
House, and was a popular and successful entrepreneur. After a fire at the
Music Hall block in 1864, Haynes moved quickly to build the Haynes
Opera House and Music Hall with the new Haynes Hotel on the other
side of the road (figs. 6.6, 6.7). In 1868 Dickens performed in the beautiful
new Opera House.

Springfield had transformed from town into city in Dickens's absence,
and Dickens himself was a different person, coming not just as a visitor
but as a performer and wildly successful novelist and personality. On this
trip he used George Dolby to prepare the way. Dolby managed every
aspect of his travel and performances, was an efficient taskmaster for his
workers, and protected Dickens from his fans. Dickens's impressions of
America were entirely different from those he had in 1842, and the three
pleasant days he spent in Springfield reflect that change. He had gained
hosts of readers in the ensuing years between visits, but he had also lost

Figure 6.7. Broadside and
Tilly Haynes. Courtesy of
the Lyman and Merrie Wood
Museum of Springfield History,
Springfield, Massachusetts.

some supporters after his publication of *American Notes* and *Martin Chuzzlewit*. When Dickens's eldest son gave a reading in Springfield in 1888, his visit prompted an article entitled "The Elder Dickens's Visits to Springfield in 1842 and 1868" in the *Springfield Republican* of 15 January 1888. Of Charles Dickens's 1868 visit, the article says, "Time heals a whole nation's wounds, and the growth and experience of 26 years sufficed to show Americans that the Englishman had written justly of them. Yet when Mr Dickens came again there were some who refused to see any good in him. Maj Ingersoll recalls that when some one at the armory proposed forming a company to call on the distinguished visitor, there was a decided rebuff on every side."

Nonetheless, there was a sold-out and enthusiastic crowd for Dickens's reading at the Haynes Opera House. Mark Twain's Dickensian description of Dickens at a reading in New York captures the power of his presence as he came on the stage to begin: "Promptly at 8 P.M., unannounced, and without waiting for any stamping or clapping of hands to call him out, a tall, 'spry,' (if I may say it,) thin-legged old gentleman, gotten up regardless of expense, especially as to shirt-front and diamonds, with a bright red flower in his button-hole, gray beard and moustache, bald head, and with side hair brushed fiercely and tempestuously forward, as if its owner were sweeping down before a gale of wind, the very Dickens came! He did not emerge upon the stage—that is rather too deliberate a word—he strode."[34]

From all accounts, Dickens kept his audience in Springfield spellbound. A Mrs. Brewer of Longmeadow, Massachusetts, wrote in her scrapbook that she "carried a copy of Dickens' works, or such as he was advertised to read from, [but] her copy was not of much use as he omitted certain parts and inserted lines not in the book. He looked on his book but once in the entire evening." Mrs. Brewer felt that the two-hour performance was all too brief, and that "he took his audience by storm and made the people laugh or cry at will." She noted that when he made a fine point that provoked his audience to laughter, he laughed, too.[35] A review entitled "Charles Dickens at Music Hall," appearing in *The Springfield Daily Republican* on 21 March, captured some of Dickens's presence for its readers: "There walks on stage a gentleman who gives you not time to think about him, and who dazzles you with twenty personalities. He is Scrooge, he is Scrooge's nephew, he is Christmas past; and before you have ceased wondering he is all the little Cratchits in a bunch, crying in full treble and exquisitely funny English accent, ''Ooray!'" The writer added that "Mr Dickens was in plain evening dress, with no signs of the foppishness of which he is accused, save for the flowers at his button-hole, and a trifle too much jewelry. . . . His face bears signs of incessant toil, and he is slightly bent. In the street he is not a remarkably noticeable man."

In Springfield Dickens received an "unusually large batch of 'home' letters full of congratulations on [his] triumphant progress through the States." Dickens had sent Dolby's wife and newborn son in Ross, Herefordshire, the present of a pony, and Dolby was gratified to receive a picture of his son's surprise gift in Dickens's mail from home.[36] Dickens spent his time in Springfield reading and replying to his many letters, resting in the comfortable hotel, and walking around the town. According to the local paper, he "spent the time rambling about the town at his own will, at one point being detected giving some money to a ragged little girl, and inspecting the boat-houses and shells which flourished in those palmy days of college regattas" (fig. 6.8).[37]

Dickens had written in despair about America to his friend William Macready in 1842, but on 21 March 1868, he wrote from Springfield that "you would find the general aspect of America and Americans, decidedly much improved. You would find immeasurably greater consideration and respect for your privacy, than of old." On the same day Dickens wrote a letter to his solicitor, Frederic Ouvry, and included the news that he intended to "take [his] leave of reading for good and all, in a hundred autumnal and winter Farewell's *for ever*."[38]

Dickens left Springfield on Monday, 23 March, for a reading in Worcester. He undertook fifteen more readings before completing his U.S. tour. Dolby wrote that "Mr. Dickens's health was becoming a graver source of anxiety every day" and was pleased that they had little travel left.[39] Dickens wrote to his daughter Mary from Portland on 29 March that he had "coughed from two or three in the morning until five or six, and have been absolutely sleepless. . . . However sympathetic and devoted the people are about me, they *can not* be got to comprehend that one's be-ing able to do the two hours with spirit when the time comes round, may be co-existent with the consciousness of great depression and fatigue."[40]

Dickens's farewell speech in New York on 20 April 1868 ends with these powerfully resonant words:

> The relations that have been set up between us . . . must now be broken, for ever. But I entreat you to believe that in passing from my sight, you will not pass from my memory. I shall often, often recall you as I see you now, equally by my winter fire and in the green English summer weather. I shall never recall you as a mere public audience, but rather as a host of personal friends, and ever with the greatest gratitude, tenderness, and consideration. Ladies and gentlemen, I beg to bid you farewell—and I pray God bless you, and God bless the land in which I leave you.[41]

In Dickens's first visit to Springfield we see a young man on his thirti-eth birthday eager to be admired and eager to admire this nascent coun-try. By 1868 he and the country had matured in myriad ways. Admirers overwhelmed him in 1842, but when he returned, Dolby protected him so much that his interactions with his public were almost entirely through his characters, presented in a dramatic, entertaining, and compelling form. Dickens gathered a "host of personal friends" in his readers, and made his readers feel like a "kindred spirit" of the author. In his readings,

Figure 6.8. Springfield and Connecticut River, ca. 1860. Courtesy of the Lyman and Merrie Wood Museum of Springfield History, Springfield, Massachusetts..

he made a more immediate connection with his audiences. The work of the young man who visited Springfield in 1842, and the frail yet dynamic celebrity who read in Springfield in 1868, reaches through the ages and continues to make his novels meaningful today.

NOTES

1. Charles Dickens, *The Mystery of Edwin Drood* (London: Chapman and Hall, 1870), 9.63.

2. Peter Ackroyd, *Dickens* (New York: HarperCollins, 1990), 350, 1019.

3. Charles Dickens, *The Pilgrim Edition of the Letters of Charles Dicke*ns, 12 vols., ed. Madeline House et al. (Oxford: Clarendon Press, 1965–2002), 2:383 (14 September 1841).

4. Juliet John, *Dickens and Mass Culture* (Oxford: Oxford University Press, 2010), 79.

5. Dickens, *Letters*, 3:42n.

6. Ibid., 3:156 (22 March 1842).

7. Patrick McCarthy, "Truth in *American Notes*," in *Dickens, Europe and the New Worlds*, ed. Anny Sadrin (New York: St. Martin's Press, 1999), 75.

8. Dickens, *Letters*, 3:vii.

9. James Spear Loring, *The Hundred Boston Orators Appointed by the Municipal Authorities and Other Public Bodies, from 1770 to 1852; Comprising Historical Gleanings Illustrating the Principles and Progress of Our Republican Institutions* (Boston: John P. Jewett and Company, 1854), 574.

10. Dickens, *Letters*, 3:345n2.

11. Ibid., 3:225 (1 May 1842).

12. Michael H. Frisch, *Town into City: Springfield, Massachusetts, and the Meaning of Community, 1840–1880* (Cambridge, Mass.: Harvard University Press, 1972), 14.

13. The Springfield Armory was closed in 1868. The armory reopened as the National Park Service's Springfield Armory National Historic Site. The campus is shared with Springfield Technical Community College. Many of the early buildings survive.

14. E. B. Hicks, "Report on the Navigation of the Upper Roanoke, by Means of Steamboats of Shallow Draught," *The Farmers' Register* 4, no. 5 (September 1836): 307.

15. Charles Dickens, *American Notes for General Circulation*, 2 vols. (London: Chapman and Hall, 1842), 1:5.173, 172, 174. Citations to *American Notes* include volume number followed by a colon, and chapter and page number(s) separated by a period.

16. Hicks, "Report on the Navigation," 308.

17. Dickens, *American Notes*, 1:5.174.

18. Dickens, *Letters*, 3:76 (22 February 1842).

19. Ibid., 3:248n3.

20. John Irving, "By the Book: John Irving," *New York Times Sunday Book Review*, 10 June 2012, 8.

21. Charles Dickens, *The Speeches of Charles Dickens*, ed. K. J. Fielding (Oxford: Oxford University Press, 1960), 166.

22. Dickens, *Letters*, 7:244 (13 January 1854).

23. Malcolm Andrews, *Charles Dickens and His Performing Selves* (Oxford: Oxford University Press, 2006), 226, 251.

24. George Dolby, *Charles Dickens as I Knew Him* (London: T Fisher Unwin, 1885), 160.

25. Frank Bauer, *At the Crossroads: Springfield MA 1636—1975* (Springfield, Mass.: USA Bicentennial Committee of Springfield, 1975), 36.

26. Edwin M. Bacon, *The Connecticut River and the Valley of the Connecticut River* (New York: G. P. Putnam's Sons, 1907), 341.

27. Dolby, *Charles Dickens as I Knew Him*, 276.

28. Dickens, *Letters*, 12:78 (19 March 1868).

29. Ibid., 12:86 (31 March 1868).

30. Dolby, *Charles Dickens as I Knew Him*, 291.

31. Ibid.

32. Wayne Phaneuf, "Springfield's Massasoit House Housed the Famous," 23 May 2011, www.masslive.com.

33. "Abolitionism & the Underground Railroad," *Our Plural History*, http://ourpluralhistory.stcc.edu.

34. [Mark Twain], "Charles Dickens," *Daily Alta California*, 5 February 1868, http://cdnc.ucr.edu.

35. "Announcement Union to Publish Dickens Work Recalls Visits to City," *Springfield Republican*, 2 March 1934, photocopy provided by Jim Gleason at the archives of the *Springfield Republican*.

36. Dickens identified Dolby as "The Man of Ross" in the Great International Walking Match.

37. "The Elder Dickens's Visits to Springfield in 1842 and 1868," *Springfield Republican*, 15 January 1888, 5.

38. Dickens, *Letters*, 12:80, 12:83 (21 March 1868).

39. Dolby, *Charles Dickens as I Knew Him*, 293.

40. Dickens, *Letters*, 12:85 (29 March 1868).

41. Dickens, *Speeches*, ed. Fielding, 383–84.

CHAPTER 7

Dickens, Martineau, and Massachusetts: The Republic They Came to See

IAIN CRAWFORD

◆

HARRIET MARTINEAU and Charles Dickens both burst into celebrity during the 1830s—Martineau with the publication of *Illustrations of Political Economy* in 1832 and Dickens with the appearance of *The Pickwick Papers* just four years later. Having consolidated these initial successes and secured their positions as major new figures in the world of early Victorian letters, both authors were then drawn to join the steady stream of English writers who set out to travel to the United States, intrigued by the social experiment underway in the New World, enthusiastic to see it for themselves, and eager to bring back their impressions to share with the readers at home. In writing about America, moreover, Martineau and Dickens not only became each other's audiences but also entered into wider transatlantic conversations that, as Amanda Claybaugh has shown, were as fundamental to the process of social reform in Britain as in the United States.[1] The divergent ways in which they responded to America, then, speak to wider cultural debates in the early Victorian period and, for the two authors themselves, foreshadowed the reasons why their relationship would later come to an untidy end when they fell into an ugly public quarrel over industrial safety policy during the winter of 1855–56.

The received narrative of this quarrel has read it as one in which Dickens gently disciplined Martineau in the pages of *Household Words*, regretfully correcting her supposed misunderstanding of the role of public policy in regulating industrial safety. I have written elsewhere to show the limitations of this narrative and to argue that, rather than simply a dispute over the details of the Factory Acts and their workings, the episode points to much wider debates in Victorian society around Utilitarian values, the role of journalism in shaping cultural discourse and public policy, and the increasing role of women authors in the press.[2]

Here, I address a longstanding critical tendency to retrofit analysis of
Martineau's and Dickens's differing responses to America so as to align
their reactions with the established account of the later dispute—a tendency most extensively represented by Jerome Meckier's reading of the
relationship between Martineau's *Society in America* and Dickens's *American Notes for General Circulation* as a textual agon in which Dickens writes
against Martineau and the alleged errors she was led into as a "hopelessly
deluded 'left-wing' meliorist."[3] In fact, what makes the early connection
over America and its anticipation of the later breakdown significant is
the ways in which it speaks beyond their personal conflict and to their
larger differences over the nature of civil society and the role of the press
in forming the public sphere. In particular, their reactions to Massachusetts and, specifically, to four aspects of its social life—the industrial community in Lowell, the position of women, education, and the role of the
press—thus offer a metonymic anticipation of their broader responses to
America as a whole, responses that in turn proved central to the agendas
they set for themselves as they returned to Britain and—both deeply
affected by their experiences across the Atlantic—moved toward the next
stages of their professional careers.

Overall, Martineau's and Dickens's reactions to the new society could
hardly have been more divergent. While Martineau recognized American civilization's limitations, particularly its continuing reliance on slavery and the cloistered role it imposed on women, her many and varied
writings about America collectively reveal a fundamentally optimistic
vision of the New World. Moreover, rather than being inspired by radical progressive thinking, as scholars have frequently assumed, hers was
a vision founded on the tenets of eighteenth-century classical political
economy.[4] Specifically, it rested on the stadial model of historical progress that she derived from Adam Smith, which comprised a theory of
history based on economic development through a four-stage series of
phases or "stades." As Nicholas Phillipson has argued, this model was
a keystone in Scottish Enlightenment thinking, developed at a point in
history when unprecedented economic change was creating tensions with
prevailing social practices. It provided "a context in which to situate the
political problems of preserving liberty in an age in which the spirit of
commerce was often at odds with laws and customs whose origins lay in
the needs of a feudal age."[5] The rapidly evolving character of American
society, with its combination of both dynamic entrepreneurship and re-
actionary cultural mores, thus made the new democracy an ideal object
of study for someone with Martineau's range of intellectual interests and

ideological commitment to classical economics and their role in shaping social development.

By contrast, it was Dickens who traveled to America with the hopes of a radical progressive whose political identity had taken shape during the turbulent 1830s. Unlike Martineau and her theory-shaped thinking, however, his politics seem more instinctual in their commitments and less guided by inherited intellectual constructs. Given that he was also treated as a public celebrity and allowed very little opportunity to explore America either so extensively or as privately in the ways that had been possible for Martineau, perhaps it was not then surprising that he found the actual experience of his visit overwhelming. Indeed, as Juliet John has valuably shown, a fundamental outcome of his brief months in America was the way in which they brought him face to face with the "reality of a mass culture he had thought he desired" but that in fact appalled him.[6] Thus, after greatly enjoying his initial experiences in Boston, the burden of being treated as a peripatetic superstar became increasingly oppressive. He grew ever more disenchanted with America and Americans, and, as he wrote home to William C. Macready on 22 March 1842, he came to a conclusion that nothing in the remainder of his visit could amend: "This is not the Republic I came to see. This is not the Republic of my imagination."[7]

Given these contrasting frames for their journeys and the profoundly different experiences they had in America, it is no wonder that Martineau and Dickens wrote in very different ways about the New World once they had returned home. Martineau published expansively out of her two-year stay in America and produced several articles and reviews as well as three major books: *Society in America* (1837), *Retrospect of Western Travel* (1838), and *How to Observe Morals and Manners* (1838).[8] She would also continue to write on American subjects for the rest of her career, appearing first in the abolitionist press and then in an ever wider series of venues on both sides of the Atlantic.[9] Collectively, the three books have played an important part in Martineau's interdisciplinary recovery over the past twenty years and have been central to the growing recognition of the range of her impact on early Victorian culture. *Society in America,* which offers an extended exploration of the political, economic, and ideological infrastructures of the new state, has come to be recognized as both a designedly innovative approach to travel writing and a fundamental contribution to the formation of sociology as a discipline.[10] *Retrospect of Western Travel,* by contrast, offers a far more personal narrative, one that follows established patterns of travel writing and blends her more intimate responses to the experience of travel through the New World with portraits of many of the leaders shaping American democracy. *How to Observe Morals and Manners,* which she began on the voyage to New York and expanded to book-length after returning to England, lays out guidelines for examining, recording, and evaluating the details of a culture, and deals extensively with the challenges of avoiding ethnocentric responses. Like *Society in America,* then, it is a central text in her contribution to the formation of sociological thinking.

By contrast with Martineau's studies of her American experience, Dickens's primary publication out of his visit was the brief and breezy picaresque account that derived primarily from his letters home and that, at least ostensibly, followed the established forms and conventions of early Victorian travel writing.[11] Less than a year after the publication of *American Notes,* he returned to the subject of America when he set two of *Martin Chuzzlewit'*s monthly numbers and part of a third in the United States.[12] Having done this, however, he wrote almost nothing further on American topics during the remainder of his career. While modern scholars, from Jerome Meckier to most recently Amanda Claybaugh and Juliet John, have valuably argued for *American Notes'*s importance in understanding Dickens's development as a writer, contemporaries were almost unanimously negative in condemning what they saw as its superficial rendering of American life and society. Even his closest American friend, Cornelius Conway Felton, for instance, when writing a largely protective account for the *North American Review,* felt compelled to point out the book's weaknesses, noting in particular that its representation of the press strained credulity: "We look upon the boundless power Dickens ascribes to the worst part of the American newspaper press with as much incredulity as we should upon the asserted wonders of any necromantic agency."[13]

In the close-knit world of English letters of the time, those who traveled to and wrote about America were generally aware of one another's books, and this was certainly the case for Dickens and Martineau. Still, although modern critical discussions have tended to assume that they had read one another's works thoroughly, a closer examination suggests that this was perhaps not in fact the case. For example, although Dickens appears not to have read *How to Observe,* the 1844 inventory of his library does show that he owned both *Society in America* and *Retrospect of Western Travel.*[14] But just how fully had he absorbed Martineau's accounts of America? The primary evidence on this question lies in his remark to Ann Warren Weston, a Boston abolitionist who wrote about a call she had paid on Dickens and his wife in early February 1842 and a discussion they had had about Martineau. Drawing from earlier work by Noel C. Peyrouton, the editors of Dickens's letters give a brief account of the meeting: "In conversation with Ann Warren Weston in Boston [he] described her work as 'the best . . . that had been written on America.'"[15] For Meckier and others, this statement indicates that Dickens was clearly positioning his own perceptions of the New World in the context of Martineau's books.

Returning to the manuscript of Weston's letter, however, and examining her complete narrative of the encounter provides a rather different picture: "We talked some of Harriet Martineau and he represented her health as dreadful—spoke well of her book, and said, bating a few errors, it was the best book that had been written on America. I said we were specially grateful to Miss M. for what she had said on the Slavery question, for as we had all the Commercial and Political influence of the country against us, the literary influence was particularly desirable. He assented I believe with something of a stare."[16] Imprecise as to which of her books he had in mind and improbable in his assessment of Martineau's errors after he himself had been in the country less than two weeks, Dickens's authority here is further undermined by Weston's recording his inert reaction to her remark about the interaction of cultural and commercial forces around the question of abolition. Rather than evidencing deep knowledge of Martineau's work, then, his observation on her book may well have owed more to politeness than to careful reading. Later that year, moreover, he would write to Frances Trollope and offer a similar and equally laudatory response to her representation of America: "No Writer . . . has so well and accurately (I need not add, so entertainingly) described it, in many of its aspects, as you have done."[17] To have commended these mutually incompatible writers on America in such similar terms may have been gracious, but it hardly evidences critical mastery of their widely contrasting visions of the New World.

Martineau in turn was no less ready to offer an opinion on a book she had not read and, with the forthrightness that so often marked her response to friends' work, she was decidedly less generously inclined toward Dickens's American writings than he had been in his comments on her text. So skeptical was she of the merits of *American Notes* that she offered judgment on it before she had even read it, writing to Henry Crabb Robinson on 29 October 1842:

Dickens's book is on the way to me. Meantime, I have seen large portions of it in the papers, & rejoice to find how far more moderate his tone is therein than in his speeches & conversation, & letters. It is absurd enough to pretend to an impression before having read the book: but I *have* an impression that it is humane, good-tempered, faithful, as far as it goes,—but superficial, rather affected & fine in parts, likely to occupy the whole world for a month or two, & then be absolutely forgotten in the superior merits of his fictions. Is this a good guess?[18]

If Dickens's undiscriminating appraisals of Martineau and Trollope may suggest a lack of due attention to either writer, Martineau's readiness to leap to judgment on partial representations of Dickens's work hardly boded well for the long-term health of their relationship. Clearly, whether or not they had actually read one another's works was no obstacle to their forming opinions of one another's writings, and it suggests that each held strong conceptions of the other—a factor that would certainly influence the fiery demise of their relationship more than a decade later.

While their manner of engaging with one another's texts suggests major differences between them, much the same was true of the ways in which their texts represented core elements of American society. These differences appear most notably in their accounts of Massachusetts and are first apparent in their divergent reactions to industrial life in New England. Although the heart of their experiences in the commonwealth inevitably lay in Boston and its surroundings, they both traveled out to visit the industrial experiment in Lowell. Having come to fame as a political economist, Martineau was particularly interested to see whether America was fulfilling the potential Adam Smith had anticipated for it in *The Wealth of Nations,* and she describes in some detail the ways in which Massachusetts industrial centers in Waltham and Lynn were enabling economic independence for the workers and creating a "society where every man is answerable for his own fortunes; and where there is therefore stimulus to the exercise of every power."[19]

Lowell offered additional interest since there she was able to witness the fusion of laissez-faire capitalism with the enlightened leadership of Unitarian industrialists endeavoring to create opportunities for the young women who migrated in from rural homes to work in the mills. In Martineau's reading of Lowell, the particular value of the industrial community thus lay in the ways in which it enabled young American women to achieve social independence as they moved into spaces created in the labor market by the migration westward of large numbers of young men. She describes the benefits these women derived from the experience most fully some years after she wrote her travel books, when she provided Charles Knight with a letter to use in his preface to a selection from *The Lowell Offering*. Admittedly, in this piece she does sound a conventional note in describing the factory girls as "well-dressed and lady-like," and she praises them for using their earnings to fulfill such gender-normative responsibilities as putting their brothers through college or paying off family debts. But she also pictures them as models of healthy independent living as she recounts young women partnering "to build dwellings for their own residence" and, emphasizing the liberating power of their active cultural lives, claims that "Their minds are kept fresh, and strong, and free by knowledge and power of thought; and this is the reason why they are not worn and depressed under their labours."[20] Even though she elsewhere expressed grave concern about the disempowering treatment of women in America through masculine codes of honor and chivalry, the visit to Lowell affirmed her faith in what she referred to as "the public mind . . . awakening to the necessity of enlarging the sphere of female industry," a faith that was fundamental to her understanding of social progress.[21] Just as she would continue to model "female industry" in her own career, so in her writing she would return time and again to the emancipatory power of employment for women, and her description of Lowell provides an early statement of what would become an enduring commitment in her life and work.

In this, she and Dickens could hardly have differed more strongly. For him, the visit to Lowell was an isolated occasion that led to his single description of industrial society in America and sole description of working women. To be sure, he does gesture toward contemporary transatlantic conversations about the nature of industrial life as he makes a passing contrast between Lowell and England's industrial towns as "great haunts of desperate misery." Perhaps constrained by writing within the conventions of travel narratives, however, he refrained from providing detailed support for his appraisal of this aspect of English life even as he claimed authority for the breadth of his judgment of its American counterpart. Martineau, herself a product of the English industrial bourgeoisie and an avid proponent of its accomplishments, might well, as she wrote to Crabb Robinson, have found this a "superficial" representation of the subject. Even more telling, however, are Dickens's and Martineau's perceptions of the female workers in the Lowell mills. While Dickens shares Martineau's favorable impression of the factory girls, his account is limited to external and conventional terms and focuses on the ways in which the workers conform to gender norms: they are

"well-dressed," "healthy in appearance," and free from all affectation, and
his definition of what makes their lives notable is limited to the presence
of pianos in the boardinghouses, the girls' subscriptions to circulating
libraries, and their production of *The Lowell Offering*. Moreover, while he
shared Martineau's interest in this publication, for him its value was not
as a vehicle for creative or intellectual expression but rather as an agent
of social discipline, since "many of its Tales are of the Mills and of those
who work in them; . . . they inculcate habits of self-denial and contentment, and teach good doctrines of enlarged benevolence."[22] Writing in
a genre where his single narrative voice dominates the reader's experience of the text, Dickens thus renders the Lowell factory girls as epito-
mizing the selflessness he so often privileges in his accounts of female
characters and simultaneously reduces both their agency and individual
autonomy.

These differences in their accounts of the Lowell factory workers
encapsulate a deeper divide in Dickens's and Martineau's understandings
of the nature of women's lives in America. For Martineau, the opportunities provided to working-class women in Lowell or to the Unitarian
intellectuals she met in Boston were the exception rather than the norm.
Indeed, as she notes in *How to Observe Morals and Manners,* the sup-
pression of women is inextricably linked to the new democracy's larger
failings to achieve its founding promise—"if women were not helpless,
men would find it far less easy to be vicious."[23] Central to her diagnosis
of these failings is the direct connection she makes between the position
of women and the continuing practices associated with slavery, especially
in the South. Challenging conventional expectations of women's travel
writing, she insists on bringing into her text material that would nor-
mally be considered inappropriate subject matter for a female author as
she describes the most extreme instance of such viciousness: the wide-
spread practice of miscegenation by "the gentlemen who, by their own
licentiousness, increase the number of slave children whom they sell in
the market." In its corrosive effects on marriage, moreover, this behavior
further undermines the standing of women, since "there is an end to all
wholesome confidence and sympathy, and woman sinks to be the orna-
ment of her husband's house, the domestic manager of his establishment,
instead of being his all-sufficient friend."[24] Appalling though she found
this, she also saw it as just one instance of larger patterns in the way
women's lives were ordered in America and so she reiterated the recip-
rocal relationship between women's rights and social progress: "Where
moral force is recognized as the moving power of society, it seems to

follow that the condition of Woman must be elevated; that new pursuits will be opened to her, and a wider and stronger discipline be afforded to her powers."[25]

In his writings about America, Dickens, by contrast, shows neither interest in the question of whether women should be granted public agency nor any sense that doing so would have broader social significance. Instead, he consistently represents American women as little more than the passive objects of male protection that Martineau had found such a problematic feature of the culture. Again, it is in Massachusetts that he finds his most favorable American exemplar, as he describes at length Laura Bridgman, the deaf, dumb, and blind resident of the Perkins Institute for the Blind and the text's sole extended account of a female subject. But "this gentle, tender, guileless, grateful hearted being" also exemplifies his larger pattern of representation as she is depicted simply as a model of benign, paternalistic treatment, and the reader is left to imagine her as eternally quiescent, safe within the walls of the protecting institution. After his account of Bridgman and a passing reference to the female inmates of the Eastern Penitentiary, whom he somewhat implausibly suggests that the prison experience "humanizes and refines" even as it proves so destructive to the male inmates, Dickens makes no further reference to women in America until he arrives at the single positive detail he offers about his voyage up the Mississippi. There, in his description of a "little woman so full of hope, and tenderness, and love, and anxiety" who is traveling home to St. Louis after giving birth in her mother's home in New York and taking her newborn baby to his father, he continues his representation of feminine experience in America, reinforcing his sentimentalized definition of women's lives as framed by their domestic roles and contained within social institutions and structures that, he blithely suggests, function purely for their benefit. Referring to his closing days in the New World, he offers a last example of this pattern, one that seems very different but that in fact affirms the same fundamental point. Describing an unsatisfactory visit to a Shaker village in Lebanon, New York, he represents the sect's prayer dancing as "infinitely grotesque" and localizes its failings into the person of its female leader, a woman kept "in strict seclusion . . . never shown to profane eyes," marked, he imagines, by the bizarre ugliness that characterizes the community as a whole, and with whose sequestration he is in "perfect concurrence."[26] Just as Martineau had found in America exemplars she could adopt for her own advocacy of women's advancement back in Britain, so Dickens represented women in the New World in terms of the cloistered femininity that the novels he had written before crossing the Atlantic had already established as his own normative pattern.

Given their sharply conflicting visions of both industrial society and women's lives in America, it is hardly surprising that Martineau and Dickens also perceived education in the New World in contrasting terms. For Martineau, America's potential to establish an educational system that would produce the educated citizenry Thomas Jefferson saw as foundational to a democratic society was simultaneously fundamental to her optimism about the nation's future and yet also rendered problematic by its present state of development, and she found both qualities exemplified in Massachusetts. On the one hand, with a characteristic refusal to make concessions on what she saw as matters of principle, she is unsparing in her comments on the failings of Unitarian Harvard. Dismissing it as merely "the aristocratic college of the United States," inaccessible to those from more modest segments of society, out of tune with the nation's needs, she notes that it is in danger of being marginalized as "more and more new colleges are rising up, and are filled as fast as they rise, whose principles and practices are better suited to the wants of the time."[27] Just as she had elsewhere criticized the Unitarian clergy in Boston for their failure to take leadership in the abolitionist movement, so here she makes a larger point about the ossification of the denomination's leading educational institution.[28] By contrast with Harvard, she looked beyond Boston and Cambridge to western Massachusetts, where she found reason to praise Amherst College and its more progressive stance, although even here she had cause to note ironically that the college authorities allow "the admission of girls to such lectures as they could understand . . . and that no evil had been found to result from it."[29] She had to move even further from New England, however, to find her most impressive examples of educational progress, which she located among those new colleges that she had earlier contrasted with Harvard and that were springing up along the frontier. From this group, she singled out Oberlin, founded by abolitionist students breaking away from the Lane Seminary in Cincinnati, which admitted women and free African Americans from its founding. In its inclusiveness of the two most important marginalized populations, Oberlin thus articulated precisely Martineau's vision of what was essential if America was to advance and fulfill its founding ideals, since the college's existence was justified by its providing "the repository from which the essential materials may be derived for the great moral contest now fierce in the United States, between the chains of mercenary violence on the one hand, and of depressed human rights on the other."[30]

Given the amount of interest in education his early fiction had already evidenced, Dickens's lack of attention to the subject in America is somewhat surprising. Yet beyond the brief remarks on *The Lowell Offering* and his description of Laura Bridgman, his one substantial comment on education in *American Notes* is limited to a single paragraph about Harvard. In it he praises its faculty, who "shed a grace upon, and do honour to, any society in the civilised world," and its exemplification of a larger national virtue of American universities that "disseminate no prejudices; rear no bigots; dig up the buried ashes of no old superstitions; never interpose between the people and their improvement; exclude no man because of his religious opinions; above all, in their whole course of study and instruction, recognise a world, and a broad one too, lying beyond the college walls."[31] For Juliet John this paragraph shows Dickens expressing a sense that intellectual life in America, and specifically in Cambridge, offers an alternative to the predations of the mass culture and indicates how much he valued the social circle he developed among the Harvard academics because it "represented culture, in particular a learned culture that saw itself serving needs beyond the commercial."[32] While it certainly speaks to Dickens's fondness for his Cambridge friends, the paragraph, like his comment on Lowell's superiority to English industrial cities, provides no evidence to support its larger claims about the Harvard faculty, let alone its assertions about the quality of American higher education as a whole. Dickens quite literally does not know what he is talking about here, and it was the superficiality of comments such as this that laid *American Notes* open to attack by reviewers on both sides of the Atlantic, Martineau among them.

While his paragraph says nothing of persuasive substance about the education the university offered, by reinforcing the value Dickens found in the personal friendships he made among the Cambridge academics, it does serve to remind us just how exceptional the first two weeks in Boston were within the larger context of his visit. For this brief early period before disillusion set in was clearly the high point in his experience of America. Not the least of its pleasures was the fact that during these weeks he was able to construct for himself the kind of close-knit homosocial group he relied on throughout his life and that he found nowhere else in the New World. Although it contributes little to the reader's understanding of either education or intellectual life in America, then, Dickens's account of Harvard does say a great deal about its author and the extent to which his time in Boston and Cambridge set the stage for his subsequent disappointment with other aspects of the new society.

Just as they had both looked at industrial life, the position of women, and the nature of higher education in the new republic and seen very different things, so, finally, Martineau and Dickens were each fascinated by, and came to markedly contrasting opinions of, the phenomenon of the American press. Given the importance she placed on the role of education in forming American society, it is not surprising that Martineau should return to the subject of the press throughout her American books, combining larger appraisals of its qualities with specific examples of papers she had read during her travels. In doing so, she worked toward creating the kind of less personalized, more comprehensive, and more nuanced assessment of a social institution that is fundamental to her whole approach to writing about the new democracy. While she can be as critical as other English travel writers about the "slough of rancour, folly, and falsehood" American newspapers present, she is also careful to cite James Madison's authority for the potential role of the press as "the utterance of the national mind." As is the case throughout her representation of America, she insists upon the new society's evolving character, noting the ways in which the press has established a structure of civic discourse that provides far greater potential than had been available when political life had been built solely around public oratory.[33] She is also at pains to emphasize the particular power the press has to assist the growth of the national mind in a culture that has not yet developed its own literature and remains dependent on models from across the Atlantic.[34] For her, a free press is essential to ensure "the wide diffusion of political power"[35] in a democracy, and she is, accordingly, particularly disturbed by the patterns of formal and informal censorship she observes across the South.[36] Set against this corruption, and paralleling the ways she represents the western frontier as the leading edge of social progress in education, she offers a series of examples of effective, socially responsible journalism not only in urban centers such as Boston but also in the newspapers she comes across in the far less developed communities of the West, from Ann Arbor, Michigan, to Cleveland, Ohio.[37]

Our understanding of Dickens's representation of the American press has in recent years been deeply enriched, first by John Drew's suggestion that *American Notes* is "significantly *about* the invasive power of the press,"[38] and second by Juliet John's modifying argument that for Dickens the press stands as representative of the larger failings of a "debased mass culture."[39] While recognizing the value of these readings, however, it is also important to realize how much they depend on knowledge that is available to us from both Dickens's letters and our awareness of his later work. If we position ourselves with the original readers of *American Notes,* what becomes strikingly evident is how few references to the press it contains and how easy it was at the time of the book's first appearance to interpret these as just one more instance of its superficiality. For, after being greeted by the dockside "Editors" in Boston, Dickens has nothing to say about American newspapers other than a single paragraph on the New York press "pimping and pandering for all degrees of vicious taste" until the very end of his account.[40] There, in the final chapter, he devotes four pages to what he describes as the "licentious Press," a "monster of depravity," which he labels a "frightful engine" that drives the corruption of American political life.[41] Issued as a declarative assertion, providing no supporting evidence, and insisting on Dickens's unmodulated judgment, this passage exemplifies Drew's point that the greatest problem with *American Notes* is that it is uncertain about its target audience.[42]

As Amanda Claybaugh has shown, however, Dickens's treatment of the American press has recently come to be seen as part of a more complex engagement in the transatlantic debate over abolition. Claybaugh's suggestion is reinforced by Joel J. Brattin's account in this volume of the ways in which the manuscript of *American Notes* reveals Dickens's careful attention to how his text should represent the whole issue of slavery. For Claybaugh, the "Slavery" chapter and Dickens's appropriation into his own text of passages from American newspapers via Theodore Weld's pamphlet *American Slavery as It Is* works as a shock tactic, defamiliarizing, particularly for southern readers, practices they had been accustomed to take for granted by recirculating them into America through the act of reprinting.[43] Brattin's chapter, meanwhile, shows strikingly how the manuscript of *American Notes* reveals the extent of Dickens's concern over the role of the press in America and, in particular, its capacity to shape public discourse around what was becoming the single most important issue facing the new society.[44] For contemporary readers and critics, however, Martineau among them, both this manuscript evidence and the innovative effects of recirculating the language of the American press clearly remained invisible, unrecognized, and thus unavailable to counter the negative appraisals of the text's more overt failings that defined its initial reception on both sides of the Atlantic.

But if *American Notes* offers a vision of the nation largely devoid of newspapers and made its points about the press only indirectly, *Martin Chuzzlewit* indicates just how much the visit to America had influenced Dickens's understanding of the role of the press. The novel shows his readers an America that fully embodies Drew's definition of the press's

invasive properties, and, as it does so, it once again confirms Dickens's
vision of Massachusetts as the exception to his larger disillusioned view
of the United States. From young Martin's landing in New York to his
near-death experience in the swamps of Eden, newspapers are his constant companion, beginning with Colonel Diver, editor of the *New York
Rowdy Journal,* who takes him up and introduces him to the New World,
its "bubbling passions," and the power of the press to make the population "yield to the mighty mind of the Popular Instructor." Favorably
likening this control over public opinion to slavery, with both numbered
among "the ennobling institutions of our happy country," the New York
journalists preside over a society that has become dependent on them for
its sources of information: "'We are a busy people, sir,' said one of the cap-
tains who was from the West, 'and have no time for reading mere notions.
We don't mind 'em if they come to us in newspapers along with almighty
strong stuff of another sort, but darn your books.'"[45]

Although none of the American scenes in *Martin Chuzzlewit* are set
in Massachusetts, the text draws on the commonwealth to counter this
dark vision of semiliterate barbarism. Its strongest voice against the awful
power of the American press is assigned to Mr. Bevan, a character perhaps modeled on Cornelius Felton, the Eliot Professor of Greek Literature at Harvard, an embodiment of the tradition of classical learning, and
the author of the most positive review *American Notes* received. Despite
Felton's disputing Dickens's claims for the power of the American press
in that review, his fictional avatar is made to voice the author's constant
complaint about the level of public discourse in the United States. For, as
Bevan notes, "the great mass, asserts a spurious independence, most mis-
erably dependent for its mean existence on the disregard of humanizing
conventionalities of manner and social custom," while the elite "leaves
the public weal to such fortune as may betide it in the press and uproar
of a general scramble," and journalism operates to maintain social mores
as their lowest common denominator: "If another Juvenal or Swift could
rise up among us to-morrow, he would be hunted down. If you have
any knowledge of our literature, and can give me the name of any man,
American born and bred, who has anatomised our follies as a people, and
not as this or that party; and has escaped the foulest and most brutal slan-
der, the most inveterate hatred and intolerant pursuit; it will be a strange
name in my ears, believe me."[46] Massachusetts, then, provided the one
voice of opposition to a larger national trend in the press, even if its representative in the novel can only lament the culture's failure to generate
any broader resistance to its worst tendencies.

As Bevan's comment suggests, Dickens himself returned home with a new sense of the power and potential of the press, and in this he and Martineau had come to a similar realization. As she wrote to Lydia Maria Child on 10 January 1838, for instance, "The design for the newspaper on behalf of Woman rather flags, owing to our not having perfect confidence in the proposer of the plan. When I have any further light, you will be sure to know. The scheme is too important to be perilled by being put into any but the best hands."[47] Although nothing more is known about this project, that Martineau was thinking about a newspaper "on behalf of Woman," and that she was writing about it to a Massachusetts friend with whom she had stayed early in her visit, both evidences her interest in engaging with the mass media to advance a particular cause and shows the importance of the connections she had made in America to such a project and its social agenda. Although she would not completely fulfill this ambition for more than a decade, the long career that she began in 1852 as one of the most important leader writers for the *Daily News* can surely be traced back to what she learned about the power of the press during her visit to America in the mid-1830s.

For his part, Dickens's new sense of the press and of his potential role in it is evident from a letter he wrote to Lady Holland on 8 July 1842, just days after his return from America. Seeking her support and, through her, financial backing from the liberal elite, he proposed taking over the floundering *Courier* and putting it to work in support of the progressive cause:

> I need scarcely say, that if I threw my small person into the breach ... I could command immediate attention; while the influence I have with Booksellers and Authors would give me a better chance of stamping it with a new character, and securing for it, after a reasonable trial, good advertisements, than almost any other man could possess. . . . I feel a perfect confidence that I could establish an organ for the party which would do good service, and which would have the inestimable advantage of taking a certain position at once, instead of struggling for years before it became known.

Had he not been away, he suggests, he would have communicated with the party leaders earlier "and made proposals to them for saving the Paper—nailing the true colours to the mast—and fighting the battle staunchly, and to the Death."[48] While the specific project was not realized, its articulation is doubly revealing: on the one hand, it suggests the urgency with which Dickens, back from America, desired to become engaged in the work of fostering political progress through the press. On the other, in its enthusiastically self-confident language, his letter anticipates the heroic role he imagined for himself as editor, a role he would seek through various iterations before he discovered the extraordinary influence and commercial success he could achieve using weekly journalism in the forms of *Household Words* and its successor, *All the Year Round*.

Alike in many ways and yet so fundamentally different in others, Martineau and Dickens both returned from America with a heightened sense of the power of the press to shape the public sphere. Although their underlying differences over the nature of industrial society and, above all, women's social agency and engagement in public discourse would eventually lead to their friendship's ugly demise, for both of them the visit to America and, in particular, the time they spent in Massachusetts proved vitally formative to their understanding of the power of the press to shape these issues—and of the opportunity the press could provide them to advance their own beliefs. The republic they came to see, and especially the commonwealth that made such an impact upon them, thus helped to form crucial elements of the underlying conflict that would come to its bitter public resolution years after their journeys across the Atlantic, as they negotiated the shifting frontier of mid-nineteenth-century journalism and moved toward their own high noon in its columns.

NOTES

1. Amanda Claybaugh, *The Novel of Purpose: Literature and Social Reform in the Anglo-American World* (Ithaca, N.Y.: Cornell University Press, 2007).

2. Iain Crawford, "Harriet Martineau, Charles Dickens, and the Rise of the Victorian Woman of Letters," *Nineteenth-Century Literature* 68 (2014): 449–83.

3. Jerome Meckier, *Innocent Abroad: Charles Dickens's American Engagements* (Lexington: University Press of Kentucky, 1990), 122.

4. Valerie Kossew Pichanik, *Harriet Martineau: The Woman and Her Work, 1802–1876* (Ann Arbor: University of Michigan Press, 1980), 80–81; Caroline Roberts, *The Woman and the Hour: Harriet Martineau and Victorian Ideologies* (Toronto: University of Toronto Press, 2002), 36–37.

5. Nicholas Phillipson, "Language, Sociability, and History: Some Reflections on the Foundations of Adam Smith's Science of Man," in *Economy, Polity, and Society: British Intellectual History 1750–1850*, ed. Stefan Collini, Richard Whatmore, and Brian Young (Cambridge: Cambridge University Press, 2000), 71.

6. Juliet John, *Dickens and Mass Culture* (Oxford: Oxford University Press, 2010), 76.

7. Charles Dickens, *The Pilgrim Edition of the Letters of Charles Dickens*, 12 vols., ed. Madeline House et al. (Oxford: Clarendon Press, 1965–2002), 3:156 (22 March 1842).

8. Harriet Martineau, *Society in America*, 3 vols. (London: Saunders and Otley, 1837); *Retrospect of Western Travel*, 2 vols. (London: Saunders and Otley, 1838); *How to Observe Morals and Manners* (London: Charles Knight, 1838).

9. See Harriet Martineau, *The Martyr Age of the United States of America: With an Appeal on Behalf of the Oberlin Institute in Aid of the Abolition of Slavery* (Newcastle upon Tyne, Eng.: Finlay and Charlton, 1840).

10. See, for example, Michael R. Hill, "A Methodological Comparison of Harriet Martineau's *Society in America* (1837) and Alexis de Tocqueville's *Democracy in America* (1835–1840)," in *Harriet Martineau: Theoretical and Methodological Perspectives*, ed. Michael R. Hill and Susan Hoecker-Drysdale (New York: Routledge, 2001), 59–74; and Maria Frawley, *A Wider Range: Travel Writing by Women in Victorian England* (Rutherford, N.J.: Fairleigh Dickinson University Press, 1994), 171–82.

11. Charles Dickens, *American Notes for General Circulation*, 2 vols. (London: Chapman and Hall, 1842). Citations to *American Notes* include volume number followed by a colon, and chapter and page number(s) separated by a period.

12. Charles Dickens, *Martin Chuzzlewit* (London: Chapman and Hall, 1843–44). Citations to *Martin Chuzzlewit* include chapter and page number(s) separated by a period.

13. [Cornelius Conway Felton], "*American Notes for General Circulation.* By Charles Dickens," *North American Review* 56 (January 1843): 230.

14. Dickens, *Letters*, 4:721.

15. Ibid., 3:ix.

16. Anne Warren Weston to Deborah Weston, 4 February 1842, Boston Public Library, Anne Warren Weston Correspondence (1834–1886), Ms.A.9.2v17, p. 32, http://archive.org/stream/lettertodeardebooowest128.

17. Dickens, *Letters*, 3:395 (16 December 1842).

18. Harriet Martineau, *The Collected Letters of Harriet Martineau*, 5 vols., ed. Deborah Anna Logan (London: Pickering and Chatto, 2007), 2:135 (29 October 1842).

19. Martineau, *Society in America*, 2:252.

20. Charles Knight, ed., *Mind amongst the Spindles: A Selection from The Lowell Offering, a Miscellany, Wholly Composed by the Factory Girls* (London: Charles Knight, 1844), xviii, xx, xxi.

21. Martineau, *How to Observe Morals and Manners*, 177.

22. Dickens, *American Notes*, 1:4.164, 155–56, 161–62.

23. Martineau, *How to Observe Morals and Manners*, 178.

24. Martineau, *Society in America*, 2:155, 338.

25. Martineau, *How to Observe Morals and Manners*, 37.

26. Dickens, *American Notes*, 1:3.74, 1:7.261, 2:4.113, 2:7.217.

27. Martineau, *Retrospect of Western Travel*, 2:94.

28. Martineau, *Society in America*, 3:281–83.

29. Martineau, *Retrospect of Western Travel*, 2:84.

30. Martineau, *The Martyr Age*, xiv.

31. Dickens, *American Notes*, 1:3.63.

32. John, *Dickens and Mass Culture*, 86.

33. Martineau, *Retrospect of Western Travel*, 1:40, 194; 2:53.

34. Martineau, *Society in America*, 3:205–9.

35. Martineau, *How to Observe Morals and Manners*, 198.

36. Martineau, *Society in America*, 2:141, 2:344–45.

37. Ibid., 1:153–54.

38. John M. L. Drew, *Dickens the Journalist* (Houndmills, Eng.: Palgrave Macmillan, 2003), 63.

39. John, *Dickens and Mass Culture*, 101.

40. Dickens, *American Notes*, 1:6.210.

41. Ibid., 2:10.293–94.

42. Drew, *Dickens the Journalist*, 64–65.

43. Claybaugh, *The Novel of Purpose*, 79.

44. Joel J. Brattin, "Slavery in Dickens's Manuscript of *American Notes for General Circulation*," this volume.

45. Dickens, *Martin Chuzzlewit*, 16.194, 199, 207.

46. Ibid., 17.210–11, 16.209.

47. Martineau, *Letters*, 2:14 (10 January 1838).

48. Dickens, *Letters*, 3:262–63 (8 July 1842).

Selected Works by Charles Dickens

✦

AN ASTERISK before a title indicates that the novel is available in facsimile via the Project Boz website, http://dickens.wpi.edu. Project Boz plans to provide high-quality searchable facsimiles of every page of every Dickens novel in its original serial form, including wrappers, illustrations, and advertisements.

Sketches by Boz, Illustrative of Every-Day Life and Every-Day People (collected essays and sketches, 1836; later revised and expanded)

The Village Coquettes (comic opera, 1836)

Sunday under Three Heads (political pamphlet, 1836)

The Strange Gentleman; a Comic Burletta in Two Acts (1836)

The Posthumous Papers of the Pickwick Club (novel in monthly parts, April 1836–November 1837)

Is She His Wife? or Something Singular; a Comic Burletta in One Act (1837)

*Oliver Twist; or, The Parish Boy's Progress (novel serialized in the monthly magazine *Bentley's Miscellany,* February 1837–April 1839)

Sketches of Young Gentlemen (1838)

The Lamplighter (play, 1838)

The Memoirs of Joseph Grimaldi (edited by Dickens, 1838)

*The Life and Adventures of Nicholas Nickleby Containing a Faithful Account of the Fortunes, Misfortunes, Uprisings, Downfallings and Complete Career of the Nickleby Family (novel in monthly parts, April 1838–October 1839)

Sketches of Young Couples (1840)

*The Old Curiosity Shop (novel in weekly parts, April 1840–February 1841)

Barnaby Rudge: A Tale of the Riots of Eighty (novel in weekly parts, February–November 1841)

American Notes for General Circulation (travel book, 1842)

A Christmas Carol (Christmas book, 1843)

The Life and Adventures of Martin Chuzzlewit, His Relatives, Friends, and Enemies. Comprising All His Wills and His Ways: With an Historical Record of What He Did, and What He Didn't: Showing, Moreover, Who Inherited the Family Plate, Who Came in for the Silver Spoons, and Who for the Wooden Ladles, The Whole Forming a Complete Key to the House of Chuzzlewit (novel in monthly parts, January 1843–July 1844)

The Chimes (Christmas book, 1845)

The Cricket on the Hearth (Christmas book, 1846)

The Battle of Life (Christmas book, 1846)

Pictures from Italy (travel book, 1846)

*Dealings with the Firm of Dombey and Son: Wholesale, Retail, and for Exportation (novel in monthly parts, October 1846–April 1848)

The Life of Our Lord (retelling of the New Testament for his children, probably written in 1846; not intended for publication; published in 1934)

The Haunted Man and the Ghost's Bargain (Christmas book, 1848)

The Personal History, Adventures, Experience, and Observation of David Copperfield the Younger of Blunderstone Rookery (Which He Never Meant to Be Published on Any Account) (novel in monthly parts, May 1849–November 1850)

Mr. Nightingale's Diary: A Farce in One Act (with Mark Lemon, 1851)

A Child's History of England (published at irregular intervals, January 1851–December 1853)

*Bleak House (novel in monthly parts, March 1852–September 1853)

*Hard Times: For These Times (novel in weekly parts, April–August 1854)

*Little Dorrit (novel in monthly parts, December 1855–June 1857)

"The Lazy Tour of Two Idle Apprentices" (with Wilkie Collins, five-part semiautobiographical account of a holiday journey, 1857)

The Frozen Deep (with Wilkie Collins, play, 1857)

*A Tale of Two Cities (novel in weekly parts, April–November 1859; also published in monthly parts, June–December 1859)

*Great Expectations (novel in weekly parts, December 1860–August 1861)

The Uncommercial Traveller (collected essays and sketches, 1861, later revised and expanded)

*Our Mutual Friend (novel in monthly parts, May 1864–November 1865)

"Doctor Marigold's Prescriptions" (Christmas story, 1865)

"The Signal-Man" (ghost story, 1866)

"George Silverman's Explanation" (short story, 1868)

*The Mystery of Edwin Drood (novel in monthly parts, April–September 1870, unfinished)

ABOUT THE CONTRIBUTORS

DIANA C. ARCHIBALD, an associate professor of English at the University of Massachusetts Lowell, was co-curator of the 2012 exhibition *Dickens and Massachusetts*. Her editorial work includes co-editing the June 2013 issue of *Dickens Quarterly*, editing a special issue on anti-Americanism in nineteenth-century British literature for *Symbiosis*, and editing a *Dickens Quarterly* special issue on "Dickens and America." Her first book is *Domesticity, Imperialism, and Emigration in the Victorian Novel* (2002). She wrote "Recent Dickens Studies: 2005" for *Dickens Studies Annual*, and has published a variety of articles on Dickens.

JOEL J. BRATTIN, a professor of English literature at Worcester Polytechnic Institute, has published extensively on the evolution of Dickens's texts, especially Dickens's manuscript revisions. Brattin wrote *Our Mutual Friend: An Annotated Bibliography* (1984) and edited *Our Mutual Friend* for the Everyman Dickens Edition (2000). He organized and hosted the first International Dickens Symposium in Worcester in 1996, and has contributed to each of the subsequent symposia organized by the Dickens Society. He has also served as president of the Dickens Society.

CHELSEA BRAY is a Boston College MA candidate in English literature with a particular interest in Irish Studies. Her current research examines representations of female identity and sexuality in eighteenth- and nineteenth-century British and Irish fiction. Bray received a BA from Boston University with a degree in English and credits her undergraduate advisor, Natalie McKnight, for introducing her to the sparkling world of Charles Dickens.

IAIN CRAWFORD is an associate professor of English at the University of Delaware. His work on Dickens has appeared in journals including

Dickens Quarterly, Studies in English Literature, 1500–1900, Studies in the Novel, and *Victorian Periodicals Review,* and his current book project is a study of the long and complex professional relationship of Charles Dickens and Harriet Martineau, focusing on its implications for the development of the Victorian press and the emergence of the nineteenth-century professional woman of letters.

ANDRÉ DeCUIR is an associate professor of English at Muskingum University in New Concord, Ohio. He teaches Romantic and Victorian literature, history of the British novel, and special topics courses in Dickens and other Victorian writers such as the Brontës and Wilkie Collins. His current topic of research is the impact of the visual arts on Victorian writers, and his articles on Dickens have appeared in collections such as *Gender and Reform* and *Dickens in the New Millennium.*

NATALIE McKNIGHT is dean and professor of humanities at the College of General Studies, Boston University. She has published three books on Victorian fiction: *Idiots, Madmen and Other Prisoners in Dickens* (1993), *Suffering Mothers in Mid-Victorian Novels* (1997), and *Fathers in Victorian Fiction* (2011). McKnight co-edits *Dickens Studies Annual* and is the archivist for *Dickens Quarterly.*

LILLIAN NAYDER is a professor of English at Bates College. She is the author of *Wilkie Collins* (1997), *Unequal Partners: Charles Dickens, Wilkie Collins and Victorian Authorship* (2002), and *The Other Dickens: A Life of Catherine Hogarth* (2011), and has edited a volume on *Dickens, Sexuality and Gender* (2012). She is writing a biography of Charles Dickens and his brothers as well as a historical novel centered on Letitia Austin, Dickens's younger sister, and their sister-in-law Harriet Dickens.

KIT POLGA recently retired from teaching at Springfield Technical Community College. After raising four children, she returned to academia as an Ada Comstock Scholar at Smith College in 1992, and then earned an MA degree at the University of Kent in Canterbury. She has presented papers on "Dickens's Contributors to *Household Words,*" "Dickens and the Morality of Imagination" (published in *Dickens Quarterly*), and "Dickens's Voice in *Household Words.*" She is an active member and former trustee of the Dickens Society, and an enthusiastic member and past president of the Dickens Fellowship of Worcester, Massachusetts.

INDEX